CarTech®

838 Lake Street South
Forest Lake, MN 55025
Phone: 651-277-1200 or 800-551-4754
Fax: 651-277-1203
www.cartechbooks.com

Edit by Bob Wilson
Layout by Hailey Samples

ISBN 978-1-61325-471-4
Item No. CT653

Library of Congress Cataloging-in-Publication Data

Names: Foster, Patrick R., author.
Title: 1001 Jeep facts / Patrick Foster.
Other titles: One thousand one Jeep facts | One thousand and one Jeep facts
Description: Forest Lake, MN : CarTech, [2019]
Identifiers: LCCN 2019008684 | ISBN 9781613254714
Subjects: LCSH: Jeep automobile–Miscellanea. | Jeep automobile–History. |
LCGFT: Trivia and miscellanea.
Classification: LCC TL215.J44 F6493 2019 | DDC 629.222–dc23
LC record available at https://lccn.loc.gov/2019008684

Written, edited, and designed in the U.S.A.
Printed in China

10 9 8 7 6 5 4 3 2 1

DISTRIBUTION BY:

Europe
PGUK
63 Hatton Garden
London EC1N 8lE, England
Phone: 020 7061 1980 • Fax: 020 7242 3725
www.pguk.co.uk

Australia
Renniks Publications Ltd.
3/37-39 Green Street
Banksmeadow, NSW 2109, Australia
Phone: 2 9695 7055 • Fax: 2 9695 7355
www.renniks.com

Canada
Login Canada
300 Saulteaux Crescent
Winnipeg, MB, R3J 3T2 Canada
Phone: 800 665 1148 • Fax: 800 665 0103
www.lb.ca

TABLE OF CONTENTS

DEDICATION

To the greatest Jeep men of all time: designers Bob Nixon and Vince Geraci. These two men led teams that were responsible for creating some of the most legendary vehicles ever produced, and I'm proud that they are among my best friends as well. God bless you both!

ABOUT THE AUTHOR

One of America's best-known automotive journalists is Patrick Foster, a dedicated historian/author who has been writing for more than 25 years. Patrick is a feature writer and columnist for *Hemmings Classic Car.*

Patrick has written 27 books and contributed material to several others. He has won numerous writing awards including the AACA's prestigious Thomas McKean Memorial Cup Award, an Outstanding Periodical Article for the year by the Society of Automotive Historians, and numerous International Automotive Media Council (IAMC) Awards. In 2011, Patrick was honored with the Lee Iacocca Award, perhaps the most coveted award in the car hobby, for excellence in automotive writing.

ACKNOWLEDGMENTS

I would like to thank Bob Wilson of CarTech Books for giving me the opportunity to author this book. I'd especially like to thank legendary Jeep designers Jim Pappas, John Sgalia, Bill St. Claire, John Starr, Jack Kenitz, Eric Kugler, George Krispinsky, Thelma Sibley, Susan Tassi, Phil Payne, and the late Jim Angers and Claude Trambley for their insight and for always being there when I needed them.

Thanks also to my good friends Frank Pascoe, Ron Konopka, and Jack Wildman of AMC/Jeep Styling; Joe Cappy and Gerald Meyers, both former CEOs of American Motors; Dean Greb; and the late Chuck Mashigan and Cruse Moss. I also want to thank Dan Clifford and Jay Cowperthwaite for suggesting some good facts. Special thanks go to Steve Magnante for all his help. You guys are the best!

A QUICK NOTE ABOUT THESE FACTS

I've been involved with Jeep vehicles for decades; first as a mechanic, then as a successful salesman, and finally as a journalist. In my time with Jeep I've accumulated one of the largest collections of Jeep literature in the world, which I consulted while writing this book. However, having noted all of the above, I have to tell you that you may find a few errors in the text. It's practically inevitable when you spend a year writing more than 80,000 words that your fingers accidently type 1962 when you really meant to type 1963, used the wrong word to describe a component, or just plain made a dumb mistake. I've written four previous Jeep books and hopefully am getting better as I age (like a fine wine?). So, if you find any errors, please accept my apology now, and send me a letter in care of the publisher so I can correct any future editions. Thanks!

Military Jeeps

Legend and Lore

 Until the first Jeep was created, there had never been another vehicle like it. Sure, the army had earlier used four-wheel-drive trucks; the first of them was during the Mexican Punitive Expedition of 1916–1917 when it brought a fleet of Jeffery four-wheel-drive trucks to Mexico to chase Pancho Villa. The trucks proved to be sturdy and capable but were heavy, and their small engines limited the top speed to about 18 mph! The big trucks found their place in the battlefields of World War I France, where they hauled ammunition and guns to the front lines. However, the army knew it needed something smaller, lighter, and more agile for the coming war.

Here, President Franklin Delano Roosevelt reviews troops from a Jeep MB.

In the years prior to World War II, the army also tried two-wheel-drive Ford Model Ts, but they proved to be unacceptable. When the cars were stripped down, with fenders, tools, and the spare tire removed, their performance was decent, but with a heavy machine gun and other equipment along with passengers and ammunition, the Ford cars got stuck in sand and mud. The army also tried motorcycles, but not surprisingly they got stuck worse than the cars.

Two soldiers even built a platform vehicle called the Belly Flopper, which had a machine gun mounted up front and room for two men to lie on their stomachs as they drove forward during the attack. The thing was uncomfortable to use and couldn't be driven on the road for any length of time (they had to be trucked to the battle-field), so although they were a decent assault vehicle, they didn't make the cut. The army was looking for a scout car that could be used for many tasks, not just as an assault vehicle.

This three-man crew appears to be on reconnaissance with a hefty machine gun in case of trouble.

 Most people know that Jeep Corporation didn't invent the Jeep; neither did its forerunners Willys-Overland and Kaiser Jeep. The first such vehicle was produced by a now-defunct company known as the American Bantam Car Company. In 1940, bidding against Ford Motor Company and Willys-Overland, the Butler, Pennsyl-vania–based Bantam won an army contract to design and build a prototype of a new military scout car. On the verge of bankruptcy, the company then instituted a crash program to try to win the pro-duction contract.

5   Bantam was a weird little company. It was founded originally to produce the British Austin Seven, a tiny, tinny, 13-hp runt of a roadster, under license. It soon went bankrupt because it was undersized, underpowered, and overpriced, whereupon it was resurrected as American Bantam, building a tiny, tinny, 19-hp runt with about the same results. By 1940, the company was essentially bankrupt, which made it desperate to find any kind of work in order to stay in business. Thus, when the army went looking for a scout car, Bantam grabbed on like a drowning man to a life preserver.

6   During 1940, the army sent invitations to bid on the new vehicle to 135 US manufacturers, including automobile and truck builders, plus specialty firms that produced vehicle bodies, chassis, or major components. It was the largest number of firms contacted by the army for a motor vehicle contract, and it expected to receive a large number of bids because the award was up to $175,000 for the initial prototype plus 69 additional vehicles with any changes the army required. However, in the end, only two companies submitted proposals: small-car builders American Bantam and Willys-Overland. Later, as the program matured, Ford joined the bidding.

7   Bantam initially thought it would be able to sell modified versions of its passenger cars to the army. The military even tested several of the Bantams, but in the end decided it need a new vehicle designed from the ground up. Not only that, but the army's required design specifications for the first Jeep went beyond the technology of the day in 1940, which meant that it either had to change the specs or give up the program (eventually the army changed the requirements).

Initial specifications included a low body height, seating for three, a 20-hp engine, four-wheel-drive, a wheelbase of not more than 75 inches, and the capability of at least 50 mph on a hard surface, all of which could be achieved. However, the army also said that the vehicle had to weigh no more than 1,300 pounds and be able to haul at least 600 pounds, or almost half its own weight. These last two demands couldn't be met using technology of the day, at least not in time to meet the army's other

requirements that the prototype use as many off-the-shelf components as possible and be ready for testing in 49 days!

The vehicle that is considered the first "Jeep" is the prototype made by Bantam Motors, seen here in 1941. Note the cycle front fenders; this is the only Bantam Jeep with this feature.

 Bantam was broke and had long since laid off its engineering staff, so in order to actually come up with a Jeep design, it had to hire a freelance engineer. Independent engineer Karl Probst, a brilliant former Packard engineer, took the job despite his own misgivings. Bantam had told him that he would only be paid if they actually won the contract. But Probst was a true patriot and understood the importance of designing the right vehicle for the army.

Once Probst agreed, he packed a bag and immediately drove to Bantam's plant in Butler, Pennsylvania. Miraculously, he managed to design the entire vehicle, create blueprints, and assign cost estimates in just three days.

 As noted earlier, army specifications called for an overall weight of 1,300 pounds for the vehicle. When Bantam president Frank Fenn asked engineer Probst about the weight specification, Probst calmly

replied, "Of course we can't make that weight target, but neither can anyone else." He was smart. From long experience designing cars and components, Probst knew that what the army was asking for was impossible, so he simply didn't worry about it. In the end, the Bantam military car weighed around 1,850 pounds.

10 Bantam didn't actually call its first vehicle a Jeep; the company dubbed it the Bantam Pilot Model. It later became known as the Bantam Mk I. The company produced 69 additional vehicles incorporating many improvements. These vehicles are known as the Mk II models (aka the Bantam BRC-60). The Bantam Pilot Model doesn't seem to have survived (at least it's never been found), but a highly skilled British enthusiast crafted a new one from scratch a few years ago, and it appears to be a perfect duplicate.

11 When the army opened the competitive bids for the initial prototype vehicle along with 69 follow-up vehicles, Bantam's bid was $2,445.51 per vehicle for a total of $171,186. Willys-Overland actually bid less than that amount. So why didn't Willys-Overland win the initial contract? Because Willys' management had to admit that they couldn't meet the army's stated deadline for delivering the vehicles in 49 days; they said they needed 75 days.

Because the army wanted this new vehicle as quickly as humanly possible, it had set a penalty of $5 per day for every day past the 49-day deadline specified in the contract. That single factor allowed Bantam Motors to win the initial contract for what became the Jeep.

12 Although there had never been a lightweight four-wheel-drive car before, it took Probst and a handful of Bantam employees less than two months to build the first Bantam Jeep basically from scratch. However, it was a nerve-racking effort.

They needed to figure out how to modify Studebaker axles to work on the front-wheel-drive part of the Jeep. Three weeks before the deadline, the problem still hadn't been solved, and Karl Probst privately admitted to a fellow engineer that they wouldn't make it. However, in the end, American ingenuity worked out the problems,

and the Bantam was finally completed and ready to go exactly one day before it had to be delivered to the army. Component suppliers were told that they would be allowed one hour each to road test the vehicle. Then it had to be delivered.

Teddy Roosevelt Jr. didn't live to see the end of the war. He was the son of former President Theodore Roosevelt and the cousin of President Franklin Delano Roosevelt. Teddy went in with the first wave of troops on D-day despite being so crippled by arthritis he required a cane. This photo was taken shortly after the landing, mere weeks before he died of a heart attack.

13 Imagine this: Rather than shipping it in an enclosed trailer, the Bantam prototype was driven to the army's test center at Camp Holabird, Maryland, from Butler, in western Pennsylvania. And this was in an era before major highways! It was a close call; the company met the army's delivery deadline with only 15 minutes to spare.

So vital was the contract that the vehicle was driven by designer Karl Probst and Bantam president Frank Fenn. They started out slow to break in the engine, but they soon realized they weren't going to make it in time unless they poured on the juice, so they began driving flat out across Pennsylvania.

14 Army Major Herbert Lawes, who had driven every military vehicle tested in the prior 20 years, test drove the first Bantam Jeep as soon as it was delivered to the army base. He declared, "This vehicle is going to be absolutely outstanding. I believe this unit will make history."

15 After thorough testing by the army at the Maryland proving grounds, up and down many hills and through mud, sand, and muck, the military staff requested that the 69 additional vehicles

The next series of Bantam Jeep vehicles were the BRC-60 pilot production vehicles, of which 69 were produced. The front fender is squared off and the body side is different from the Bantam Pilot Model.

ordered be fitted with engines of at least 40 hp. This forced Bantam to drop its own engine in favor of a Hercules-built four, which raised its costs for the vehicle and forced it to beef up the chassis, transmission, axles, and more.

16 Even though Bantam won the initial contract, the army asked for construction of competitive vehicles from Willys-Overland and Ford Motor Company because it worried greatly about Bantam's ability to produce the volume of vehicles that might be needed. Bantam was, after all, just about the smallest automaker in America, and it was teetering on the verge of bankruptcy.

17 The Willys prototype was called the Quad; the Ford prototype was dubbed the Pygmy. They looked similar to the Bantam, and photos of each are often misidentified.

The army felt that the Ford Pygmy was better constructed and finished than the Willys Quad and the Bantam vehicle. However, with just 46 hp on tap from its ancient Ford tractor engine, it was clearly underpowered. The Willys had 60 hp and performed well but weighed a whopping 2,520 pounds, which was too far over the army's weight requirement to be accepted.

The Ford GP proposal was well built but underpowered and did not perform as well as the Willys or even the Bantam.

The little Bantam, with just 40 hp available, had the lowest overall weight, and thus performed very well. Because of that, the Bantam remained a strong contender for the main contract for 15,000 vehicles. However, army officers still worried about Bantam's ability to deliver large volumes of vehicles in an emergency.

The first Jeep proposal by Willys was the 1941 Quad. Reportedly two were built, but neither has survived, though at least one was still around in the mid-1950s.

18 When the army expressed its disappointment with the Willys Quad's weight, Willys-Overland management realized it needed to have its engineers redesign the prototype to reduce weight or it would certainly lose the big contract. They came up with a new model called the Willys MA that weighed a few ounces less than the army's revised weight goal of 2,150 pounds.

The simplest way to reduce the weight would have been to install a lighter engine, but that would have eliminated Willys' one big advantage: power. So instead of doing that, the weight reduction was

accomplished by completely redesigning the body and chassis, cutting many pounds in the process.

Engineers also cut the length of screws and bolts used in assembly, used smaller fasteners where possible, and specified higher-strength lower-weight steel in the frame and body panels. Barney Roos even weighed the paint used on each vehicle, deciding (according to legend) that one coat would have to do.

The redesigned vehicle made the weight requirement, though one officer joked that if dust had settled on the Willys it would have gone over the limit. With its potent Go-Devil engine in the lighter chassis, Willys easily outshone both Ford and Bantam and won the contract.

Willys MA.

The Willys MA was an improvement over the Quad, and 1,555 were produced for the army. However, the MA was significantly over the weight limit imposed by the military, so Willys' engineers set to work reducing its weight.

19 Despite having invented the Jeep, Bantam Motors was given contracts for fewer than 2,800 units in all. After that, it was locked out of further orders, not even being allowed to be one of the backup, or supplemental, suppliers, as Ford was. The company was given contracts to assemble military trailers instead. After the war, Bantam did not return to building automobiles.

This Ford GP is undergoing tests at Fort Hood, Texas.

20 Okay, so the big question that everyone asks is this: Where did the Jeep name come from? Over the years, I must have been asked this question a couple of dozen times. The fact is that people can't seem to agree on it. One thing that I can verify is that the Jeep name existed years before the well-known vehicle first appeared, though it wasn't capitalized. The name came about as a slurring by soldiers of the initials GP, which is military speak for a "General Purpose" vehicle. The Jeep name had been around for years, mostly in military circles. In the 1930s, a motorized military tractor, nicknamed jeep, was used to haul big guns, along with various other military trucks and vehicles. There was even a small military plane nicknamed Jeep.

21 The only civilian use of the Jeep name prior to World War II that I've been able to find was for a fictional creature named "Eugene the Jeep" that appeared for a time in the popular cartoon strip "Popeye." Eugene the Jeep was a mysterious animal with magical abilities, including being able to get out of any situation and to go

through any obstacle. Eugene usually proved to be invaluable to Popeye and Olive Oyl, often leading them on fantastic adventures and getting them out of dangerous situations.

Initially, Willys produced its Jeep MAs alongside its passenger cars, as seen here, but by mid-January 1942 only Jeep vehicles were in production.

22 So how did the Jeep name come to be associated with Willys-Overland? In February 1941, Willys-Overland's public relations people showed off the company's new MB military scout car (the successor to the Willys MA) to a group of reporters. Journalist Katharine Hillyer was driven up and down some steep hills in a Willys MB by veteran Willys test driver "Red" Hausmann.

Visibly impressed, Hillyer asked, "What's the name of this thing?"

Hausmann replied proudly, "It's a Jeep!" using the military GP slang.

So Hillyer wrote her story using that name, and it was picked up by newspapers across the country. The Jeep name soon came to stand for the 4x4 product produced by Willys-Overland.

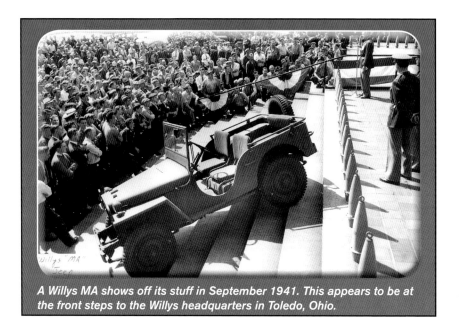

A Willys MA shows off its stuff in September 1941. This appears to be at the front steps to the Willys headquarters in Toledo, Ohio.

23 In later years, there was a great deal of controversy about who owned the Jeep name; after all, it had been created by army personnel. During the war, Willys-Overland used some clever advertising to convince people to forever link the Willys and Jeep names together. The company used headlines such as "WILLYS builds the JEEP," and you really had to squint to see the words between Willys and Jeep. After the war, everyone wanted the Jeep name, including the army, Willys, Bantam, etc.

The situation went on for years, but in the end the question was settled by James F. Holden, a lawyer. He filed a lawsuit on behalf of Willys-Overland to win the exclusive right to the Jeep name. The Jeep name has since passed on to the many successive owners of the company that builds Jeeps.

24 Fiat Chrysler Automobiles (FCA, Jeep's current parent company) is fiercely protective of the Jeep name, and rightfully so. The name was copyrighted many years ago, so whenever it appears in print it must be capitalized, Jeep. That's because Jeep is a noun, and never an adjective or verb. It's not supposed be used to classify a variety of vehicles, such as "jeep-like vehicles" and cannot be used to describe

a vehicle that's not a genuine Jeep; in other words, you can't advertise a Ford Explorer as a Ford Jeep or a Ford jeep (unless you like talking to angry lawyers). You should never say or write that you went "jeeping"; the correct way to describe an off-road adventure is to say you went four-wheeling. Got it?

These are American troops of the Patton's Fifth Army liberating the town of Vergato, Italy.

25 The new Jeep had several nicknames: Jeep, Peep, Blitz-Buggy, and the GI's Friend. Soldiers often bestowed their Jeeps with names. One Willys Jeep, which saw action on Guadalcanal, was dubbed *Old Faithful* by the Marines who used it. *Old Faithful* was officially retired on October 13, 1942, and enshrined in the Marines Corps Museum at Quantico, Virginia. Reportedly, the vehicle was awarded a Purple Heart for wounds received in battle (two shrapnel holes in the windshield).

26 Jeeps were used not only as scout cars but were assault vehicles as well. One of the most daring examples was when a fleet of heavily armed Jeeps from British General Montgomery's camp were ordered to raid General Rommel's supply line.

Traveling at night and hiding during the day, they managed to sneak their way around the German main force, ending up well behind German lines. There they waited on a hilltop overlooking Rommel's main supply route. Before long, a convoy of tanker trucks appeared, hauling fuel for Rommel's tanks. Firing up their Jeeps, the commandos came swooping down, hell-for-leather, toward the enemy. Driving flat out, their heavy machine guns blazing and spitting bullets frantically, the Jeeps weaved in and out of the German column, wreaking a hellish destruction. Within seconds the German force was reduced to nothing more than a long line of blazing trucks and dead soldiers.

The Jeeps then made it back to their own lines under cover of darkness. Rommel's forward advance stalled as a result of being low on fuel and supplies.

Equipped with a 50-caliber machine gun, a Jeep was a highly effective assault vehicle.

27 Another example is the story of two newspaper correspondents who slogged through the jungles of Burma's and India's rugged Manipur Hills, thought to be completely unpassable by vehicles, in a Willys Jeep. When they finally arrived in Imphal, capital of the Indian state of Manipur, an army officer who met them said that their sense of geography must have been mixed up because "There isn't a single road across those jungles and hills."

"Shh," replied one of the journalists, "Our Jeep hasn't found out about roads yet, and we don't want to spoil it."

28 Beloved war correspondent Ernie Pyle wrote in the *Washington Daily News*, "Good Lord, I don't think we could continue the war without the Jeep. It does everything. It goes everywhere. It's as faithful as a dog, as strong as a mule, and as agile as a goat. It constantly carries twice what it was designed for and still keeps going." Ernie Pyle later died when his Jeep was riddled with bullets by a hidden Japanese machine-gun pit.

29 Not surprisingly, during World War II enterprising US soldiers found many uses for the Jeep. Any GI needing warm food could place C-ration cans on the hot manifold of a Jeep engine and after a short drive, have a nice, hot dinner. If he wanted a warm shave, he could drain a little water from the Jeep radiator and lather up with it.

Some soldiers used their Jeeps to provide power to sawmills for cutting firewood or floorboards for their tents.

Jeeps carried men and supplies to the front lines and carried the wounded back to aid stations. Equipped with a 50-caliber machine gun, it was a terrifying assault vehicle. Fitted with a standard chaplain's pack, its hood could be used as an altar at field church services. Ingenious GIs sometimes fitted Jeeps with railroad wheels to use them as locomotives to haul train loads of supplies in areas where the locomotives had been destroyed.

This is an example of the result of battle: wounded men being cared for by medics. These caring men were able to be close to the front because their Jeep vehicles provided the all-terrain mobility that was lacking in earlier conflicts.

30 The Jeep was never meant to haul big cannons; the army had purchased special heavy-duty trucks for that. But during several invasions in which the trucks were blown up, quick-thinking soldiers hooked up their Jeeps to howitzers and small artillery pieces

and dragged them across the beach to where they were needed. The doughty Jeeps had more than enough power for the job, and their four-wheel drive provided the needed traction.

31 Once the war started and it was obvious that the armed forces would need hundreds of thousands of Jeeps, companies that previously hadn't bothered to bid suddenly became interested in building vehicles for the military. Radio maker Crosley Corporation came up with a peanut-sized "Jeep" vehicle, and taxi builder Checker Motors submitted a bid to produce a standard-size vehicle much like the Willys. A few prototypes of each were built, but no big contracts were forthcoming. It's not known how many, if any, have survived to this day.

Jeeps were shipped by the thousands to Allied forces around the globe.

32 When World War II ended, the military was forced to decide how many Jeep vehicles to ship back to America. Many were worn out or had mechanical problems and were not worth the expense of

transporting. Most of these were left behind, as were thousands wrecked in combat or in noncombat road accidents. Virtually all of the vehicles sent to Russia (many of which were the Bantams) were never returned to the United States. I wonder how many are still there.

33 For its part, Willys-Overland realized that if every army Jeep was brought back to the United States and sold as surplus, it would destroy the market for the only vehicle they would have to sell in the first year or two of postwar production. So, they asked the army to give our allies as many of the old Jeep vehicles as they needed and encouraged them to scrap any heavily damaged ones. Many other Jeeps were simply abandoned and left for the locals to use.

One Jeep Corporation vice president later called this whole-sale abandonment "the greatest free sample in history" because by introducing foreign locals to the Jeep, it helped establish Jeep's highly successful postwar export business. It also created a huge market for spare parts, which benefited Willys-Overland for years. Even in the 1970s, Jeep Corporation stocked many parts for Willys MBs because of the ongoing demand.

A casualty of war, this Jeep MB appears to have been hit by shellfire during an amphibious invasion.

34 In 1949, when it was becoming obvious that war might come to the Korean Peninsula, the military brass realized they needed new Jeeps because many of the World War II units were seven or eight years old and had been roughly used and needed replacing. Besides, the military wanted a tougher, more modern vehicle for the harsh Korean weather conditions.

Willys-Overland created a Jeep vehicle that was updated with a 24-volt electrical system, a 1,200-pound payload, deep-fording capability, and installation of standardized military components including instruments, switchgear, and generators to make stocking replacement parts easier. The army designated the new vehicle the M38; Willys-Overland dubbed it the model MC. These vehicles were produced during 1950 to 1952, at which time they were replaced by a heavily modified version.

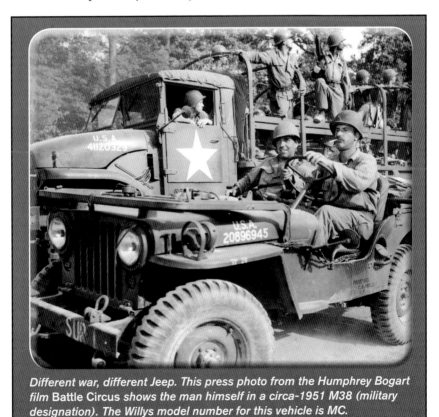

Different war, different Jeep. This press photo from the Humphrey Bogart film Battle Circus shows the man himself in a circa-1951 M38 (military designation). The Willys model number for this vehicle is MC.

Actor Alan Alda played Dr. Hawkeye Pierce on the TV show M.A.S.H., *which was based on the movie* Battle Circus. *If you watch the opening scenes of each one, you will see that they are nearly the same.*

35 The army wanted more power, more room, a better ride, and more carrying capacity. To answer those concerns, a new military Jeep appeared for 1952. Although it looked different from the M38, for some reason it was considered an improved and updated version of that vehicle, so it was given the military designation M-38A1,

which translates to M38, 1st alteration (or modification). For internal company purposes, Willys called it the model MD.

Later, a civilian version was introduced as the CJ-5, which became among the most ubiquitous of all civilian Jeeps and probably the most recognizable of them all.

Superseding the M38 was the M-38A1, shown here undergoing testing at the army's Aberdeen Proving Grounds in Aberdeen, Maryland.

36 Why the army considered the M-38A1 to be a modification of the M38 defies logic. The new Jeep had a different frame, engine, and body. Even though the basic Go-Devil block was retained, Willys engineer A. C. Sampietro devised a new "F-head" cylinder head for it.

Similar to the type used by Rolls-Royce at the time, the Willys F-head put the intake valves in an overhead valve (OHV) position but retained the exhaust valves in the block. This provided much better breathing through the larger valves, boosting engine output to 72 hp, which was a solid 20-percent gain. Torque increased by

9 ft-lbs as well. Top speed, previously about 60 mph, was now 65 mph, and fording depth was increased by half a foot, to 36 inches.

Amazingly, the new M-38A1 even weighed about 100 pounds less than the M38, despite having more interior room, more cargo room, and a longer wheelbase. The army appreciated the lower weight because it made it a little easier to transport.

To better illustrate the differences between the old and the new, here are the military M38 (on the left, aka Willys MC) and its replacement, the M-38A1 (on the right, aka the Willys MD).

37 For its first four military Jeep production vehicles, Willys used the in-house designations MA, MB, MC, and MD. There was no ME and, thankfully, no MF (I wonder what pundits would have done with that designation). There were, however, other military Jeep vehicles that came later, including the M-38A1C, which was modified to carry the army's 105-mm or 106-mm recoilless rifle, and the M-38A1D, which was designed to carry battlefield nuclear weapons.

38 The 1953 Willys Jeep Model BC (Bobcat) was an experimental vehicle built using shortened and lightened M38 and M-38A1

body parts and components. The engine was the L-head Go-Devil with an aluminum head and brackets, and the body was stamped from aluminum sheet. A two-seater with a small storage area in the rear, the Bobcat weighed about 1,500 pounds, which meant it was ideal for air transport, and even probably more agile than the M-38A1.

This December 1953 photo shows a civilian Model CJ-3B modified with a sloping hood to increase operator visibility. It was planned for both civilian and military use.

39 In later years, Jeep produced some offbeat military vehicles, such as the M606, which is a militarized version of the civilian "high-hood" CJ-3B, the M606A2, and the M606A3, which were militarized versions of the CJ-5. All of these were created in order to satisfy demands for a lower-cost but still highly capable military vehicle.

40 Another unusual "military" Jeep is the CJ-V35/U, which was a militarized CJ-3A that was intended for use during beach landings. It featured either a 12- or 24-volt generator to power radios and a heavily waterproofed electrical system. It could be fitted with intake and exhaust snorkels for deeper water running. These are extremely rare today.

41 Another post–World War II military Jeep is the M170, which is a long-wheelbase (101 inches) military ambulance based on the M-38A1, but with wide door openings and a full-length soft top. Inside, it is fitted for carrying patients from frontline areas.

42 Soldiers in World War II developed a deep, personal affection for Jeeps. One story often told is of an officer who came across a young soldier next to a Jeep that had been destroyed in an air raid. The distraught young man was crying uncontrollably over losing his Jeep.

"Don't worry, son," said the officer. "We'll get you another Jeep."

"You don't understand," replied the trooper. "I loved *this* one."

43 Okay, so the second most-asked question about Jeep is this: What's the correct pronunciation of Willys? Is it Willeez? Or is it Williss? I actually spoke with a member of the Willys family a couple of years ago, and they confirmed that the correct way to say it is Williss. It rhymes with Phyllis.

44 Where did the name Willys-Overland come from? The original name of the company was Overland (it was founded by the Standard Wheel Company, which was an auto industry supplier), and it built a car by using the Overland brand name. The Overland nameplate was picked because it sounded perfect for a rugged car, which is what the company felt the Overland was. John North Willys took over the business when it got into financial trouble, and in time, he renamed it Willys-Overland. Why? Because he liked the way it sounded.

45 By 1958, sales of Willys military Jeeps to the US Army had dwindled to almost nothing. In response, company engineers began to design new vehicles, such as the Mechanical Mule. But an easier and more profitable idea was to focus more attention on selling Jeeps to foreign governments.

One large customer was the Turkish Army, which placed an order for 1,600 Jeeps with the provision that they had to be assembled in Turkey. No problem, said Willys. The company was

an old hand at setting up overseas assembly. By 1961, the assembly plant in Turkey was in operation and produced the 1,600 vehicles, which (by looking at old photos) appear to have been the rare Model 606, a militarized version of the CJ-3B high-hood model. The Turkish army was so pleased with its Jeeps that it decided to order an additional 4,000 units.

By the way, Willys-Overland earned double profit on this order: one by selling the parts to build the Jeeps and another by charging a royalty per vehicle built. That's why Willys usually made more money in overseas markets than it did in the United States.

46 An old joke that soldiers used to tell was that after they died they wanted to be buried in their Jeep. Why? "Because there's never been a hole made that my Jeep can't get me out of," they said.

Body and Interior

47 Willys-Overland wanted to make certain that everyone knew who built the Jeep MA, so up front, just over the grille, the Willys

The president of Willys-Overland was Joseph W. Frazer. His employees nick-named him "Jeeps" Frazer because he managed to win the big contract for army Jeeps, thus ensuring Willys' survival. The vehicle is a Willys MA.

name is stamped in large letters. The company put its name on the rear of the body of the MB until around March 1942, when it was told by the army to stop the practice. Ford Motor Company also wanted to take credit for its efforts building Jeeps, so it stamped the Ford name on the rear panel of the MB body until April 1942, when it too was told to stop the practice. The army made both companies switch to a plain rear panel.

48 The body design of the production-model World War II–era army Jeep, the MB, is sort of a composite of the Willys MA body shell and the Ford GP hood. The military preferred the Ford's flat hood over the Willys' rounded one because the flat surface was useful for spreading out maps, using as a dinner table, serving as a chaplain's altar, etc.

49 The ubiquitous stamped grille was actually designed by Ford. It soon became standardized on Willys and Ford Jeeps because it was found to be quicker and cheaper to produce than the slat grilles seen on the earlier Willys products. That said, however, some 25,808 early Willys MBs were produced with the slat-style grille. I wonder how many have survived.

50 Here's something weird: The famous Jeep seven-slot grille, known throughout the world, wasn't used on World War II Jeeps because it hadn't been created yet. The MB grille is a nine-slot design. The seven-slot grille showed up first in mid-1945 with production of the civilian Jeep CJ-2A. It was also used on early "pilot" model civilian Jeeps as well as prototypes.

51 Even the Bantam Motors production models switched to the Ford-style flat hood. However, Bantam retained its unique slat grille and unique headlamp layout, probably because it never was given the chance to produce the standardized Jeep MB. In all, Bantam produced only 2,605 of its BRC-40 model.

52 To illustrate the difference in size and resources of Willys-Overland versus Ford, Willys purchased its Jeep bodies from

American Central Manufacturing of Connersville, Indiana, which produced them to the Willys design. This was because Willys-Overland lacked the financial reserves to buy body tooling. On the other hand, deep-pockets Ford Motor Company could easily afford to produce its Jeep bodies in-house at the Lincoln plant. Although at first glance the two appear identical, there are a number of minor differences between them.

A story persists that Jeep bodies were also produced in York, Pennsylvania, but to date I haven't seen enough hard evidence to convince me of that. One thing is true, however: With Jeep vehicles, anything is possible.

53 One nice touch seen on army Jeeps is that the headlamps swivel up and backward to provide a convenient under-the-hood lamp for adequate lighting for any needed field repairs in the engine bay. All you need to do is remove one wingnut and twist the lamp around. Question: Why don't we have this feature on modern Jeeps?

54 Any GI will tell you that the standard Jeep front seats are very uncomfortable after a while. However, they're much preferred over the back seat, which is situated right over the rear axle, guaranteeing a rough ride and supposedly even bringing on a case of the piles. Officers usually rode in the front passenger seat and left their underlings to suffer in the back seat. Generals who liked to be in control would even drive, letting their "driver" have the front passenger seat.

55 The military Jeep body was built of low-carbon steel, which was 18 gauge for the exterior body panels and 16 gauge for the floor. The body was bolted to the frame via 16 bolts. Initially, the builders inserted rubber dampers between the body and the frame at the bolt holes to help insulate noise. After a while, wartime restrictions on rubber were instituted because India was under Japanese occupation, and that was where most rubber came from. The situation forced Willys to change to fabric shims. As a side note, the wartime shortage of rubber was also the impetus to the invention of synthetic rubber.

56 The World War II–era army Jeep didn't come with the tailgate that's so familiar to Jeepers. Although a tailgate would have been a useful feature, adding one would have raised the vehicle's cost and forced the company to add extra bracing to the body, which in turn would have increased the weight. The fold-down tailgate didn't appear in production until mid-1945, when the first civilian Jeeps began to trickle down the assembly lines.

57 Although both the Bantam and Willys Quad prototypes had one-piece windshields, the army decided to standardize the two-piece windshield seen on the Ford GP vehicles. Willys basically copied the design for its MA vehicles. All the prototypes had fold-down windshields, but in my opinion Ford appears to have been the inspiration for the standardized design.

58 As World War II progressed, Willys-Overland began developing and experimenting with a two-passenger baby Jeep featuring a

This 1943 photo shows two experimental Jeep MB-Ls flanking a stock MB in Toledo. The MB-L (for "Light") used cut-down bumpers, plywood body panels, and was stripped of extraneous equipment to reduce weight. They held just two passengers.

body that would be lightweight and cheap to build because it was made out of plywood! The tiny Jeep included several other ideas to save weight and cost, such as leaving off the headlamps and most of the gauges. Several prototypes were constructed, but after testing, the army ultimately rejected it.

59 Determined to win as much wartime business as it could, in 1942 Willys management delivered to the army an experimental six-wheel Jeep, configured as a 6x6 cargo truck and built on a lengthened and beefed-up Willys MB chassis. Capable of hauling 1 ton of cargo or troops, it's not certain what became of the prototype.

In an effort to gain business, Willys engineered this 6x6 Jeep truck. However, the army already had many other truck suppliers and decided not to use it.

60 During the war, an amphibious Jeep was also produced: the GP-A (for amphibious). Popularly known as the Seep (for sea-going Jeep), it was designed and built by a joint venture of four-wheel-

drive truck specialist Marmon-Herrington and boatbuilder Spark-man and Stevens. This was not a Willys-Overland project.

Built around a Ford GPW, it was hurried into production before adequate testing was completed. The Seep's much heavier weight put a strain on the 4-cylinder engine, hurting on-road acceleration and performance. In the water, a propeller was used to power the vehicle, but here too the little Seep was slow.

It also suffered from insufficient freeboard, a result of underestimating the GPW's weight during the design phase, so it could easily be swamped in stormy waters. In the European theater, it wasn't popular with GIs because they found it wasn't very good for the rivers there, which often had steep banks that the Seep had difficulty overcoming.

Seep production was stopped after some 12,778 were produced. A lot of the vehicles were shipped to Russia, where they were better suited to the country's low-lying rivers.

61 Not all Jeeps are created equal, at least in the eyes of today's collectors. Among military vehicle buffs the early slat-grille Jeeps are worth more money that the later stamped-grille type, mainly because of their rarity. According to published sources, the stamped grille went into production in March 1942. Interestingly, there's not a big price differential between the Willys MB and the Ford GPW. It probably comes down to the fact that Ford guys like Ford Jeeps and Willys guys like Willys Jeeps.

62 In many wartime photos of Jeep vehicles, you notice a vertical metal bar attached to the front bumper and rising to a height of about 5 feet or so. Probably you have wondered what it's for. It seems that right after the Normandy invasion German soldiers came up with a nasty trick: They strung metal wires across the roads so that anyone driving in an open Jeep would have their neck snapped. It wasn't long before enterprising GIs began welding the thick bars to the front of their Jeeps in order to break the wires before they could kill any more soldiers.

63 In the postwar era, the next-generation 1950–1951 military M38 Jeep (aka the Willys MC) received improvements that included a 24-volt electrical system, a one-piece windshield, and a tailgate. The tailgate was easy to add, of course, because it had been developed for the civilian CJ-2A. After the M-38A1 (aka the Willys MD) appeared in 1952–1953, many of the MCs were sold as surplus because the army realized the new M-38A1 was superior.

64 Ever hear of an M-38E1? It was a prototype military Jeep developed by Willys-Overland that bridged the gap between the flat-fender M38 and round-fender M-38A1. Designed in 1951, it combined the body tub of an M38 with unique front fenders that were flat on top but rounded on the edges. To provide the increased power that the military was asking for, it was equipped with the tall F-head four-banger. In order to make that engine fit, the hood is tall but has a rounded appearance much like the M-38A1.

Another military prototype was the 1953 Jeep Bobcat. Similar in size to the earlier MB-L, this model was likewise a two-seater but lightened to make it easier to transport by air.

The M-38E1 came within a whisker of being produced for the army, but in the end the M-38A1 was created and became the new standard army Jeep. The M-38A1 offered everything the M-38E1 did as far as mechanical improvement, but provided much more interior room with less weight.

65 Driving a World War II–era army Jeep in the winter was cold. The soft top gave little protection from freezing weather. Although a fair number of Jeeps were given homemade enclosed bodies built by enterprising GIs, a serious effort to "winterize" the Jeep didn't occur until after the war when US occupation forces contracted with vehicle builder Steyr in Austria to refurbish Jeeps and build enclosed cabs for them. The new cabs were extremely well built, and that wasn't surprising because the Austrian company that had built them had previously produced military trucks and staff cars for the German army.

66 Mention military Jeeps and most people think of the Jeep MB of World War II. Realistically, the category also includes the M-series trucks based on the civilian Forward Control Jeeps. There were four basic models: the M-676 was a standard two-door pickup, the M-677 was a four-door crew cab pickup, the M-678 was a van/carryall, and the M-679 Ambulance was similar looking but without rear side windows. Production began in 1964. These vehicles, when you can find one today, are highly collectible.

67 Perhaps the rarest military Jeep of all is dubbed the CJ-4M, a military prototype based on the proposed civilian CJ-4 and related to the M-38E1. How many were built? Perhaps as few as one or two. Photos you may see on the internet show a dark-colored military prototype with a snorkel kit, which may be the civilian model with a new paint job, as well as a long-wheelbase ambulance-type vehicle. So far, only one CJ-4 has been found, and it's the original CJ-4 serial number 01 civilian prototype. The vehicle still exists. None of the military versions have turned up so far.

Engine and Drivetrain

68 All of the initial Jeep prototypes were powered by 4-cylinder engines because using a 6-cylinder engine would have resulted in a vehicle that was much too heavy to meet the army's strict weight requirements. Bantam fitted its vehicle with a 40-hp Continental engine that was popular in lift trucks; the Ford GP was fitted with a Ford tractor engine good for 40 hp. Willys used the same four-banger that was in its passenger cars. The Willys' mill was a rugged, durable 134.2-ci engine that developed 60 hp at 4,000 rpm and 105 ft-lbs of torque at just 2,000 rpm, which meant it was ideal for lugging along in low range yet also capable of fairly high road speeds. The Willys engine's compression ratio was 6.40:1, meaning the doughty little Jeep could easily run on low-quality gasoline without knock or pinging.

69 The Willys engine originated in the 1926 Whippet, a line of popular, low-priced cars built by Willys-Overland during the late 1920s and early 1930s. Developing just 30 hp at the time, the little flathead mill was fine by the standards of 1926, but sadly out of date by 1938, when it was still being used in the new Willys 48 small car.

By that point, output had been boosted to 48 hp, but the engine was noisy, rough-running, and had a well-earned reputation for being short lived. The engine tended to wear out its bearings, burn pistons, and throw rods. It had a lot of problems.

70 That bad reputation was holding down sales. Who wants to buy a car with a tired, weak engine? So during 1939, the company's management ordered the engineering department to do something about it. Engineering vice president Barney Roos, assisted by an extremely capable young engineer named Floyd Kishline, decided to go through the engine and fix the problems one by one.

The two men found many; in the end they had to redesign the engine block to give it full-length water jackets for better, more even cooling; design a new cylinder head; engineer a new carburetor and intake and exhaust manifolds for better breathing; design

better valves, water pump, bearings, pistons, air cleaner, timing gears; and much, much more. It involved a lot of work and a lot of testing, but in the end, Roos and Kishline created essentially a new engine without the extreme expense of all-new tooling.

Engine output rose from 48 hp to 60 hp, a solid 25-percent improvement, and the engine ran much smoother and quieter. At the same time, durability was vastly increased. Prior to the redesign, a stock Willys 4-cylinder engine run at full throttle usually burned out in about four hours; that's how bad the engine was. By the time Roos was finished with it, the redesigned engine ran 100 hours or more at peak rpm with no damage.

The Roos-Kishline redesign effort made the Willys engine the most powerful and most durable four-banger in America. They called it the Willys Go-Devil. It went on to become a legend and remained in production for decades.

71

The MB's transmission is a T-84 3-speed manual gearbox that was produced by Warner Gear. The transfer case is a 2-speed unit

Army test drivers were told to drive the test Jeeps until something broke, then report the problem to Willys, which would then engineer a stronger replacement part. The result was a light but extremely strong vehicle that could be produced for a relatively low price.

manufactured by Spicer Manufacturing Company, which later was renamed Dana Corporation. Some sources report that the Brown-Lippe company also supplied transfer cases to Willys-Overland.

72 The Spicer 25 front axle used on the wartime Willys Jeep MB is a full-floating design combining the stability of a hypoid design with steerable front knuckles at the outer ends of a rigid axle housing. This combination provides good maneuverability and outstanding durability in off-road situations.

73 As sturdy as the Willys Jeep was, during early prewar days the test drivers at Camp Holabird were tougher, running the test vehicles around the clock with specific instructions to keep pounding them until something broke. One test Jeep suffered a cracked frame at 5,184 miles; another had its engine cylinders so badly worn out by 5,011 miles that the engine had to be replaced. The army had no spare engines on hand, so a couple of enterprising mechanics from Willys-Overland pulled the engine from a civilian Willys car in the parking lot!

Other problems that showed up in early testing included transfer case main bearing failures, steering pin failures, and several spring and suspension failures. The army testers forwarded their report to the Quartermaster General, who told Willys it better fix the problems if it wanted to keep the contract. Barney Roos, Willys vice president of engineering, conferred with suppliers and with Willys' own manufacturing people and ordered them to beef up the weak parts ASAP.

74 A report found in the files of Willys-Overland refers to a wartime effort to produce a Jeep without a carburetor. Exactly how that would have worked isn't mentioned, and I wonder if the test reports on that effort are stowed away in some obscure file at Jeep.

75 In addition to all of the Jeep vehicles it produced for World War II, Willys also produced 83,000 Go-Devil engines that were mounted and used as stationary power units and electrical generators. The company also produced the Robomb (rocket-bomb), which was the US Army's answer to the German V-1 and V-2 rockets.

The military chose the Willys Jeep MB to be the standard Jeep for the armed forces and contracted with Ford to produce them. The Ford units are dubbed GP-W (for General Purpose) Willys. The MBs and GP-Ws are nearly identical and were designed for easy shipping.

76 By 1952, the Go-Devil was once again out of date and in need of replacing. The new Jeep M38 (Willys MC) weighed about 2,750 pounds and fully loaded could weigh just under 2 tons, which is a very heavy load for 60 hp to pull. So, when the M-38A1 was being developed, increased horsepower was ordered.

Willys management was still extremely frugal with capital invest-ments and didn't want to shell out the money for an all-new engine, so it instructed its engineers to somehow squeeze more juice out of the aging Go-Devil. Willys' chief engineer Barney Roos and engineer A. C. Sampietro (Floyd Kishline had left the company) went to work on the little mill. Sampietro designed a new F-type cylinder head for the Willys mill that boosted output to 72 hp, another 20-percent boost.

77 Okay, so you're asking: What exactly is an F-head? It's an engine with one valve in the block, similar to an old-style L-head (or flat-head) engine, and one valve in the head, similar to an OHV engine. It provides much better breathing compared to a flathead engine and

thus more power. It's a relatively cheap way to boost power in an old-style engine.

78 The little Willys Whippet 4-cylinder engine, introduced for 1926, remained in production through at least 1971 for the United States, and even longer in export markets. It became the Go-Devil engine in 1938 after Willys' engineers went through it with a fine-tooth comb, ironing out all its bugs. Then it received another large power boost with the introduction of the F-head Hurricane version in the 1950s.

It was offered in nearly all of the postwar Willys vehicles. After Kaiser Motors took over the company, it was kept in production as the standard engine on all Kaiser Jeep CJ Jeeps, and even for the DJ-5 and DJ-6 models, as well as the Jeepster Commando series, despite it being sorely out of date by then. I asked a retired Kaiser Jeep vice president why the company continued to produce the hoary old Hurricane for so long when it was out of date, and he replied, "We did it simply because it was very cheap to make." Oh.

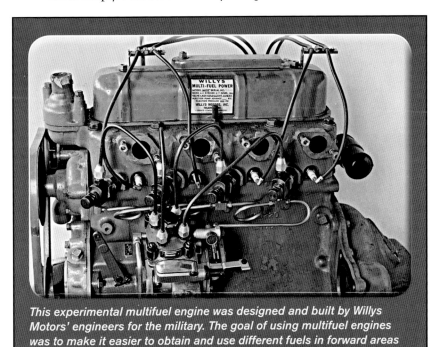

This experimental multifuel engine was designed and built by Willys Motors' engineers for the military. The goal of using multifuel engines was to make it easier to obtain and use different fuels in forward areas where gasoline might not be available, but diesel or kerosene was.

79 The 1950–1951 military M38 Jeep (also known as the Willys MC) still had the classic flat fenders up front but was given a stronger Spicer 44 rear axle and sturdy timing gears in the engine, rather than a timing chain as used previously.

80 Military Jeeps used a variety of engines over the years, but the most unique has to be the 3-cylinder Cerlist diesel engine fitted to the FC-based M-series Forward Control trucks. This unique engine produced 85 hp and 170 ft-lbs of torque and was fuel efficient and durable. The army chose them because they were also multifuel engines that could run on diesel, kerosene, jet fuel, or gasoline.

Suspension and Brakes

81 Initially, the main use that the army had in mind for the Jeep was to serve as a scout/combat car capable of carrying a 50-caliber machine gun into battle, along with at least 3,000 rounds of ammunition for it. Those were part of the army specifications. Because of the weight of the ammunition and gun and the kick of the gun as it was fired, the rear floor area of the Jeep had to be heavily reinforced to withstand the strain, and the suspension had to be beefed up to carry the weight.

82 The Jeep MB's axles were produced by Spicer, the same company that manufactured the transfer case and today is known as Dana Corporation. For the wartime Jeeps a Spicer Model 25 axle was used up front with a Spicer Model 23-2 in the rear. And talk about customer loyalty and longevity: To this day, Dana is still a major supplier of axles to Jeep.

83 Military Jeeps used a Ross Model T-12 cam and lever–type steering gear with a cam ratio of 14-12-14. Although early civilian Jeeps use essentially the same setup, these vehicles came with different tie-rod ends and a different mounting for the bell crank.

84 The military Jeep MB sat on a ladder frame that was built by Midland Steel, a company that was in business from 1893 to 2003. One of the easiest ways to tell a Willys MB from a Ford MB is to look at the front crossmember. The Willys Jeep used a round or tubular crossmember; the Ford vehicle used a U-section design.

85 Army Jeep brakes were four-wheel drums, 9x1.75 inches, mainly because disc brakes hadn't been invented yet. The parking brake was a drum type working on the transfer case. The brakes were supplied by Bendix, a reputable firm still in business today. Jeep wheels were ruggedly built steel 16x4.5 inchers fitted with 6.00x16-inch tires. Understandably, whitewall tires were not available.

86 The military Jeep's suspension was as tough as possible according to the engineering standards of the day and included heavy-duty semi-elliptic leaf springs at all four wheels. The vehicle's ride was stiff, to put it kindly, but suspension failures were rare.

87 To provide important extra strength and robustness to the Jeep's suspension system, heavy-duty anchor and shackle spring attachments were specified.

88 The Jeep MB maximum gross vehicle weight (GVW) was 3,250 pounds, and its maximum payload was 800 pounds. Surprisingly, in light of how small the Jeep was, the vehicle was rated to pull a 3,500-pound trailer at highway speeds, with a maximum drawbar pull of 900 pounds.

Numbers Crunching and Press Commentary

89 After testing the first few prototypes from Ford, Bantam, and Willys during 1941, the army decided to give each of the companies a contract for 1,500 more vehicles. The 4,500 total vehicles would be tested further, and a winner would be chosen that would receive the big contract everyone wanted: 16,000 Jeep vehicles. Apparently, more vehicles were ordered because in the end Ford built more than 3,500 of its GP prototypes (the exact

number is still debated); Bantam produced 2,674 of its MK II and its improved Bantam BRC-40; and Willys built 1,555 of its MA, making the Willys prototype (aka pilot cars) the rarest of the early Jeep vehicles.

90 According to company records, regular production of the Willys MA Jeep commenced on June 5, 1941, with serial number 78401; it ended on September 19, 1941, with serial number 79907.

A small notation to the records says that the company also produced serial numbers 85501 to 85550, which may be experimental units with four-wheel steering or some other low-volume prototype variation. They may also be Willys civilian pickup trucks beefed up for military duty because Willys was eager to sell the army its pickups, and it's known that a small number were built.

91 The contract that Bantam, Ford, and Willys were struggling to win was set at 16,000 vehicles. In the final round, Ford bid $782.59 per vehicle, Bantam came in at $788.32. Willys made the low bid of just $748.74 per vehicle. Despite presenting the lowest bid (and for a superior vehicle, no less), the Quartermaster recommended accepting the Ford bid! He claimed that Ford was the only builder that could deliver the vehicles in quantity and on time.

At this point, William S. "Big Bill" Knudsen, the former GM president who was now in charge of military vehicle procurement, stepped in and refused to accept the Ford bid, saying that in his opinion Willys was a competent source of supply for the vehicles, and he was not about to reject the low bid. Because Knudsen was considered to be the world's foremost authority on vehicle production (one of the reasons he was asked to oversee it for the military), the question was settled, and the contract went to Willys.

Within days, an additional 2,600 Jeep vehicles were added to the order with instructions that it had to be completed by January 18, 1942. War seemed ready to break out at any time, and the army was rushing to prepare for it.

92 A memo in Willys-Overland files provides the following information concerning the production of the Willys Model MB military Jeep:

- 1941 series production began on November 6, 1941, with serial number 100001.
- 1942 series production began on January 1, 1942, with serial number 108640.
- 1943 series production began on January 1, 1943, with serial number 199970.
- 1944 series production began on January 1, 1944, with serial number 293801.
- 1945 series production began on January 1, 1945, with serial number 402501.

When the Allies liberated Paris, they drove in triumphantly in Jeeps that were quickly thronged with grateful Parisians.

93 Once America became involved in the war, Ford Motor Company was given production contracts to supplement the vehicles being produced by Willys. Ford was instructed to produce a standardized vehicle using the Willys blueprints, so the Ford product,

previously known as the GP (General Purpose) was designated the GPW (General Purpose Willys).

Both Willys and Ford were allowed to supply vehicles to Allied forces. Huge quantities of Jeeps were shipped to Great Britain, Africa, India, and China; pretty much anywhere forces were fighting for freedom. More than 80,000 Jeeps were sent to Russia, which were used to spearhead the ultimately devastating mobilized campaign against the German army.

94 Company records indicate that during 1943, Willys-Overland produced 91,777 Jeep vehicles; of that total, 1,000 were special firefighter units.

The flag of free France flew again over the Eiffel Tower as victorious GIs liberated our oldest ally.

95 According to an official report issued by Kaiser Jeep Corporation, Willys-Overland Company and its successor companies' military Jeep production from 1940 through 1963 was as follows:

- Willys MA 1,800 vehicles built 1940–1941
- Willys MB 368,714 vehicles built 1941–1945
- Willys MC (aka M38) 60,345 vehicles built 1950–1952
- Willys MD (aka M-38A1) 90,529 vehicles built 1952–1963

That's a total of 521,388 Jeeps plus the two Willys Quad prototypes. Some reference sources claim the MD went out of production in 1955, not 1963. The memo referenced above may include M-170 models in the MD totals because the M-170 is basically a lengthened and reengineered Jeep MD.

96 Popular legend has it that Ford built more Jeeps during World War II than Willys did. You'll even see it stated as fact in many books, and I can't count the number of times people have told me this as fact. However, if you compare the numbers for 1940 to 1945, Willys produced 370,514 production models (MA and MB) while Ford built 283,767 units (GP and GPW). So Willys was clearly the leader.

97 Although the military Jeep MB quickly earned a reputation for being able to go anywhere, less is said about how fast it was. Top speed was reported to be about 60 mph, which doesn't sound very fast today, but it was considered outstanding back then, especially for a four-wheel-drive vehicle that was classified as a quarter-ton truck. Many civilian trucks had a much lower top speed, even 6-cylinder jobs with two-wheel drive. Earlier four-wheel-drive army trucks were lucky to do 40 mph. The Quad trucks of World War I topped out at about 20 mph. So it's no wonder the military was impressed by the little Jeep.

98 As things turned out, the Jeep arrived just in the nick of time. Willys MB production began on November 18, 1941. A mere three weeks later, Japanese bombers launched a sneak attack on the US Navy base at Pearl Harbor, Hawaii, even as representatives of the government of Japan were in Washington, supposedly negotiating

to prevent a war that they had already decided to start. The level of treachery and dishonesty that was displayed by the empire of Japan is unequaled in history.

99 Jeep vehicles were meant to haul military supplies to the front, so it's not surprising that there was a lot of demand for Jeep trailers during World War II. Several companies were contracted to produce them. Nash Motors built many, as did Bantam Motors. Willys-Overland built 78,731 Jeep trailers between 1942 and 1944.

100 In many books about Jeep history you see photos of the American Motors Mighty Mite, but you don't see it here. Why not? Because the Mighty Mite is completely unrelated to Jeep. It's not a Jeep and has no business being in a Jeep book. You also do not see the M-151 Mutt in this book because it too has no relationship to Jeep. The M-151 was designed and built by Ford (though Willys did build about 18,000 of them after underbidding Ford for a small contract). In fact, it was the M-151 that replaced the Willys Jeep during the late 1950s.

101 A lot of people don't know that optional equipment was offered even on the military MBs. The options included a 12-volt conversion kit for radio use, an arctic conditions kit, a hot weather kit, a front-mounted capstan drive winch, big 7.50-16 flotation tires, a deep-water fording kit, decontamination kit, and more. No, air-conditioning wasn't available.

102 One little "fact" that you often hear is that World War II Jeeps came in only one color: US Army Olive Drab. But that's not entirely true. The fact is, there were actually two more standard choices: US Marine Corps Green and US Navy Gray. In later years, the color palette for military Jeeps grew even larger.

103 Willys military Jeep production for World War II ended on August 25, 1945, with serial number 459841. Civilian production of CJ-2As began on June 16, 1945, which means that for two months Willys was producing both civilian and military vehicles. Neat.

104 One of the more interesting production years in military Jeep history is 1952. With the war in Korea, the military needed Jeeps fast. The new M-38A1 (MD) was coming into production alongside the outgoing M38 (MC). A production schedule found in Jeep's corporate files says that in 1952, Willys produced 22,561 MC Jeeps and 25,555 MDs, for a total of 48,116 military Jeeps for the United States. The company also produced 2,090 MCs and 750 MDs for the Canadian military.

105 For 1957, Willys introduced a new military vehicle: the M-274 Mechanical Mule. Basically a stripped and simplified chassis and platform, the Mechanical Mule was sold to military customers only as a low-cost alternative to a Jeep or a truck. By this point, Willys' military sales were very low and the company was trying to come up with new products to sell to the army.

106 The Willys XM-443 experimental platform vehicle is often confused by historians with the earlier M-274 Mechanical Mule, but they are completely different. The XM-443 was meant to be a

This experimental Jeep XM-443E was created as a supplement and/or eventual replacement for the Jeep MD. Willys Motors built a number of these vehicles, but the US Army declined to purchase them in volume.

direct replacement for the military Jeep M-38A1 and was created to compete with Ford Motor Company's M-151 Mutt. Although Willys built many of the XM-443s for testing and merchandising efforts, apparently none were sold to the military. It's not known if any have survived. When the army turned down the XM-443, Willys tried to interest several of its overseas customers, but to the best of my knowledge, none were ordered or built.

107 Once the M-38A1 was replaced by Ford's M-151 by the US Army, Kaiser Jeep Corporation continued to build small numbers of Jeep vehicles for military forces overseas. The company also began to offer production partnerships with various countries in which Kaiser Jeep and the client country arranged for local manufacturing of Jeep vehicles. Kaiser Jeep sold the clients all of the parts needed to build Jeeps and sent experts to help them set up local production.

Kaiser Jeep Corporation earned a royalty on each vehicle produced, as well as the profits on the parts kits. This business ended up being extremely profitable. In fact, it became more profitable than the civilian Jeep production for the United States.

108 Although many enthusiasts consider the M-422 Mighty Mite to be a Jeep, it's not. The same rule applies to the M-151 Mutt, except to note that Willys actually did build them for a short time. The M-151 was designed and originally produced by Ford Motor Company. Willys managed to underbid them on one contract in the early 1960s. Later, AM General began producing M-151s instead of Ford.

109 It's not known how many of the Forward Control–based M-series military trucks were produced, but one source claims about 3,000 in all, with 1,200 of them being powered by the Cerlist diesel engine and the rest using the Willys 226-ci 6-cylinder engine. According to legend, Kaiser Jeep had to go through its 226 engine to make it more reliable before the army would accept them in the M-series.

110 By 1964, Kaiser Jeep's US military business was tiny, so it purchased the military business of Studebaker Corporation, which had recently ended US car production. In one of the greatest deals of the 20th century, Kaiser Jeep obtained a newer plant in South Bend, Indiana, along with a contract to produce 9,369 5-ton tactical trucks, which was soon followed by a large order for 2½-ton trucks. For the first time, Jeep was building military vehicles other than Jeeps and Mechanical Mules and found them surprisingly profitable. The new operation eventually evolved into AM General, the largest tactical truck producer in the world.

111 In 1966, Kaiser Jeep Corporation added to its military business by winning a big contract to produce the M-715 series, designed to replace the ancient but respected M37 Dodge Power Wagon. Based on the civilian Jeep Gladiator pickup, the Kaiser

Once the market for Jeep M-38A1s had dried up, Willys Motors was able to continue as a major factor in military vehicles. In 1966, it showed off this M-715 military truck, which was based on the Jeep J-series Gladiator pickup. Produced in several versions, it was built from 1967 to 1969.

M-715 was offered in four basic variations: M-715 cargo/troop carrier, M-724 cab and chassis, M-725 ambulance, and M-726 utility body.

Rated at 1¼-ton capacity, it was nicknamed the "five quarter ton" truck by soldiers. It was powered by the Kaiser overhead cam (OHC) 6-cylinder engine, which gave decent performance, though the same engine did not do well in civilian vehicles, where it had a reputation for oil leaks and short life. According to popular stories, the military versions of the engines were built stronger and have improved sealing to eliminate oil leaks.

112 So how good was the wartime military business for Willys-Overland? Prior to the war, it struggled to survive. But from July 1941 to August 1945, Willys-Overland's gross receipts for Jeeps and Jeep parts totaled $464,963,926. That's an incredible amount for such a small company. It also sold the military some $60 million worth of 155-mm shells and $19 million worth of trailers. Willys also produced a great many other wartime products.

113 The Ford Mutt (aka the M-151) was a Jeep-like vehicle that the army began purchasing in the late 1950s. A unibody vehicle, it was lighter and more modern than the Willys, though it suffered from on-road handling problems. Ford thus stole the US Army business away from Willys Motors for a while, though for 1962, Willys successfully underbid Ford on its own product and won a contract to build 18,000 M-151s in Toledo.

114 Kaiser Jeep was a major player in the military vehicle business until 1970, when American Motors purchased the company and spun off the former military division into a separate company known as the General Products Division. In 1971, this entity was renamed and became incorporated as AM General. From that point on, any military vehicles produced by Jeep Corporation were incidental to the business. Jeep Corporation was to focus on civilian products and leave the military business to AM General. It did so, with a few exceptions.

From 1971 on, the military vehicle business was produced by a spin-off company called AM General. However, even then, Jeep produced small numbers of military vehicles from time to time, as this 1978 militarized CJ-5 illustrates. It is one of 65 produced for the US Army.

115 One of the most unusual military Jeeps of all time is the 1970s era DJ-5 Dispatcher in military trim. Essentially a postal Jeep in military garb, it was pitched as a low-cost staff car, rear-area dispatch carrier, and military police vehicle. Powered by the American Motors 232-ci 6-cylinder, it was fitted with a 3-speed automatic transmission. It could be ordered with left- or right-hand steering.

116 Another unusual military Jeep was the CJ-10A. A short, squat, little Jeep built for the air force to tow planes around airfields, the CJ-10A was essentially a short-wheelbase version of the export-market CJ-10 pickup and was built in limited numbers. You still see them around, and occasionally one comes up for sale.

117 So, whatever became of Jeep's military business? As noted, in 1970 it was spun off as the General Products Division, then in 1971 was renamed AM General Corporation. AM General is still in business as a privately owned company and is headquartered in South Bend, Indiana, the old hometown of Studebaker's military business. AM General's best-known product today is the military Humvee, which comes in many variations.

118 Want to have a laugh? Watch the otherwise outstanding war movie *Patton*, starring George C. Scott. Although mostly accurate, you quickly notice that some of the World War II Jeeps are actually postwar models that were repainted Olive Drab. The producers probably hoped you wouldn't notice.

119 *Popular Science* magazine came up with 1,001 possible peacetime jobs for the Jeep. Having had to come up with 1,001 facts about Jeep for this book, my sympathy goes out to them!

120 Despite claims of "Surplus Jeeps Selling for As Little As $25," the actual selling prices of most surplus Jeeps averaged $400 to $600, according to an article written by US Army Lieutenant Colonel Manuel Conley. The key words in any selling headline is "As Little As," because the ones that sold for that amount (assuming any actually were, which I doubt) were probably only good for scrap.

121 I almost forgot the 2007 military Jeep J-8. It's easy to not know what a J-8 is because they were only produced in Egypt by a joint-venture company known as Arab American Vehicles (AAV). Originally set up in conjunction with American Motors, AAV produced the Wrangler and the prior-generation Cherokee for Middle East markets. Its original purpose was mainly to produce military vehicles for the Egyptian army. Originally it assembled the CJ-6, but it expanded in later years to other models, including a brawny version of the Jeep Wrangler TJL series (long wheelbase) called the J-8 (aka J8 MILSPEC). The neat thing about them is that they offered unique models such as an ambulance, pickup, and extended-wheelbase two-door.

Willys and Kaiser Jeep Wagons, Pickups, Forward Controls, and FJs

Legend and Lore

122 When it came time to begin designing new civilian vehicles for the postwar era, Willys had neither a design office nor any staff to do the work; just a few men in the engineering department who had some experience in design. Because of this, industrial designer Brooks Stevens from Wisconsin was given the job of creating the designs for the postwar lineup, although he got it almost by accident. He'd written a magazine article presenting ideas for postwar Jeep-based civilian vehicles, and by chance Willys-Overland's vice president of engineering Barney Roos saw the article. Roos had been worrying about finding a designer, and it was clear that the war would be over soon, so he contacted Stevens and, after an interview, put him on retainer to design new vehicles for Willys-Overland.

The first all-steel station wagon from an American producer was the 1946 Willys Jeep station wagon. Designer Brooks Stevens was instructed to keep the body lines flat and shallow. The steel sides were painted to resemble wood.

123 Prior to the war, Willys hadn't produced the bodies for its American automobiles; it had purchased them from an outside supplier to save the cost of tooling and body-making machinery. Because of that, there wasn't an easy way for the company to

go back into production when the war ended. Ford and General Motors owned their own body-building companies, so they got back into production fairly quickly. But in Willys' case, the independent companies that produced automobile bodies weren't interested in working for such a small firm when they could easily get more lucrative contracts from bigger automakers.

This forced Willys to abandon the traditional passenger car business in favor of building something, anything, that it could produce on its own. For the time being, that would have to be the ex-military Jeep.

124 Willys management realized that the company couldn't survive for very long by building only the small Jeeps, so they put Brooks Stevens to work designing a series of new, larger vehicles. The first of the "senior" Jeep vehicles to be put into production was the Willys Jeep station wagon, introduced for 1946. The Willys wagon was quickly followed by the Willys Jeep Panel Truck, which was a station wagon with steel sides rather than windows and with a regular monotone paint job rather than the faux wood scheme used on the station wagons.

This Willys wagon is on the assembly line in Toledo, Ohio. This appears to be the body-drop section of the plant.

125 People are often surprised to learn that all of the 1946 Willys Jeep station wagons and panel trucks are two-wheel drive only. Folks naturally assume that anything called a Jeep must have four-wheel drive. Nope. Willys management realized that, at that time, the market for four-wheel-drive vehicles was much smaller than the market for conventional cars, and they did their best to convince people that the Willys Station Wagon was simply a family car with utilitarian styling.

126 The third new senior Jeep model to be introduced was the Willys Jeep pickup truck, which was offered initially as a 1/2-ton model with two-wheel drive, or as a 1-ton four-wheel-drive model. Each of these trucks were powered by the Go-Devil four-banger engine.

127 At first, Willys tried to emphasize the Willys-Overland company name for the wagons, rather than the Jeep brand. This was partly because it wanted to maintain Willys as a viable brand name in the event that it reentered the passenger car market (which

These new Jeep vehicles are coming off the assembly line and ready to be driven to a storage lot.

management certainly planned to do as soon as it was possible). And this was partly because at the time the company felt that the public would only accept the Willys Universal (aka CJ-series) as a "real" Jeep. However, in time, the immense popularity of the Jeep brand convinced Willys to refer to its senior vehicles as Willys Jeep station wagons and trucks, which it did successfully.

128 Have you ever wondered why the postwar senior Jeep vehicles look the way they do? It wasn't by accident; designer Brooks Stevens was instructed to keep the body lines flat and shallow, with no complex curves or deep-drawing shapes. The president of Willys-Overland at the time told him to design body panels that could be stamped out in a refrigerator factory because there was no other steel pressing equipment available.

129 Although many enthusiasts consider the Willys postwar station wagon to be a truck, the company usually referred to it as a passenger car. It was hard for management not to compete in the traditional car market. After all, the company had once been the number-three automaker in the world. Management wanted to keep a toe in the passenger car business at any cost, realizing it would help them when they were finally able to add passenger cars to the product line.

130 Many enthusiasts and historians believe that Willys came up with the idea of putting four-wheel drive in its station wagon all by itself, but that's not the case. During 1948, the US Army asked Willys management if they could design, engineer, and build such a vehicle. The military was even then looking for more four-wheel-drive vehicles for various jobs that the MB couldn't perform. In response, Willys engineers produced a prototype four-wheel-drive wagon for the army.

Although it doesn't appear that the army thought enough of it to ask for more (in other words, offer a production contract), Willys felt the concept was a good one and rushed it into production for 1949. It gave the company and its dealers another product to sell, something that had no real competition.

As a direct result of building an experimental four-wheel-drive station wagon prototype for the US Army, Willys was able to introduce a new four-wheel-drive wagon for 1949.

131 Regardless of what anyone may say, the first sport utility vehicle (SUV) was the 1949 Willys Jeep 4x4 station wagon. It was built from the ground up as a family station wagon, and it came with factory-installed four-wheel drive. It was engineered for hard off-road driving. In light of the immense size of the worldwide SUV market today, the Willys Jeep four-wheel-drive station wagon is one of the most historic vehicles on the planet.

132 When the Willys Jeep pickup debuted in late 1947, it was offered in five basic versions: bare chassis, cab and chassis, pickup, box truck (with a box bolted on), and platform stake truck. These were available in a two-wheel-drive 1/2-ton version or as a 1-ton version equipped with four-wheel drive.

Do trucks get any prettier than this? The 1956 Willys Jeep 1-ton pickup was a sturdy beast and ruggedly handsome.

133 The next line of senior Jeep vehicles to appear were the Forward Control (FC) models. The first of these, the FC-150, arrived in December 1956 as a 1957 model. The FC-150 pickup was rated at 5,000 pounds gross vehicle weight (GVW) and was based on a beefed-up CJ-5 chassis. It rode an 81-inch wheelbase and had a close-coupled pickup body. Power was supplied by the Willys Hurricane 4-cylinder engine.

Willys Motors went out on a limb, style-wise, when it introduced the Jeep FC-150 (the FC stood for Forward Control). With a short CJ wheelbase and a 4-cylinder F-head mill, it was built for difficult work, mainly off-highway.

134 The next FC model to arrive was the FC-170 pickup truck, which was built on a much longer 103.5-inch wheelbase and powered by the sturdy Kaiser-Willys 226-ci 6-cylinder engine. The FC-170 pickup came with a long cargo bed.

The FC-170 heavy-duty pickup, introduced for 1957, boasted a longer wheelbase and larger engine than the FC-150 series. All FC trucks produced in the United States were four-wheel-drive units.

135 Both FC models were also offered in cab-and-chassis and cowl-and-chassis versions so that buyers could arrange to have any sort of specialty body installed on it. Many went into service as farm trucks and tow trucks.

136 The rarest civilian FC trucks are the FC-170 Dual Rear Wheel versions, which were produced for just three years in the United States. For 1959, the factory produced just 335 of them; for 1960 it built 402 units; then for 1961, another 320 were built.

137 The best year for FC truck production in the United States was 1957, when 6,637 FC-150s and 3,101 FC-170s were produced in the Toledo factory, for a total of 9,738 FC trucks built during the calendar year.

138 Although they were never especially popular in the United States, the Jeep Forward Control truck models ended up being one of the longest-lived Jeep vehicles in production. The reason for that is that after being produced from 1956 to 1965 in the United States, the tooling was sold to Mahindra & Mahindra, a Jeep affiliate and assembler in India. That company produced many FC variants over the ensuing decades, including a very popular bus model that was in production into the late 1990s, for the local market.

139 Mahindra & Mahindra expanded the FC truck model range to include an FC-160, FC-360, and FC-460, along with a passenger bus, cargo van, paddy wagon, ambulance, and army personnel carrier. Production continued in India into the 1990s, and sales brochures often appear for sale on eBay. They are quite an interesting collectible item.

140 Willys was always looking for ways to grow its sales volume without incurring much tooling expense. In that spirit, in 1961 the company began producing the Willys Jeep FJ-3 Step Van for the US Post Office, which used the small trucks for mail delivery. The FJ-3 chassis was essentially a two-wheel-drive DJ-5 modification, and to save the cost of tooling the body was produced by an outside company, Highway Products, in Ohio. A larger-body van was sold through Willys Jeep dealers as the Jeep FJ-3A, and these were popular with package delivery firms and laundry companies.

141 Jeep manufactured the FJ-3 chassis at its plant in Toledo, Ohio, and then shipped them to Highway Products' small factory. Highway Products then installed the van body on the chassis and arranged for delivery to the US Post Office or, in the case of an FJ-3A, to a dealer.

The FJ line of commercial vans was available in two series. The FJ-3 was a short-body unit built for the US Post Office; the FJ-3A (seen here) had a longer body and was pitched to commercial users such as package delivery, florists, dry cleaners, etc.

142 By 1966, a new version of the FJ series was introduced, dubbed the FJ-6, which was followed by the slightly modified FJ-6A in 1967. These vehicles are much less common today than the FJ-3 models, and they appear to have been sold exclusively to the US Post

Office. Nowadays both the FJ-3 and FJ-6 are collected by people who love the unusual. Sadly, many of them have been hot rodded or heavily modified, which is a shame considering their rarity.

143 Most people don't know it, but the FJ series wasn't the only Jeep-based van. During the 1960s, Jeep's Spanish affiliate, a company by the name of Viasa, produced a line of unique Jeep vehicles that included a panel van, passenger van, and van-based pickup. The bodies were tooled and produced locally, and they look like no other Jeep product ever produced. Picture a Ford Econoline, only bigger, squarer, and much-sturdier looking.

This is a nice, circa-1957 Jeep 1-ton pickup in its natural environment: off-road.

Body and Interior

144 As mentioned earlier, the first of the "senior" Jeep vehicles to be produced was the station wagon. Designed by Brooks Stevens, it generated quite a bit of talk within the industry because it was the first all-steel station wagon. Prior to its introduction, station wagons had used expensive, hand-built wooded bodies, and thus the vehicles were priced at where usually only people with high incomes could afford them. The Willys Station Wagon, in comparison, was priced at $1,495, undercutting the Chevrolet's $1,605 price; a big difference in

Here is the Willys wagon for 1948, showing no substantial change and still extremely popular today.

those days. That price differential continued: In 1947, the Chevy wagon was priced at $1,893 versus $1,616 for the Willys wagon; in 1948, the Chevy wagon was tagged at $2,013, compared to $1,645 for the Willys wagon.

Another price factor was that the Willys steel-bodied wagon required much less maintenance than the wood-bodied wagons, which had to be sanded, stained, and varnished on a yearly basis. More than 6,000 of the sparkling new Willys station wagons were sold during the first year of production.

145 One thing that traditional wood-bodied wagons had going for them was style; their gorgeous wooden body panels looked rich and elegant. To give its customers a good measure of that glamour, Willys treated every one of its new station wagons to a paint scheme that mimicked the look of wood paneling. The base paint job for the sheet metal was a pretty color called Luzon Red, which was a deep,

rich maroon. Then the factory applied crème paint in a pattern that imitated the look of pine wood borders, and the larger flat body sides were painted brown to imitate stained birch. The effect was terrific. It gave the Willys wagons a beautiful look at the price of a little paint rather than costly wood and varnish. And all the owner had to do to keep it looking nice was wax it every year.

146 The reason that the Willys wagon is so slab sided is simple: Willys had no body-stamping equipment so the automaker specified a design that could be stamped out on equipment used to make refrigerators. The actual depth of the "draw" was limited to a maximum of 4 inches. That specification eliminated the ability to stamp out deep fenders or complex shapes. Everything had to be shallow and simple, but the talented Brooks Stevens made it all look fabulous.

147 The Willys station wagon came only in a two-door model because that was the least expensive way to produce it and was also the industry custom for passenger wagons of the time. Years later, some of Willys' overseas affiliates added four-door versions of the station wagon, which were quite attractive and very useful, but none of these were ever offered in the United States. In time, Willys decided to invest in an all-new design, which became the Jeep Wagoneer.

The Willys Station Wagon for 1949 was still a very attractive vehicle with its wood-look paint job and rugged reliability.

148 The standard Willys station wagons were considered six-passenger vehicles: three on the front bench seat and three on the rear bench. An optional sideways-facing third seat could be ordered to make the wagon accommodate seven passengers. The rear seats are easily removed to allow more space for carrying cargo.

149 Although it is quite compact on the outside, the Jeep station wagon boasts a full 98 cubic feet of cargo room inside with the rear seats removed. The company bragged that you could use it to carry a broken washing machine or chair to the repair shop. Farm families especially appreciated the utility values of the station wagon, which could work on the farm all week and then take the family into town on Saturday.

150 The versatility of the Jeep station wagon body was truly remarkable. In its initial version it was a stylish family wagon, and then, with the side windows not cut out and with the rear seats

The two-wheel-drive Jeep panel delivery truck was an inexpensive and cheap-to-operate truck. This is a 1948 model.

omitted, it became a panel truck. With side windows, plain paint, and only the front seats installed, it was a low-cost utility wagon that contractors loved. It was later offered in ambulance and fire/rescue versions as well.

151 Although the list of available options for the Willys wagons was usually limited, it did include such dress-up items as front and rear bumper guards, wheel trim rings, whitewall tires, fog lamps, and a spotlight. A heavy-duty air cleaner was also available.

152 Although today we tend to think that the Willys trucks and wagons look rather quaint, when they first appeared they seemed marvelously new and modern. The prewar Willys trucks had looked like everyone else's trucks only smaller, and the wagons, while stylish, were small, wood bodied, and a little pricey. So, when the all-new Willys postwar vehicles debuted, they were like nothing else on the road. The public loved them.

153 Like many American cars and trucks of the time, the Willys senior Jeep vehicles came with vacuum wipers and a booster-type fuel pump to help them keep operating even when the engine was under load. However, on long hills the wipers do tend to slow down, and sometimes even stop. Let your foot off the gas for a second and they sweep once or twice before stopping again. It's a little tedious, but it only happens on steep hills, or if the vacuum motor is worn.

154 The 1946 Jeep wagons came in one color only: Luzon Red. With the 1947–1948 Jeep models, color choices such as Wake Ivory, Tunisian Red, Normandy Blue, Olive Drab Green, Manila Blue, and Mahogany Brown were introduced into production.

155 You may see old Jeep station wagons with a grille badge that includes either a "4" or a "6." This was used to identify the engine (i.e., a 4-cylinder or a 6-cylinder). This practice began during 1948 production.

156 Question: How do you turn a station wagon into a sedan? In the case of Willys, you do it with new paint and a different engine. In 1948, Willys-Overland introduced a new vehicle called the Jeep Station Sedan, which it described as ". . . a luxurious, comfortable, and beautiful passenger car . . ."

However, one look and you can easily see it was merely the carryover Willys station wagon with a monotone body paint offset by an attractive canework striped area on the upper doors and body sides, a fancier interior, and the new Willys 6-cylinder engine under the hood. A 3-speed plus overdrive manual transmission was standard equipment, along with a bright chrome T-bar overlaid on the grille. It looked very sharp, and with its 6-cylinder engine it could handle the highway better than the standard wagons. It was priced

This sales brochure for 1952 illustrates the canework body side trim available with the Deluxe station wagon that year. Willys customarily offered the wagon in a variety of trim levels in an effort to expand sales volume.

$245 more than the regular station wagon, and it probably didn't sell all that well. Have you ever seen one?

157 By sometime in 1949, what had been the Station Sedan was now referred to as the Station Wagon and was distinguished from the faux-wood wagon by unique paint with a contrasting side panel, along with its standard 6-cylinder engine. Willys often struggled with nomenclature as it tried to present the image of having a full line of vehicles.

158 Do you have difficulty identifying the year of a Jeep station wagon by sight? Here are a few tips that can help you: The 1947 and early 1950 models have a plain body-color painted grille and flat front fenders. The 1950–1953 models have five horizontal chrome grille bars and rounded, pointy front fenders. The 1954– 1963 models have three horizontal grille bars, all evenly spaced except for the 1956 models, which have two of the bars near the top of the grille and one bar near the bottom. Why only that one year? No one seems to know.

Willys-Overland had this interesting display outside its headquarters building in Toledo, displaying all the variations of the senior Jeep line.

159 Here's another way to help identify years: For 1951, Willys station wagons were given a wraparound rear bumper to replace the thin, straight-bar bumper previously used. The new bumper provided added protection for the rear body sides. It also enhanced the look of the vehicle, at least in my opinion.

160 People often wonder where the Forward Control (FC) Jeep's styling came from because it's so unusual. The designer was Brooks Stevens, who was still on retainer with Willys Motors. The styling was quite controversial at the time, with people either loving it or hating it. One magazine writer referred to it as "the Helicopter Look" because it vaguely resembled some of the military helicopters that were around at the time.

161 During the time he was busy creating the FC styling, Brooks Stevens envisioned a whole lineup of FC vehicles, including a short-wheelbase pickup, long-wheelbase pickup, delivery van, and family van/wagon that would have been the first minivan on the market. Only the two pickup trucks were produced for the civilian market in the United States. But as noted earlier, Mahindra & Mahindra added several other bodystyles built on the FC platform.

162 Any restorer of Jeep wagons or trucks knows that rust is usually a big problem. Part of the reason is that rust-retardant materials and spray applications of that era were not as robust as they are today.

Another problem is that Willys (and Kaiser) often tried to avoid the expense of tooling up for large stampings and instead used a series of smaller stamping and then weld them together. For example, they made a fender in two or three parts and welded them together. Although it looks fine when new, the first rust to show on a Jeep is usually wherever those welded parts meet because moisture seeps into and on the unprotected metal and starts the cycle of corrosion.

163 From 1947 to 1964, Willys offered a variety of special-bodied Jeep wagons and trucks. A buyer could order a cargo box for the back of the pickup or a service body fitted with various lockable storage compartments. Rack bodies and stake bodies were also

offered. From 1955 to at least 1961 a special Cargo Personnel Carrier vehicle was available, with an open cab and 10-passenger personnel carrier body fitted with sideways-facing seats.

164 The first Jeep to wear the "Commando" name wasn't the 1967 Jeepster; it was a factory-built fire truck on the Willys truck chassis. Featuring an open cab (the factory simply cut the roof off), it was fitted with a 500 gallon-per-minute pumper along with a heat exchanger to keep the engine cool while sitting stationary at fires. These vehicles were produced in small numbers from 1955 to about 1961.

165 Jeep also offered two distinct ambulance models based on the senior models. The first was a conversion of the standard panel delivery truck, with litters and medical supplies fitted into the rear area, and a rooftop vent installed to keep things cool inside. The second version was fitted with a much larger custom body produced by Mil-Ner that featured a raised roof and much more interior space.

166 One special version of the Willys wagon was the Hy-Rail produced from about 1949 to 1957 by Fairmont Railway Motors (the company is now known as Harsco Rail with vehicles sold under the Hy-Rail name). It was fitted with special steel wheels to enable it to be driven on railroad tracks by maintenance crews. The body was really special: It was converted to four doors! It's not known how many were produced, but the company is still in business.

167 Another interesting Jeep variation is the 1954–1955 Economy Delivery, a stand/drive delivery truck of the type used by bakeries, florists, and package delivery companies. The Willys Jeep Economy Delivery was powered by the 72-hp Hurricane 4-cylinder engine, and it featured a large, tall, and roomy body built by an unknown outside vender.

168 Countless other variations of the Willys Jeep wagons were built around the world. A 1955 US-market catalog illustrates two types of truck/wrecker that were offered in the truck line, either

of which used the standard Willys truck bed rather than a special platform, which was an important money-saving feature.

169 The Willys Jeep FC-170 was one tough truck even in standard form, boasting a 7,000-pound GVW and a curb weight of 3,490, meaning it could carry just over 3,500 pounds of cargo. And it could be ordered beefed up to haul even heavier loads.

170 How's this for the ultimate Willys truck option: an integrated backhoe. The factory offered it, and with it, a Jeep truck could easily dig a 12-foot hole. The digger was able to swing 160 degrees and offered load buckets up to 36 inches wide. The backhoe weighed 2,250 pounds, so it must have slowed the truck considerably. The trucks were fitted with beefed-up cooling systems to handle the heavy work. These vehicles are rarely seen today, but some have survived in the hands of dedicated Jeep collectors.

171 If you look closely at the cabs on Jeep Forward Control trucks, you notice that some of them have rear quarter windows and some don't; the panels just aft of the doors are plain sheet metal. Those quarter windows are part of the Deluxe Cab option, which also included dual sun visors, armrests on both doors, cowl trim, foam rubber seats, a cigarette lighter, and front panel kick pads. The Custom Cab option was a popular choice, so you see more FC trucks with it than without.

172 Forward Control trucks offered several body/chassis options including a stripped chassis, with full drivetrain and steering but no body whatsoever, so a buyer could order a special body for it. One step up from that was a chassis and cowl option, which included the cowl, an instrument panel, and a windshield, but no body. A closed cab and chassis were also available. It's not known how many were produced.

173 For 1958, Jeep introduced a new version of the two-wheel-drive passenger station wagon that played off the name of the television show *Maverick*, which Willys Motors sponsored. The Jeep

Maverick Special was a two-wheel-drive Willys station wagon with a special two-tone paint job and some extra chrome trim, greatly upgraded interior trim, the 4-cylinder Hurricane engine, and a new semi-elliptic leaf-spring suspension system that was said to provide a much smoother ride. To improve handling, a front stabilizer bar was standard, as were four Captive-Air tires (and no spare tire).

The Maverick Special was priced at a bargain $1,895. Although most books say that the Jeep Maverick first appeared in 1959, it actually debuted in 1958 and was continued with minor changes in 1959.

The 1958 Maverick Special was a two-wheel-drive Jeep station wagon powered by the F-head 4-cylinder engine and fitted with nice interior trim. Note the smooth, high-dome roof panel.

174 The 1959 Jeep Maverick Special differs from the 1958 version mainly in the roof panel, which is flatter and ribbed on the 1959, versus tall and rounded on the earlier model. The base price was increased, to $1,995, although even then it still remained the lowest-priced full-size family station wagon on the market.

175 The Jeep Maverick name was dropped after 1959, but the series/model designation was continued in a series of stylish two-wheel-drive wagons that are identified by their attractive "missile" side trim and two-tone paint, along with fancy interior trim. Although the factory referred to them simply as the "two-wheel-drive station wagon," collectors today refer to these wagon as the "later Mavericks."

By 1960, what had been the Maverick Special was now simply the station wagon. The exterior trim was new, and the roof panel by now had been replaced with a flatter one with roof strengthening "bows" stamped in.

176 In 1960, Jeep introduced an interesting new model called the Jeep Traveler, which was a Willys station wagon body fitted with a conventional front seat and two sideways-facing rear bench seats. Interior trim was in the Traveler was plain, and a sideways-opening rear door was fitted. Aimed at hotels, resorts, and anyone else who needed to transport a number of guests to and from the train station, these unique vehicles were produced through 1964.

Engine and Drivetrain

177 The Willys Jeep station wagons and trucks never offered a fully automatic transmission, so don't bother looking for one. A conventional 3-speed manual transmission was standard equipment, along with overdrive. When looking to buy a vintage Jeep wagon or truck, always try to find one with overdrive so you can drive the vehicle on the highway. It still won't be quite fast enough for today's crazy traffic, but at least you'll have a fighting chance.

178 The engine used in the original senior Jeeps of 1946–1947 was the 134.2-ci Go-Devil 4-cylinder engine rated at 63 hp. To say that the senior Jeep was underpowered would be generous, but thankfully the national highway system hadn't been built yet, so average cruising speeds were still rather low. These vehicles today should probably not be taken on a major highway unless they have overdrive.

179 In late 1947, Willys introduced an L-head 6-cylinder engine for the two-wheel-drive wagons and panel trucks. The engine displaced 148.5 ci and produced just 72 hp, only 9 more than the Go-Devil 4-cylinder, but it offered buyers a little more torque and

The city of Pittston, Pennsylvania, included this circa-1951 four-wheel-drive Willys Jeep pickup in its fleet for service duty around the city.

much greater smoothness. Not having to work as hard as the four-banger, the new six was also much quieter.

180 Willys continued to offer only the 4-cylinder engine in its 1/2-ton and 1-ton pickups through 1948. This limited sales appeal because many buyers insisted on having a more powerful 6-cylinder engine under the hood of their new truck, and Willys couldn't provide that until late in 1948. Even then Willys seemed a bit stingy with them, always trying to push the low-priced 4-cylinder versions instead.

181 The new 148.5-ci 72-hp inline 6-cylinder engine introduced in late 1947 was the smallest 6-cylinder mill in America. Willys called it the Lightning Six, and it was a pretty decent little engine.

182 As noted earlier, when looking for a vintage Jeep wagon or truck to purchase, a good strategy is to find one with overdrive, since

This 1953 Willys Jeep Sedan Delivery is a handsome vehicle for a basic work truck, but not many have survived intact. Many were foolishly converted to four-wheel drive by later owners who didn't realize the value of an original, stock vehicle.

that will give you a fighting chance when you take it on the highway. A 6-cylinder engine with overdrive is the best choice by far. Don't bother trying to find a Willys Jeep with air-conditioning because it wasn't offered in the product lineup until 1964. By that point, Jeeps were no longer sold under the Willys brand name.

183 When sales of Willys-Overland vehicles began to slow dramatically toward the end of 1949, the company knew it had to do something to increase interest in them, as well as inspire its dealers to greater sales efforts. So, for 1950 it offered two series of Jeeps: The first series were basically carryover models that were essentially unchanged from the 1949 versions. The second series of senior Jeep vehicles, introduced in April 1950, received new, more powerful engines along with a few styling updates.

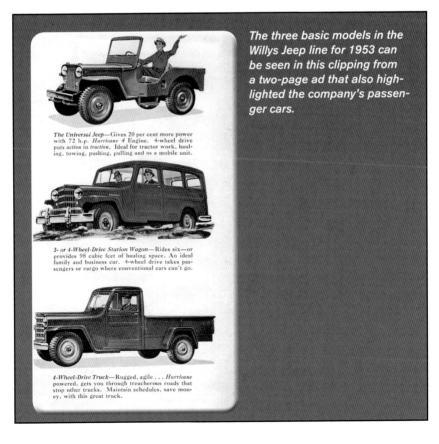

The three basic models in the Willys Jeep line for 1953 can be seen in this clipping from a two-page ad that also highlighted the company's passenger cars.

The Universal Jeep—Gives 20 per cent more power with 72 h.p. *Hurricane 4* Engine. 4-wheel drive puts *action* in *traction*. Ideal for tractor work, hauling, towing, pushing, pulling and as a mobile unit.

2- or 4-Wheel-Drive Station Wagon—Rides six—or provides 98 cubic feet of hauling space. An ideal family and business car. 4-wheel drive takes passengers or cargo where conventional cars can't go.

4-Wheel-Drive Truck—Rugged, agile . . . *Hurricane* powered, gets you through treacherous roads that stop other trucks. Maintain schedules, save money, with this great truck.

The Go-Devil four was replaced by the new Hurricane four, which offered 75 hp in the senior Jeeps, a lusty 20-percent increase. Because that number was actually higher than the horsepower of the Lightning L-head six, it increased that engine's displacement to 161 ci, while increasing output to 75 hp.

184 The last regular-production two-wheel-drive Willys pickup trucks were produced in late 1951, although it appears that some were built on a special-order basis in later years (probably built for fleet orders). The little Willys two-wheeler pickup had simply never caught on with the public, probably because there was so much competition in the light-duty pickup market. The Willys four-wheel-drive pickup, on the other hand, was almost the only four-wheel-drive light-to-medium pickup on the market for many years. It was attractively priced when compared to the aftermarket four-wheel-drive conversions offered by a handful of specialty companies.

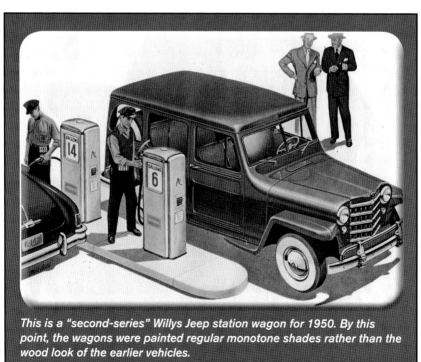

This is a "second-series" Willys Jeep station wagon for 1950. By this point, the wagons were painted regular monotone shades rather than the wood look of the earlier vehicles.

185 Willys panel truck models didn't receive a 6-cylinder option until 1951. Company executives viewed them as simple utility vehicles, driven mainly in town at slow speeds. To appeal to small businesses, Willys highlighted the 4-cylinder panel trucks' fuel economy and low purchase price, both of which were possible mainly with the 4-cylinder engine.

186 The F-head 134.2-ci 4-cylinder engine debuted in the 1950 Model 473 wagons with 75 hp, 5 hp more than in the Jeep Universal (CJ) series. This was possible because it was fitted with a different cylinder head that gave it a slightly higher compression ratio: 7.4:1 versus 6.9:1 in the Universal.

This photograph, taken March 30, 1950, shows legendary Willys Engineering boss Delmar "Barney" Roos with the new Willys F-head 4-cylinder engine.

187 One of the key benefits of Kaiser Motors taking over Willys-Overland was that it was able to introduce its own 226-ci 6-cylinder engine into the 1954 senior Jeep vehicles. The Kaiser 226, called the Super Hurricane, proved to be a better, stronger engine than the Willys six. It helped keep the senior Jeeps competitive power-wise for several more years. In later years, the Kaiser 226

mill was the basis for the Willys Tornado-OHC (overhead cam) 6-cylinder engine, which was introduced as an option in some of the 1962 Jeep senior models.

188 Designed and originally built by Continental Motors, the Kaiser Super Hurricane 226-ci engine was rated at 115 hp (40 hp more than the Willys six) and a very impressive 190 ft-lbs of torque.

189 Civilian versions of the Jeep Forward Control models offered two engines: The FC-150 series came with the 72-hp Hurricane four and the long-wheelbase FC-170s came with a 105-hp version of the 226-ci Super Hurricane six.

190 For the 1962 model year, Willys Motors introduced the new 140-hp Tornado-OHC 6-cylinder engine for the senior Jeeps (the station wagons and pickups). It was a historic engine, the first mass-produced overhead cam six from an American producer. It was powerful and reliable, although it tended to suffer from oil leaks, at least initially.

191 In scientific tests, Willys Motors was able to prove that the Tornado-OHC 6-cylinder engine was also the most fuel-efficient six on the market, based on a comparison of fuel economy per cubic inch of engine displacement. The combination of high horsepower and superior fuel economy made the Tornado-OHC six perhaps the most remarkable 6-cylinder engine from an American company since the Hudson Hornet with its 308-ci flathead six.

192 Although it debuted in the 1962 senior Jeep models, the new Willys Tornado-OHC six was actually designed for and became standard equipment on the all-new Wagoneer, Gladiator, and Panel trucks, which were being readied for introduction with the 1963 model year.

Willys management realized that the larger, new J-series vehicles would need a much more powerful engine than the basic Kaiser 226 mill. This same potent OHC six was later used in the Jeep M-715 series military trucks as well.

193 How's this for a standard axle ratio: 5.38:1! That was the standard ratio for the Jeep FC-150 series trucks, and it was needed because of the low horsepower rating of the 4-cylinder engine, the only engine offered on the FC-150 series. Because of its standard 6-cylinder engine, the more powerful FC-170 line of trucks came with a 4.88:1 axle ratio, which was still a rather high numerical gear set.

194 Like the Willys wagons and trucks, the FC truck series never offered an automatic transmission, even as an option. The first Jeep to offer an automatic transmission was the all-new J-series Wagoneer, Gladiator, and Panel trucks.

Suspension and Brakes

195 When it comes to chassis specifications, the postwar Willys senior vehicles hold few surprises. Brakes were non-assisted drums all around, and their size was 10x1.75 inches on the 4-cylinder station wagons and 11x2 on all trucks and 6-cylinder station wagons. Although they were more than adequate in their era, you have to be careful when driving a senior Jeep on the highway nowadays because they can't stop nearly as quick as a vehicle with modern four-wheel power disc brakes. It's something to keep in mind while cruising the highway: Always leave yourself plenty of room for stopping. Never tailgate, because if the driver in front of you goes into a panic stop, you probably won't be able to avoid rear-ending him or her.

196 The front suspension used on the first-generation two-wheel-drive senior Jeep wagons and trucks was an independent type of suspension called Planadyne. Designed by Willys chief engineer Barney Roos, it used a seven-leaf transverse-mounted spring. It was relatively cheap to make, durable as hell, and simple to service. It also worked very well.

197 The wheelbase measurement for the Willys station wagons was 104 inches until 1955 and 104.5 after that. Interestingly, 104 inches is the same as the 1941–1942 Willys American. Yes, the postwar senior Jeep chassis was based on the prewar chassis, although

beefed up and improved. There's no reason why it shouldn't have been done that way, since the initial senior Jeep vehicles were two-wheel-drive just like the prewar vehicles. Besides, Willys management was always loath to invest in new tooling if they could reuse existing tooling. It's one of the many ways that the company kept its costs down and its profits up; a necessary thing when you're a small automaker in a land of giant automakers.

198 Even though the initial Willys station wagons were offered as two-wheel-drive vehicles only, Willys-Overland engineers provided them with plenty of ground clearance because it was expected that many of the vehicles would be sold to farmers, who would drive them off-road and through fields. The Jeep station wagons have a generous 8.25 inches of clearance at the rear axle, which is more than many SUVs have today.

199 The four-wheel-drive Willys trucks were rated as 1-ton units, and the company referred to them as heavy-duty vehicles; the two-wheel-drive trucks were rated as 1/2-ton units, and the

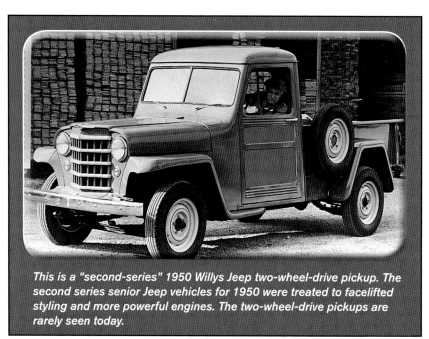

This is a "second-series" 1950 Willys Jeep two-wheel-drive pickup. The second series senior Jeep vehicles for 1950 were treated to facelifted styling and more powerful engines. The two-wheel-drive pickups are rarely seen today.

company referred to them as medium-duty vehicles. Either of them could be purchased in different gross vehicle weight (GVW) ratings via optional springs and heavier-duty suspensions.

200 The Willys Jeep Forward Control trucks were fitted with Bendix 11x2-inch brakes with a total braking area of 176.5 square inches. The standard parking brake was a lever and cable type that worked on the rear brakes, although a driveshaft parking brake was available as an option.

201 The 1957 Forward Control FC-170 truck sales catalog lists the standard axles as being the Hotchkis type, with a full-floating axle situated up front and a semi-floating type of axle out back. Front load capacity was listed as 3,700 pounds; the rear was rated at a hefty 4,500 pounds. So even in their base, standard form, the FC-170s were tough, rugged trucks.

202 Willys added a line of two-wheel-drive trucks for 1948, with GVWs of 4,700 and 5,300 pounds. These bore the industry classification of "medium-duty" trucks. The company didn't offer a lighter-duty truck until 1949, when a line of two-wheel-drive 1/2-ton pickups debuted.

203 Willys engineers preferred the Ross type of cam and lever steering systems. They considered them rugged and simple, and that's how the FC trucks came. The overall steering ratio was 32:1, and power steering was never offered by Willys on the FC series trucks.

204 Hefty tires are important on any trucks, especially ones that are designed for hard work and heavy loads. The standard tires on the FC-150 were 7.00x15 four-ply; the FC-170 used hefty 7.00x16 six-ply tires. Other sizes were available as a factory option to suit any kind of load or work situation.

205 During most of the years of their production, the FC-170 trucks offered the greatest standard ground clearance of

any vehicle in the Jeep product line (a very generous 8.9 inches of ground clearance). They were built for rugged duty on- and off-road, and many of them were put into service with construction companies and contractors.

Numbers Crunching and Press Commentary

206 Willys-Overland sales volume (or gross income) fell dramatically in 1946, to just over $60 million, compared to the 1945 sales volume of $179.3 million. That was an almost two-thirds drop in pay, and the reason was that in mid-1945, orders from the US military for Jeeps, rockets, and other war materiel slowed dramatically when it became obvious that the war was drawing to a close.

In many cases, especially after Germany surrendered, existing defense contracts were canceled or the order volume was drastically reduced. During 1945, the company also struggled to get its civilian vehicles into production to replace the reduced volume of wartime business for Jeeps, landing gears, rockets, trailers, etc. In July 1945, Willys was producing both civilian and military Jeep vehicles on the same assembly lines, although the volume of civilian production was very low.

207 In the first two years after the end of World War II, Willys-Overland could sell just about every Jeep Universal CJ-2A it could build, because pent-up demand for civilian vehicles was so tremendous. Company officials realized that once supply caught up with demand, however, the market for Jeep Universals would slow considerably. Thus, they hurried to put the new "senior Jeep" wagons into production so they would have something new and profitable to sell. They were able to overcome shortages of sheet metal and vehicle parts and components in reasonable time. Production of the all-new Willys station wagon was commenced on July 16, 1946, starting with serial number 10001.

208 It's a good thing that Willys decided to introduce the new family station wagon, commercial panel truck, and pickup truck models because in 1949 production of the Jeep Universal

CJ models, which was running at a pace of more than 60,000 per year in the three years prior to 1949, fell to just 31,491, which was an almost 50 percent drop. Without having the larger Jeep models to sell, Willys-Overland would in all probability have gone out of business. By auto industry standards it was still a small company, although it had grown considerably during the war years.

209 How many times can the name of a company change? The answer is as many times as the ownership of the company changes hands. In the case of Jeep, the owner changed on numerous occasions.

For example, from 1953 to 1963, the Jeep's parent company had three different names. First it was Willys-Overland. After Kaiser Industries took over the company in mid-1953, new owner Kaiser Motors changed the name to Willys Motors. In mid-1963, the Kaiser people decided to change the name once more, to Kaiser Jeep Corporation. In earlier years, the company had also been known as Willys-Overland Corporation and Willys-Overland Motors.

210 Standard equipment on the 1946–1950 Willys station wagon included an ashtray on the dashboard, two ashtrays in the rear seat area, front and rear interior lights, two sun visors, armrests front and rear, dual horns, and safety glass all around. Believe it or not, many of these things were considered options on some other vehicles. During the 1950s especially, cars and trucks were advertised in "stripped-down" form at a really low price, but most buyers knew they would have to spend hundreds more on options and accessories to bring the vehicle to the point that they could enjoy it.

211 With a mere 63 hp and just 105 ft-lbs of torque trying to propel a vehicle with a curb weight of 2,925 pounds, you are certainly not going to be setting any speed records or lighting up any tires. The station wagons (and the Jeep trucks) tend to be a bit leisurely going, to put it kindly. It's no fault of the vehicle; it was designed for the roads and highways of the era, which moved at a much slower pace than today's traffic. On the popularity of the Willys wagons, trucks, and CJs, the company was able to reach as

high as number four in sales of US vehicles in export markets, a strong addition to America's trade balance, and a healthy addition to Willys profits.

212 At the end of World War II, Willys' new president, James Mooney (a former GM executive), took a dim view of the postwar economy. In 1946, he predicted that high taxes, along with materials shortages and high inflation, were going to make the postwar era a time of struggle for all American families. Postwar conditions, he said, ". . . will pinch average family budgets and force retrenchment of spending in many directions." This led the company to focus on its 4-cylinder vehicles rather than 6- or 8-cylinders. So, when America instead experienced the greatest growth in its history, the Willys vehicles were out of touch with what the majority of new car customers wanted power-wise.

213 Have you ever wondered why you don't see many of the handsome 1947 Willys Jeep trucks? It's because fewer than 5,000 of them were produced that year. According to company records, just 2,642 of the two-wheel-drive trucks and 2,346 of the four-wheel-drive units were produced for the 1947 model year. Because of the way they were used and the rough roads on which they were driven, these trucks tend to have much lower rates of survival than the station wagons, so very few of them still exist. Certain parts for them are also difficult to find.

214 For 1951, Willys-Overland introduced three colorful new station wagon models. The Grand Canyon was painted Canyon Glow brown with gray accents, and the interior came fitted with Weskit Check fabric in maroon and gray trim.

The Jamaica station wagon was painted two shades of Jamaica Green, with Jamaica Green tattersall weave upholstery.

The Caribbean wagon was painted Caribbean Blue with attractive contrasting Potomac Grey body bands and an interior in blue Weskit fabric.

215 During 1953, Willys-Overland celebrated its 50th year in business. Would you like to know how Willys CEO Ward Canaday celebrated the historic event? He sold the company for just over $60 million to Henry J. Kaiser, the owner of Kaiser Industries Corporation and Kaiser Motors (formerly known as Kaiser-Frazer Corporation). Mr. Kaiser offered Canaday an executive position with the company, but Canaday declined. He kept the Willys-Overland name and used it as a sort of real estate trust for himself and some of his friends. Kaiser renamed its Kaiser Motors subsidiary Willys Motors.

The US Post Office purchased a fleet of two-wheel-drive Jeep station wagons to use as delivery vehicles. Built with right-hand steering, they would seem to have made an ideal delivery vehicle, but the Post Office never reordered them, eventually switching to the larger Jeep FJ-3 post vans.

216 Always looking for ways to innovate during 1953, Willys introduced yet another pioneering vehicle: the four-wheel-drive panel truck. At the time, panel trucks were considered simple work trucks that were bought for the lowest price possible and used around town for light delivery duties. However, Willys managers had realized that construction companies, oil companies, utility companies, and many others often needed a hauler that had the ability to go anywhere it was needed, on- or off-road, and thus the 4x4 panel truck came into being. It was never a big-volume seller, but it was a highly profitable vehicle for the company.

217 Henry J. Kaiser needed to acquire Willys-Overland in order to prop up his own failing Kaiser-Frazer Corporation, one of the large independent car companies in the postwar era. As noted previ-

ously, Kaiser renamed the firm Willys Motors. Although the Kaiser car went out of production two years later, the Willys Jeep vehicles helped the company to survive, albeit under the Willys Motors name. This wasn't the last time a car company was saved by Jeep.

218 The well-loved Willys station wagon remained available to US consumers at least through the 1962 model year, when it was mostly replaced by the Wagoneer. Production continued in Toledo, although after 1962 most of the vehicles were shipped to overseas markets.

219 Despite the oddball styling, the automotive press generally loved the new FC pickups, viewing them as rugged, fresh, and innovative. Unfortunately, the FC's styling didn't catch on with the buying public, and the FCs were rather slow sellers.

220 The Willys 226 OHC six that was introduced on the 1962 Willys senior models was so powerful compared to the prior six that *Four-Wheeler* magazine dubbed it "Willys New 140-Hp BOMB." The engine had really been developed for the Wagoneer and Gladiator vehicles that were introduced toward the end of 1962 as 1963 models.

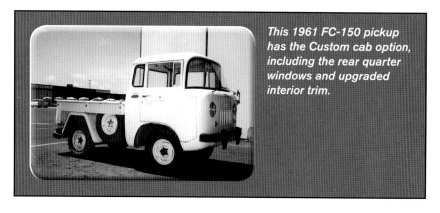

This 1961 FC-150 pickup has the Custom cab option, including the rear quarter windows and upgraded interior trim.

221 The Jeep FC series was built in the United States through the end of 1965, at which time the line shut down and tooling was sold to Mahindra & Mahindra in India.

Jeep CJs and DJs

Legend and Lore

222 The first postwar "civilian" Jeep was a modified military Jeep MB that was put into production in mid-1945. It was the first Willys vehicle for sale after the war; the larger (or senior) Jeep station wagons and trucks came later.

To create the civilian Jeep Universal CJ-2 prototype, Willys engineers simply pulled a military Jeep MB off the assembly line in June 1944 and modified it with the various improvements and enhancements that they thought most civilian users wanted. The spare tire was moved off the rear panel and onto the vehicle's side, and a small tailgate was cut into the Jeep's rear panel. Moving the spare tire thus reduced the Jeep's overall length by 9.5 inches.

The civilian CJ-2A Jeep went into production in mid-1945 and was a modified version of the World War II Willys MB.

223 Willys-Overland assembled at least one CJ-1 Jeep prototype (probably more) before incorporating a series of improvements that resulted in a vehicle dubbed the CJ-2. It's believed that at least 40 of these CJ-2 "preproduction" civilian Jeep vehicles were produced between 1944 and 1945; some were built as experimental projects, some as pilot line models, and the rest as preproduction vehicles.

224 One of the rarest Jeep vehicles of all time is the AgriJeep (not to be confused with the later Farm Jeep). The AgriJeep was an early preproduction model that is easily identified by the unique brass nameplates that were affixed to the hood sides. These ultra-rare vehicles were probably given the name AgriJeep during the time when management was still thinking of marketing the post-war Jeep CJ primarily as a farm vehicle. Many suggestions for various other uses were sent to Willys by people who were interested in purchasing a Jeep vehicle after the war. In addition, experimentation by Willys engineers eventually proved that the Jeep Universal was suited to many more tasks than first thought.

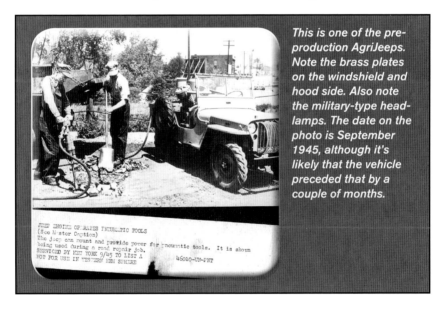

This is one of the pre-production AgriJeeps. Note the brass plates on the windshield and hood side. Also note the military-type headlamps. The date on the photo is September 1945, although it's likely that the vehicle preceded that by a couple of months.

225 In mid-1945, Willys-Overland engineers made a few more changes to the Jeep CJ-2 preproduction vehicles, including a switch to standard-size headlamps. Voila! The new production Jeep CJ-2A was born. Some 1,824 of these vehicles were produced for 1945. But if you look at early postwar Willys Jeep press photos and at least one of the early sales folders, you see that they show a CJ-2 fitted with the small headlamps rather than the larger ones used in production. This is another example of Willys trying to save a buck.

226 One of the enduring urban legends is of the "Jeep in a Crate." In this myth, someone knows someone who found a company that had bought a warehouse load (or shipload, or etc.) of brand-new war-surplus military Jeep MBs that are literally "still in the crate" with each part coated in Cosmoline to protect it from rust. Supposedly the purchase price was super cheap, on the order of $50, because the Jeep was in pieces and, not only that, before you could even begin to assemble the thousands of parts that went into the vehicle you had to clean off all that sticky Cosmoline.

I've heard this story told in countless variations, always by someone who knew a guy who knew someone. The problem is, so far no one has stepped forward to say he or she knows where the Jeeps are, or that they actually bought one that way. Of course, we know that the Jeeps were *not* shipped disassembled to the last part, nor were they all coated in Cosmoline. The wartime Jeeps were shipped either completely assembled sans tops or were in crates with only the wheels, tires, tops, and a few other parts attached. Many of the mechanical parts did have a coating of light oil to prevent rust.

227 The US Army did arrange to have Jeep vehicles shipped in crates, broken down to just a few large parts and components. The actual assembly was relatively easy, and some of the photos in my files show the Jeeps being assembled on beaches and desert areas, hardly the types of places where you would try to put together a vehicles that is in thousands of pieces.

228 Another Jeep legend, about the postwar era, and which is mostly true, is the one about some people who bought a new Jeep plow vehicle just before a snowstorm and earned enough money by plowing during the storm to pay for the Jeep. That's probably a bit of an exaggeration, but a person could almost do it, providing the storm was extra severe and long lasting.

In any case, it was very common for people in the 1950s and 1960s to earn more than a full payback in their first winter of plowing, and that says a lot.

229 In 1951, Willys introduced a specialty model called the Farm Jeep. It was a civilian CJ with farm attachments that included a factory-installed hydraulic lift, a drawbar, heavy-duty suspension, and an engine governor. Other options were available. If you go looking to buy a vintage Farm Jeep (they are very rare and hard to find), don't be taken in by ordinary CJs that have been equipped with aftermarket hydraulic equipment. To make certain you're looking at the real deal, check the vehicle identification number (VIN). A genuine Farm Jeep can be identified by its special serial number prefix 451-GC1.

230 Another Willys vehicle that also debuted in 1951 was the Jeep Tractor. Built for work in the fields, it was a CJ that was stripped of lights, windshield, front shock absorbers, spare tire, tailgate, speedometer, and even the horn; all items that were considered to be unnecessary for the sort of work the Jeep Tractor was designed for. It had factory-equipped work equipment that included a power takeoff, hydraulic lift, governor, heavy-duty suspension, and front bumper weight. The Jeep Tractor was meant for off-road use only. Not many of these vehicles were sold.

231 Somewhere along the line the famous "Jeep Wave" was born. To do it, you leave your thumb on the steering wheel while you lift your fingers to give a quick little wave to an oncoming driver in a Jeep. But please note, the Jeep Wave is limited to Jeep CJ and Wrangler vehicles only. If you happen to be driving a Patriot or Compass or any other jeep that's not a CJ or Wrangler and try to give the Jeep wave at a person in a Wrangler, that driver might give you a one-finger salute in return. You've got to understand: It's a Jeep Thing.

232 Not surprisingly, many famous people have owned Jeep vehicles over the years. One of my favorite Jeep enthusiasts was President Ronald Reagan, who kept a well-used and slightly battered Jeep CJ-6 for his personal use on his California ranch. President Reagan kept that CJ-6 until it got so battered that his wife, Nancy, bought him a new CJ-8 Scrambler to replace it.

President Ronald Reagan was a longtime Jeep owner and enthusiast, and for many years he drove this well-worn CJ-6 on his ranch in California. Eventually, his wife got tired of seeing him driving such a battered vehicle and bought him a new Jeep Scrambler.

233 Do you remember Roy Rogers, the singing cowboy of television and movie fame? He and his wife, Dale Evans, owned a classy little CJ that they called *Nelly Belle,* which they kept on their ranch. It even had the name *Nelly Belle* painted on the front.

234 Here's a good trivia question for you: When is a Jeep not a Jeep? Answer: When it's a Ford Jeep! In 1967, Ford Motor Company bought Kaiser Jeep's Brazilian subsidiary, Willys-Overland Brazil (WOB), which by that time had become the largest automaker in South America. Willys-Overland Brazil produced Jeep vehicles and Aero Willys cars. (After Willys car production in American was ended in 1955, the company shipped the automaking tools and dies to its Brazilian affiliate, which began producing an updated model of the Aero Willys cars). After Ford Motor company took over WOB, its Jeeps were renamed Ford Jeeps and continued to be marketed that way until Jeep Corporation bought back the rights to the name many years later.

235 Do you remember the television program *Mork & Mindy?* In the show, Mindy drove a beautiful Jeep CJ, and the vehicle appeared in the opening credits and in some episodes of the show. It was that popular TV show that made young comedian Robin Williams a household name.

Remember the **Dukes of Hazzard?** *Everyone dialed in to catch a glimpse of Catherine Bach.*

236 Another famous Jeep enthusiast was Cincinnati Reds baseball great Pete Rose. In 1979, he went into a Jeep dealership and bought 10 Jeep CJs. He gave most of the Jeeps to members of the team and kept one for himself. That's what you call class.

237 As a longtime Jeep salesman in the 1970s and 1980s, I can recall telling many prospective Jeep buyers that "Nothing can kill a Jeep, except rust!" During the 1960s and especially in the early to mid-1970s, the factory rust protection on the Jeep CJs was essentially two coats of paint and a prayer. The dealership where I worked was located in New England, where they use a lot of salt on the roads during winter, and rust-through was a big problem for all vehicles, but especially Jeeps. Because of this, we sold a lot of aftermarket rust-proofing jobs and undercoating.

The 1977 CJ-5 Renegade was one of the most popular vehicles in the Jeep lineup.

238 Willys-Overland and successor Willys Motors had some pretty interesting chief engineers over the decades. The first one was Delmar "Barney" Roos, the man who studied the basic Bantam design and then created his own version that was tougher and more powerful. Roos was also the man who oversaw the complete redesign of the prewar Willys Whippet 4-cylinder engine that transformed it into the sturdy and spectacular Go-Devil engine that powered the World War II army Jeeps.

After Barney Roos came A. C. (Achilles) Sampietro, nicknamed Sammy Sampietro. He created the F-head design for the Willys 4- and 6-cylinder engines, and he's also credited with engineering the Forward Control Jeeps, along with the legendary Jeep Wagoneer and Gladiator lines that debuted in late 1962.

239 Perhaps the greatest Jeep chief engineer was my friend the late Roy Lunn, who joined American Motors in 1971 with the mandate to reengineer and modernize the existing Jeep line. Previously

Lunn had worked for Ford Motor Company, where he assembled and directed the team that designed the fabulous GT40 racing cars, which were the Fords that won at Le Mans, beating Ferrari and all the other European makes that had for so long dominated that race.

After he went to American Motors, Lunn created an entirely new chassis to install under the Wagoneer and Gladiator truck models. He also created the engineering that allowed Jeep Corporation to introduce a new line of engines, transmissions, and the incredible Quadra-Trac four-wheel-drive system in the 1970s.

240 Let's take a look at one statistic that illustrates just how low Jeep had sunk in the US retail market: During the 1969 calendar year, Kaiser Jeep Corporation sold about 37,000 Jeep vehicles in the United States. Even that tiny number was trending downward in spite of the fact that the four-wheel-drive market was rapidly expanding, with a promise to continue to do so. Ford, Chevy, International, and Dodge were all doing well in the four-wheel-drive market while Jeep was losing its once-strong hold.

The problems were many, but they were mainly centered on the fact that Jeep vehicle engineering and technology had been allowed to become old and stale, and also because the Jeep retail network of dealers was small and weak. Once American Motors took over in 1970, it began to offer Jeep franchises to its existing dealers, who were much stronger financially than most of the old Jeep dealers, and retail sales began to grow. It took time to reach a profitable level of sales, so the civilian side of the Jeep business continued to lose money until 1972, when it finally turned the corner.

241 The Jeep XJ-001, built on an 81-inch-wheelbase CJ-5 chassis, was introduced in April 1970. It was an exciting concept vehicle that envisioned a small Jeep two-seat four-wheel-drive sports car powered by a V-8 engine, a fiberglass body, and full-time four-wheel drive. Designed during 1969 by Kaiser Jeep Styling under Jim Angers, it might have reached production if AMC hadn't bought the company during 1970.

Unfortunately for fans of the XJ-001, American Motors had no interest in producing it because the concept vehicle didn't fit into

AMC's product plans for Jeep. The only existing Jeep XJ-001 prototype was accidently destroyed while being transported to an auto show. The truck that was carrying it was involved in an accident, rolled over, and caught fire. Burned beyond repair in the fire was the XJ-001.

242 In 1976, Jeep Corporation unveiled an additional model in the Jeep CJ series: the CJ-7. Built on a longer 93.5-inch wheelbase, the CJ-7 boasted a much larger door opening, allowing passengers easier entry and egress, along with enough chassis length to allow engineers to fit an automatic transmission and full-time four-wheel drive underneath. These two moves opened up CJ ownership to a vast new group of people who either didn't know how to drive a manual transmission or simply preferred the convenience of an automatic. Being equipped with full-time four-wheel drive also eliminated the annoying need to exit the vehicle to switch the front hubs.

The 1976 Jeep CJ-7 was an addition to the CJ line and replaced the CJ-6 in the US market. The longer wheelbase provided room for an optional automatic transmission as well as larger door openings and greater interior room.

243 Years ago, I spoke with a highly placed American Motors product planner who had worked on the CJ-7 program. He

told me that the people involved in creating the CJ-7 considered it to be a replacement for the Jeep Commando more than anything else because, like the Jeep Commando, the CJ-7 was a more civilized Jeep aimed at families rather than traditional off-roaders. It retained the feel of the classic CJ-series but allowed modern conveniences to be offered.

244 Over the years, Willys-Overland and its successors have produced the CJ-2A, CJ-3A, CJ-3B, CJ-5, CJ-5A, CJ-6, CJ-6A, CJ-7, CJ-8, and CJ-10 models. You probably noticed that two numbers are missing: the CJ-4 and the CJ-9. The company actually produced one or two CJ-4 prototypes, but thus far no information has surfaced about a possible Jeep CJ-9, even in prototype form.

While researching this book, I spoke with two former heads of Jeep styling, and neither recalls any CJ-9 program, nor can they say why the company skipped that number before going on to produce the CJ-10.

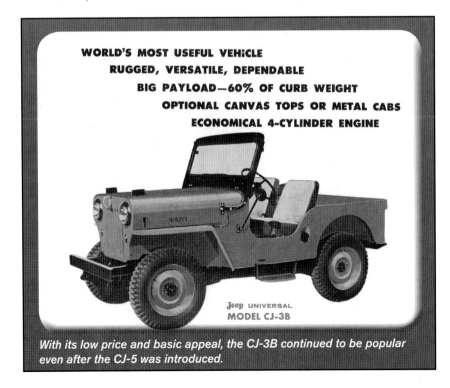

WORLD'S MOST USEFUL VEHiCLE
RUGGED, VERSATILE, DEPENDABLE
BIG PAYLOAD—60% OF CURB WEIGHT
OPTIONAL CANVAS TOPS OR METAL CABS
ECONOMICAL 4-CYLINDER ENGINE

Jeep UNIVERSAL
MODEL CJ-3B

With its low price and basic appeal, the CJ-3B continued to be popular even after the CJ-5 was introduced.

245 The Jeep CJ-4 was a prototype program that began in June 1951 when a new experimental vehicle was hand-built by Jeep engineers to create a platform that could offer improvements to the Jeep vehicle, especially increased power from a new engine. The CJ-4 combined a CJ-3A body tub with flat fenders that were rounded and curled at the edges, along with a tall, rounded hood that looked much like that on a CJ-5.

This development program was an early effort to modify the CJ-3A enough to fit a Willys F-head 4-cylinder engine under the CJ Universal hood in order to provide the extra power that Jeep customers were beginning to demand. In the end, however, the company developed and produced the M-38A1 for the military and settled on building the new CJ-3B for civilians. The CJ-3B received the new F-head engine, but the vehicle's styling was less integrated than that of the CJ-4. The even-more-improved CJ-5 civilian Jeep came later, at the tail end of 1954.

246 Okay, so you want to know what a CJ-10 is? It was a modified Jeep CJ cab with a hardtop that was mounted on a Jeep J-10 pickup chassis. It was produced from 1981 through at least 1983 almost exclusively for overseas markets. A unique styling feature was that the headlamps were rectangular and mounted in the fenders rather than in the grille, which gave the vehicle a more massive, rugged appearance. The CJ-10 was developed mostly for the Australian army, which placed orders for them. Seeing an opportunity to expand its civilian model range, Jeep Corporation decided to go into regular production of the CJ-10 for export markets, and apparently it was fairly successful. In Australian brochures it was called the One-Tonner.

247 Jeep Corporation also produced a shortened version of the CJ-10 powered by a Nissan diesel engine. These were built in small quantities for the US Air Force, which used them as aircraft tugs. Because they were used stateside, you see them for sale every now and then, and the prices are still reasonable.

248 Jeep reportedly also offered a CJ-10A model, which was a two-wheel-drive version of the CJ-10. This model was also reserved for overseas markets, primarily in Asia and Pacific areas. Why Jeep didn't introduce the CJ-10 in both two- and four-wheel-drive versions to the US market is a mystery; it probably would have outsold the aging Jeep J-10 and J-20 by a large margin.

249 A civilian Jeep that you probably never heard of is the CJ-7 Llanero. Built in Venezuela during the 1980s and sold only in that country, it featured a stepped steel roof with a sideways-opening rear door and two sideways-mounted bench seats in the rear that enabled it to carry six passengers, with four of them seated out back and the other two seated up front. For many years, Jeep vehicles were manufactured in Venezuela for the local market, which they dominated, often having 50 percent or more of all four-wheel-drive vehicle sales in that country. It appears that Jeeps are no longer produced in that country.

250 After World War II ended, Philippine automobile mechanics began fixing wrecked and abandoned army Jeeps and using them as taxis around Manila. The vehicles, which came to be known as Jeepneys (probably meant as a play on the slang Jitney or taxi), proved to be so popular with the public that owners began to lengthen the vehicles to carry more passengers. Eventually all the surplus, abandoned, and wrecked Jeeps in the Philippines were used up, so Sarao Motors started building new Jeepneys. The company continued in business for many years before finally ceasing production. Today, the Jeepney is a national symbol of the Philippine Islands, just as the Checker cab is a symbol of New York City.

251 Perhaps the rarest Jeep in the United States is a special Philippines Jeepney built for American Motors CEO Roy D. Chapin Jr., who arranged for AMC to purchase Jeep from Kaiser Industries. During a visit to Jeep Philippine operations, Chapin purchased a new Jeepney body and had it shipped to the United States, where his engineers placed it on a new custom-built Jeep chassis. This is what you do when you have the money.

252 Another overseas CJ is the Jeep Renegado, which is a CJ-5 Renegade built in Mexico during the 1980s by Jeep affiliate Vehiculos Automores Mexicanos (VAM). The hood lettering on it says "Renegado." Jeep Corporation's Venezuelan affiliate also built a Renegado model for the local market.

253 You may be wondering what exactly a Jeep CJ-8 is. It's the official model designation for the Jeep Scrambler pickup, produced for the US market from 1981 to 1985. In overseas markets, the CJ-8 was also offered in a hardtop model called the World Cab. It could be ordered with sideways-facing rear bench seats to carry up to six passengers plus two up front.

This is President Ronald Reagan with his circa-1982 Jeep Scrambler SR, a big improvement over the old CJ-6 he formerly used.

254 Another popular version of the CJ-8 was the CJ-8 Van, which looked similar to the World Cab but without the windows in the rear section of the cab. It was produced as a cargo truck that could haul loads anywhere they were needed.

255 Legend has it that Jeep CJ-3Bs and CJ-5s are still being produced in certain overseas markets. That's not entirely true, but it's also not entirely false either. India's Mahindra & Mahindra, a longtime Jeep affiliate that produced Jeep vehicles under a license and royalty agreement, built small vehicles that were based on the CJ-3B and CJ-5 into the 1990s. Today, the company offers the Mahindra Thar, which looks very much like a Jeep CJ-5/CJ-7 and is powered by a common-rail diesel engine.

256 When the new Jeep CJ-7 model debuted for 1976, many long-time Jeep enthusiasts disliked it because it didn't have the "traditional" scooped-out door opening or offer luxuries such as automatic transmission, power steering, power brakes, or air-conditioning. However, the public in general went ape over the new Jeep, and before very long Jeep CJ sales took off like a skyrocket. In a surprisingly short time, the CJ-7 outsold the CJ-5. At the same time, CJ-5 sales maintained their regular sales pace, so most of the sales of CJ-7s ended up being additional volume for Jeep Corporation.

257 Because the original Willys Jeep CJ-5 had been announced in late 1954, American Motors chose to celebrate its 25th anniversary during 1979. To do so, the company marked the event by

Having been introduced in late 1954, by 1979 the CJ-5 celebrated 25 years in production. American Motors marked the occasion with this Silver Anniversary CJ-5 with special paint and trim.

announcing a special limited-edition Silver Anniversary CJ-5 painted in a unique and special silver paint that was not offered on other CJs, along with black and silver striping, and special interior trim. One of the Jeep designers who worked on the team that created the Silver Anniversary CJ-5 told me that all of them were produced in Jeep's Canadian plant because the Toledo plant was unable to paint that particular shade of silver. I've not been able to verify that.

258 Speaking of special Jeep vehicles, in 1982 Jeep introduced a one-year-only special model to commemorate the 30th anniversary of the legendary Jeepers Jamboree off-road event that travels the Rubicon Trail in Northern California. It's one of the toughest but most scenic and exciting off-road trails in America. The Jeep Jamboree edition featured Jamboree hood decals, a special black-vinyl spare tire cover with the Jamboree logo on it,

Jeep celebrated the 30th anniversary of the Jeep Jamboree with this special-edition CJ-7 model. Painted Topaz Gold, only 2,000 were produced.

special Topaz Gold paint, custom interior trim with gold accents, chrome-styled wheels, chrome front bumper and rear bumperettes, padded roll bar with saddle bags, Ramsey winch, AM-FM-stereo CB radio, off-road driving lights and overhead lights, a fire extinguisher, grille guard and brush guard, and much more. Only 2,500 of these special Jeeps were produced, and for some reason, Jeep Corporation never produced another Jamboree edition.

259 Introduced in late 1954, the Jeep CJ-5 was finally dropped from the US market after the 1983 model year. The official reason that it was discontinued was to reduce complexity in the company's production lines, because the new Jeep Cherokee and Wagoneer XJ series vehicles had debuted. However, a more likely reason is that it was a result of lawsuits resulting from a series of rollover accidents involving CJ-5s in which people were killed or seriously injured. The ensuing bad publicity caused a slowdown in CJ sales. There was also a huge amount of bad publicity as a result of doctored road test results that were documented by the *60 Minutes* television program. The high-end Jeep CJ-7 Limited model was dropped at the same time, mostly because it had proven to be a very slow seller.

260 You might remember a 1977 Jeep concept vehicle called the Concept Jeep II that debuted in 1977 as part of an American Motors traveling road show called Concept 80 and wonder why that cute little Jeep was never produced. It was a small CJ vehicle that was similar in appearance to the CJ-3A and was powered by a small 4-cylinder engine (it probably would have used a Renault engine) for maximum fuel economy. I saw it in person at its New York unveiling and sat in it with American Motors vice president of design Dick Teague, who was very excited about the project. The reason that the little Jeep wasn't put into production is simple: Extensive market testing revealed that traditional Jeep buyers *hated* it. They felt that it was too small and toylike; that it looked too "cutesy"; and they also wanted a much bigger, more powerful engine.

Body and Interior

261 To create the first postwar Jeep vehicles, the engineers at Willys-Overland had to create a new grille in order to fit the larger civilian-type headlamps. They settled on the now-classic seven-slot grille, discarding the MB's nine-slot opening. The headlamps were flush-mounted rather than recessed, as in the MB.

262 The initial run of CJ-2A production models were fitted with headlamp rings that were body color (probably due to the shortage of chrome in the postwar era). But during 1946, the switch was made to bright rings, giving the little Jeep a dash of style and pizzazz.

263 Willys management realized that most buyers of the postwar Jeep vehicles were purchasing them for their utilitarian value. With that in mind, the company developed a range of work-use attachments and options for the new Jeep. The CJ-2A offered the following options:

- Draw Bar
- Rear Power Takeoff
- Front Power Takeoff
- Hand-operated Windshield Wiper (yes, you read that right)
- Engine Governor
- Two-passenger Rear Seat
- Front and Rear Soft Tops
- Inside Rearview Mirror
- Radiator Screen and Brush Guard
- Front Bumper Bar Weight (to act as a counterweight when the vehicle had a heavy rear attachment or was used as a farm plow)
- Engine Oil Filter (although this might seem unusual, having the oil filter as an extra-cost option was actually a standard industry practice at that time)
- Pintle Hook
- Spare Wheel, Tire, and Carrier (again, this was not unusual in the American truck market at that time)

- Heater
- Front Passenger Seat (this remained an option into the 1970s!)
- Engine Starting Crank
- Propeller Shaft (aka driveshaft) Weed Guard

264 The new Jeep CJ-2A was changed in detail to better suit civilian requirements. The side-exiting MB muffler was replaced by one that exited behind the rear wheel. The "ranger tool" indents in the body were eliminated as of serial number 29500. Most electric components were sourced from Auto-Lite, a major Jeep supplier for years.

265 The Jeep CJ-2A was the first model with a seven-slot grille, which would become a style mark of Jeep vehicles and was eventually trademarked by American Motors. The Jeep grille shape, with seven slots, is protected by law from being copied. Several companies have come up with similar-looking grilles but made sure to keep them legal by using five or six slots rather than copying the seven-slot design.

This 1947 CJ-2A was restored to original condition some years ago and fairly represents the CJ-2 series vehicles. Note the gas tank under the seat.

266 The postwar Jeep CJ-2A was considered an open roadster and didn't come with any sort of top as standard equipment. However, most people ordered one of the optional tops. In the early days, that would have included a full soft top or half soft top, both made of a sturdy, waterproof duck material.

267 Here's an interesting tidbit: The original Jeep CJ-2A came with a single stop/tail and license light on the left rear of the vehicle and a reflector on the right rear.

268 Early Jeep CJs came with a fairly comprehensive tool kit that included a screw-type jack, a 6-inch screwdriver, 6-inch combination pliers, a socket wrench for the lug nuts, spark plug wrench for servicing the engine, and even an oil can with a bracket mounted on the dashboard.

269 Not surprisingly, among the first changes to "civilian-ize" the MB was to install more comfortable seats, which had come in for major complaints during the war and to offer a choice of body colors. For 1945, two paint colors were offered, and both of them had a farming theme: Harvest Tan and Pasture Green.

270 To maintain interest in its new product, in mid-1946 Willys began to offer even more color choices for the CJ-2A, adding Harvest Red, Michigan Yellow, Normandy Blue, and (due to popular demand, believe it or not) Olive Drab Green.

271 The civilian Jeep CJs also switched from a fuel fill under the driver's seat to a fuel filler that was situated on the driver's body side, in the space where the entrenching tool used to reside. This was a much safer spot for it and made it easier to fill the tank.

272 To clean up the Jeep's interior a bit and help make gear shifting easier, the postwar Jeeps initially came with a column-mounted shifter for its 3-speed manual transmission. However, this modern feature was dropped in early 1946, and the floor shifter was reintroduced. This may have been done due to customer demand for the floor shifter.

273 As noted earlier, optional equipment offered in the postwar Jeeps included a rear pintle hook for towing trailers and pulling farm implements. You could specify either a single pintle or a double pintle hook, depending on the equipment.

274 One popular 1950s Jeep option that took up most of the rear seat area was an arc welder that was powered by the optional power takeoff. With this equipment and a portable power source, a welder could work on welding jobs far off the highway, in places such as oil fields, coal mines, farms, and construction sites.

275 Jeep got away with things that were not acceptable to ordinary automakers. One example is the Jeep's exterior bodywork. For most years of production, the finish on CJ and DJ vehicles was not up to ordinary automotive standards, with rough weld jobs that often produced noticeable warping on adjoining body panels, along with sloppy joint welding, mounds of excess weld material in corners, and more. There was nothing inherently bad about this (it didn't affect the durability or capability of the vehicle), but to anyone accustomed to the usual Grade A autobody finish, it seemed unsightly. I recall as a young Jeep salesman pointing out these "defects" to my boss, who looked at me as if I were a dummy and replied, "It's a Jeep. You don't worry about those things." Oh.

276 Need an easy way to distinguish a CJ-3A from a CJ-2A? One way is to look at the windshield; if it's a single pane of glass and has air intake vents on the panel underneath, it's a CJ-3A. If it has two panes of glass and no vents, it's a CJ-2A. Got it? Another obvious identifier is the windshield wipers. They're mounted at the top of the windshield on the CJ-2A and at the bottom of the windshield on the CJ-3A.

277 Ever hear of a Hotchiss Jeep? These were essentially modifications of US models and were assembled in France by Hotchiss-Delahaye. Hotchiss was a longtime munitions manufacturer that was founded in the United States and later moved operations to France, while Delahaye was a proud French luxury car builder. The company assembled several different Jeep models for

civilian and military use from the 1940s to the 1960s that wore a Hotchiss emblem in the upper grille most years.

278 Because the Jeep CJ-2A came with a standard fold-down windshield, Willys engineers mounted the wiper motor on the upper part of the windshield. And talk about utility: On the first Jeeps, only the driver's side was powered. As mentioned earlier, the passenger-side wiper was an option and had to be manually operated by the passenger using a small crank.

279 In Spain, you might spot some really odd Jeep vehicles, including a 1975 CJ-3B with a 4-cylinder diesel engine. Or you may see what they called a CJ-6, which was really a lengthened CJ-3B that was also diesel powered. To confuse things, at the same time there was also a CJ-6 that looked just like the US model CJ-6.

280 Willys offered an interesting pair of Jeep specialty vehicles for 1955: the CJ-5 Crash Wagon, which was outfitted with a 40-gallon foam-type fire extinguisher, a 50-foot hose, a handheld

Jeep offered a fully equipped fire truck through its dealer network. Based on the CJ-2 chassis, it targeted airports, large factory complexes, and small towns that couldn't afford a regular fire truck.

foam fire extinguisher, and a CO2 type of fire extinguisher. Created to serve as a firefighting vehicle in hard-to-reach locations such as forests or construction sites where water wasn't available, the Crash Wagon was also sold to airports, oil refineries, and industrial plants.

Also offered during the 1955 model year was the CJ-3B Jeep Fire Engine, which came with a 200-gallon tank trailer, ladder, and other equipment. It was a low-priced alternative to buying an expensive fire engine and was marketed to small towns and factories.

281 A 1955 Jeep catalog shows two interesting options for the CJ-5. One was a heavy-duty mobile air compressor that took up so much interior space that the only seat left was the driver's seat. The package included a separate 4-cylinder engine to provide power to the air compressor, along with a big air storage tank. Also offered, as mentioned earlier, was a 300-amp mobile arc welder for welding jobs out in the field.

Introduced in late 1954, the all-new CJ-5 was roomier, better styled, and better riding than previous Jeep CJs.

282 One thing you have to admire about Willys Motors is the way that it economized on tooling, and how it squeezed every last dollar out of it. Years after the CJ-3A body was out of production, the company brought it back as the two-wheel-drive DJ-3A and used the long-in-the-tooth basic Go-Devil 4-cylinder engine as the power source. The automaker built these vehicles into the 1960s!

283 Want to know how Willys was able to get top dollar for a plain vehicle such as the DJ-3A? The company

This 1959 Willys Jeep DJ-3A Surrey was especially designed for resort use and as a family beach car. These vehicles are very much sought after by collectors today.

dressed up some of them with a pink paint job and added a matching striped canopy top and front and rear seats. That was the formula for the Jeep Gala, which was sold in Mexico and Caribbean markets. After it proved to be successful in those foreign markets, it was introduced to the US market as the Jeep Surrey. They were also offered in blue or green with matching interiors and tops.

284 When the Jeep CJ-5 appeared at the end of 1954, it was a revelation. Here was a Jeep Universal that actually had real style. In addition to being very attractive, the earlier Jeeps were entirely functional. In fact, their appearance came about mostly as a result of their functionality. The CJ-5 had full, rounded fenders and a stylish hood; it was plainly the result of some hard work on the part of the Willys designers.

The Willys MD (aka CJ-5) was based on the military Jeep M-38A1. Here it is undergoing field testing by a Willys Motors technician.

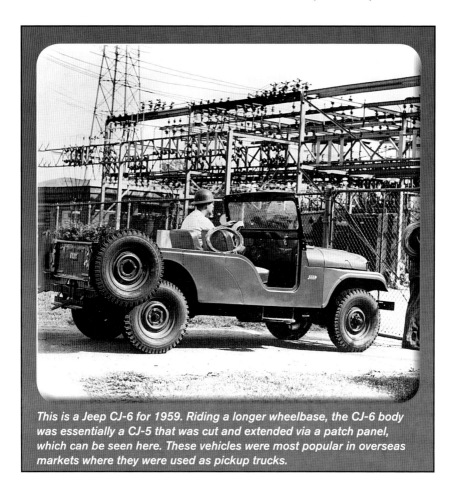

This is a Jeep CJ-6 for 1959. Riding a longer wheelbase, the CJ-6 body was essentially a CJ-5 that was cut and extended via a patch panel, which can be seen here. These vehicles were most popular in overseas markets where they were used as pickup trucks.

285 For 1956, Willys Motors introduced the CJ-6, which was essentially a CJ-5 on a 20-inch-longer wheelbase. These models appealed to customers looking for increased cargo space. They were especially popular in overseas markets where they were usually sold as a pickup truck with a half cab, either of steel or fabric.

286 To create the longer CJ-6 body, Jeep engineers welded sheet metal panels between the scooped-out door opening and the rear wheelhouse. They are easy to spot when you look at them. Although not as sturdy or attractive as a one-piece body side stamping would have been, this was a much less expensive approach than tooling up for a one-piece side.

If you're in the market for a vintage Jeep, you probably won't want to consider this 1958 CJ, which has been modified to operate as a lavatory service truck for airliners. During the year, Jeep introduced a line of airport service vehicles.

287 In August 1961, Willys Motors introduced two interesting new models to the Jeep lineup: the CJ-5A and the CJ-6A. These two vehicles were marketed under the name Tuxedo Park Mark IV and

This circa-1961 CJ-6 was built for the US Border Patrol and featured a steel cab extending all the way to the tailgate.

were dressed-up versions of the base vehicles. The Tuxedo Park Mark IV models boasted standard equipment that included chrome outside mirror brackets, chrome bumpers on front and rear, special wheel covers, a 60/40 front seat, rear wheel housing cushion pads, and whitewall tires. Although listed in some guide books as an option, technically the Tuxedo Park Mark IV's are separate models because each of them has its own distinct model number.

288 One question I often hear is How do you identify the year of a Jeep CJ-5? For most people it's just about impossible, but there are a few easily remembered identifiers that can help you to narrow it down a bit. If the CJ's windshield frame is painted black, it's a 1954–1974 vehicle (unless of course it was restored incorrectly). If the windshield frame is painted body color, it's a 1975-or-later model. Does it have a V-6 badge on the side? If yes, that narrows the year range to 1966–1971. If it has no side-marker lights, it's a pre-1969 vehicle. If the CJ has side-marker lights on the hood, it's a 1969 or early 1970. If the side-marker lights are mounted on the fenders, it a mid-1970-or-later model.

All of these tips refer, of course, to US-market Jeeps. Overseas models have a great deal of variation according to the country of its final destination.

This is a 1965 CJ-5 with a factory-optional full steel cab. Half cabs were also available.

289 There were three series of DJ vehicles in the civilian Jeep line (and even more in the Commercial, Postal, and AM General versions). The DJ-3A was the original model that debuted for 1956. The DJ-5 and long-wheelbase DJ-6 models came out for 1965. The DJ-6 remained in production for the US market for only a few years, but the DJ-5 model was still available for purchase at Jeep dealerships as late as 1973.

The 1956 model year saw the introduction of the Jeep DJ-3A Dispatcher, a line of low-price vehicles aimed primarily at the commercial market. This example is a personal-use vehicle for the lady of the house.

290 In 1965, Meyer (the snowplow manufacturer) announced a new factory option for the Jeep CJ-5: a steel hardtop cab, which it described as the first "Jeep owner-designed cab" for the CJ. It offered greatly improved styling along with larger windows and better overall quality.

291 One valid complaint that buyers had about Jeep CJs was that just about everything was optional. Even in the early to mid-1970s, the base CJ-5 didn't included a passenger seat, a rear seat, any kind of top, the passenger grab bar, a steering damper, a stabilizer bar, etc. It wasn't until the mid-1970s that American Motors finally began to upgrade the standard Jeep equipment.

292 Another complaint about Jeep vehicles was that they often didn't improve on problem areas. For example, even in 1966 (when the CJ-5 had been in production for more than 10 years), road testers of the day complained that the factory-supplied optional soft top wasn't very good. It leaked, rattled, and buffeted at highway speeds, and interior noise was almost deafening. *Road Test* magazine suggested that, because it was an option, a buyer should consider ordering the Jeep with no top and buying one from an independent supplier, which usually sold tops that were of higher quality and better fit. They estimated the cost of an outside-sourced fabric top at about $150.

To expand the little Jeep's appeal, Kaiser Jeep Corporation introduced the CJ-5A Tuxedo Park Mark IV, which boasted lots of chrome goodies plus a fancier interior. There was also a CJ-6A model produced.

293 In 1967, the city of Detroit purchased six Jeep CJ-5s specially equipped with right-hand steering and fabric soft tops as an experiment. The Jeeps were purchased to replace a fleet of motorcycles used by the city's Meter Maids for parking enforcement. Painted an eye-catching lemon yellow for maximum visibility, the Jeeps CJs offered all-weather protection that the motorcycles lacked. The cost difference was minimal; the new Jeep vehicles cost Detroit just $1,900 each, versus the $1,700 they had been charged for a motorcycle.

294 Do Jeep CJs really tip over? The short answer is yes, but so will just about any vehicle if it is pushed too hard. However, Jeep was saddled with this false accusation after *60 Minutes* ran a segment in December 1980 that showed Jeep CJ-5s tipping over in what appeared to be a series of fairly routine J turns. Once the episode aired, Jeep sales immediately began to fall off and lawsuits were launched by families of people hurt or killed in accidents involving Jeeps.

In the end, however, it came to light that the Jeeps shown on TV had been steered by robotic means at a very fast rate; far faster than a human could do. That's mostly what caused the accidents shown. To be fair, I should note that the CJ-5s are much more tippable than the longer-wheelbase CJ-7 or CJ-8.

295 Ever seen a CJ-5 Camper? They're pretty rare today. The factory offered them in 1969 and for a few years afterward. Basically, it was a two-passenger Jeep CJ-5 with an optional two-wheel camper unit that fit over and bolted into the CJ's rear seat area.

As small as it was, the little Jeep camper could sleep a family of four with two kids occupying a sleeping area overhanging the vehicle's cab and the parents on a bed that set up within the main area of the camper. Believe it or not, the little camper included a toilet, a kitchen, and even running water! These units are highly prized today by hard-core Jeep collectors.

In 1969, Jeep introduced this two-wheel trailer for the CJ-5. The base vehicle had to be equipped with the half-cab option in order for the add-on trailer to fit.

296 Most Jeep enthusiasts probably believe that CJ-5s came with a soft top as standard equipment, but as stated earlier, the truth is that for most years it was an option. Even when the option was ordered with the vehicle, the top wasn't installed by the factory; it was shipped in a box that was placed in the rear seat of the vehicle prior to shipping.

This family is out for a springtime drive in their circa-1967 CJ-5.

As a young Jeep salesman in the 1970s, I well recall new CJs arriving on the open delivery trucks, full of snow, with their optional soft tops in boxes strapped to the rear seat area. It was up to the dealer to install it. This supposedly was done to help ensure a better fit because the dealer's mechanics could take the time to fit it properly. In reality, it was probably simply another way for Jeep to speed up the assembly line.

297 Speaking of the assembly line, at one point during the 1970s, the Jeep CJ production line was reported to be the fastest in America, running at a rate of 85 vehicles produced per hour. The Jeep plant in the late 1970s ran two shifts per day plus mandatory Saturday overtime. Even then, it couldn't keep up with demand.

298 A fixed rear seat was an option on CJs and DJs, as was a fixed rear panel available in the early 1970s. If you didn't order the rear seat, you received a painted metal floor, often with the spare tire bolted to it if there was a tailgate. If the Jeep you ordered had the rear seat, the spare was mounted on the outside on the driver's side. If you ordered a fixed rear panel, the spare was mounted on the rear of the vehicle. Once the swing-out spare tire carriers became available, the outside spare was always put on the rear.

299 Jeep introduced a Levi's seat trim option for 1975, developed by a team under the direction of Vince Geraci at American Motors Styling. What most people don't know is that it's not really Levi's fabric because that's made of cotton and could never meet the wear, anti-fade, or fire-resistance standards in the automobile industry. Instead, Geraci had AMC's traditional seat fabric supplier create the material out of a spun nylon fabric that boasted excellent color retention, wear characteristics, and fire resistance. Originally created for the AMC Gremlin, it proved to be the most popular seat trim that AMC ever offered.

300 A long-time problem with the CJ-5 vehicle was getting into and out of it. The scooped-out door opening is rather narrow, and many people found it difficult to enter and exit; even in an era when

Americans were a lot skinnier than we are today. Jeep Corporation solved that problem (along with many others) when it developed the CJ-7, which debuted in August 1975 as a 1976 model. The CJ-7 had large, square-cut door openings, a longer wheelbase, and much more room behind the steering wheel. It also provided more rear seat room and even some storage space behind the rear seat.

301 With the introduction of the CJ-7, the Jeep CJ-6 model was withdrawn from the US market, although it continued to be very popular in overseas markets. Most of the CJ-6 models produced for overseas sales were built in the United States. Even in the case of the CJ-6s that were produced in certain overseas assembly plants, most of the parts were made in Toledo, Ohio, and shipped to the foreign assembly plant.

This circa-1974 CJ-6 is resting inside the American Motors Styling Studios, probably to serve as a base for a new concept.

302 When discussing overseas production of Jeep vehicles, it's important to explain the difference between the types of plants. The big plants in Mexico, Argentina, and Brazil were manufacturing plants in which most of the parts were sourced locally. Most of the

other plants, such as those in Costa Rica, South Africa, South Korea, Sweden, and other places, were called "screwdriver plants" because they only assembled the vehicles from parts kits shipped from America.

303 The 1976 Jeep CJ-7 offered a good-quality soft top, initially in black and white only. Also offered was an optional plastic hardtop that was quieter and much better looking than the squeaky metal cabs offered on the CJ-5 and CJ-6. The plastic tops also weighed less, which meant that they made the vehicle a bit less tippy. Jeep stylists attempted to come up with a similar plastic hardtop for the CJ-5. They designed several concept plastic hardtops that were very attractive, but in the end management never authorized their production.

304 Believe it or not, the roll bar didn't become a standard feature on CJs until 1980, even though it was a vitally important safety feature. Prior to 1980, it was an extra-cost option, and prior to about 1969 it was available only from aftermarket specialty shops, so a surprising number of CJs were sold without it. Jeep's attorneys finally convinced management that it would be smart to add the roll bar to the standard features list.

305 For 1980, Jeep introduced a new option: a soft top with steel doors that included keyed door locks. This option came in response to buyers' concerns about their inability to lock the soft top doors. Jeep had never developed any kind of security locks for the soft tops, probably thinking that they would do no good because an intruder could just cut into the vehicle. At that time, however, many women were purchasing new Jeeps and wanted more security.

306 When American Motors took over Jeep Corporation in 1970, the company immediately set about to grow its sales volume, which had been falling for years. To illustrate how effective it was, in February 1980 the one-millionth Jeep built by American Motors, a CJ-5 Laredo, was driven off the assembly line, just over 10 years after AMC bought the company. That averages about 100,000 vehicles a year, but actually, by 1978 Jeep annual production was more than 150,000 units and was still being ramped up.

307 Jeep introduced the Scrambler pickup for the 1981 model year. Part of the CJ series (its official designation was CJ-8), the Scrambler rode a longer 103.5-inch wheelbase, which was 10 inches more than the CJ-7 and 20 inches longer than a CJ-5. The Scrambler was meant to be a serious competitor in the burgeoning compact pickup market, although its standard four-wheel drive and relatively high price tag relegated it to being a sporty hauler that appealed mainly to Jeep traditionalists.

308 Although designed to be a pickup truck, the base Jeep Scrambler came as a basic roadster with no top. The company offered the choice of a pickup-style half-cab soft top or hardtop. Dealers could also install a full soft top, although they were seldom ordered. The Scrambler offered a wide range of free-standing factory-installed options. It could also be ordered with the Scrambler SR package, which was nearly identical to the CJ Renegade package, or the Scrambler SL package, which corresponded to the CJ Laredo.

309 Jeep enthusiasts often wished they could buy a four-door CJ vehicle, but one was never produced for the United States. Jeep affiliate companies overseas did offer them, for example, in Brazil during the 1960s and in India a little later.

This 1982 Jeep Scrambler is equipped with a hardtop and the optional SR sport appearance package.

310 Jeep Scramblers are among the hottest-selling vintage Jeeps for good reason. They're a better vehicle overall than a CJ-7 because the longer wheelbase provided better ride and better handling, plus they are more useful as haulers. Unfortunately, the Scramblers were not very popular when new, so there aren't enough of them around to satisfy demand. Thus, if you try to buy one today, you may be shocked by the high prices that nice examples can fetch.

Engine and Drivetrain

311 One weak point of the wartime MB was its T-84 transmission, so for the postwar civilian Jeeps a switch was made to the stronger T-90 transmission (and you wonder why the change wasn't made earlier!). The new T-90 was about 40 percent stronger than the T-84, important because engineers believed the civilian Jeep would often be used by farmers as a tractor.

312 Field testing of prototype civilian Jeeps began in 1944 and actually began in the field, farm fields, to be more precise. Willys-Overland owned a farm that it used as a testing area for Jeeps and its optional farm equipment. Those tests uncovered a number of areas in the Jeep that needed improvement if it was going to be used successfully as a farm tractor and all-around work vehicle. The final-drive ratio was changed to 5.38:1, which reduced its top speed but made the Jeep more suitable for slow-going farm work where low-end lugging power is needed the most.

313 Willys-Overland made sure to have all the necessary gauges in the postwar CJ-2A, including a speedometer (made by King Seeley or Auto-Lite), a gasoline gauge, plus ammeter, oil pressure, and temperature gauges (all of which were produced by long-time supplier Auto-Lite).

314 The new civilian Jeep CJ-2A engines were fitted with a heavy-duty oil-bath air cleaner manufactured by Oakes Products, along with a Purolater oil filter (part number 27078). Oil-bath filters

tend to do a little better job filtering out dirt and dust than regular dry-type air filters. They also muffle intake noise better. Another plus is that it's much cheaper to replace the dirty oil than to replace a dirty filter cartridge.

315 The CJ-2A's optional engine governor was a new precision-type nine-position unit that was manufactured by King Seeley. It was a popular work option and you see them on many older Jeeps. Useful in field plowing operations, they also are used to maintain a steady engine speed when using various work attachments offered by Willys.

316 The postwar Jeep CJ-2As also received newly revised transfer case gearing that included a 2.43:1 ratio for the low range versus the 1.97:1 gears used in military Jeep production. This was to create a more suitable farm truck and work truck.

317 The postwar Jeep CJ-2A continued to use 6-volt electrics, which was still the accepted auto industry standard at the time for both cars and light trucks. The improved 12-volt electrical systems came later, with the 1957 CJ-3B beginning with serial number 35522. It

This handsome CJ-2A is reportedly a 1949. The flat hood was possible because of the low height of the flathead 4-cylinder engine.

was typical of Jeep to introduce changes in mid-production to use up existing parts inventory prior to the change.

318 The civilian Jeeps were also fitted with a new radiator, fan, and fan shroud for improved cooling, again to make them more suitable for slow-going farm work or heavy-duty construction work. A stronger clutch was also specified by Jeep engineers.

319 By the time the war ended, the sturdy Willys Go-Devil engine was considered to be the toughest 4-cylinder, but even so it received some needed modifications when it was given a new, sturdier crankshaft, a modified cylinder head, a new intake manifold, and a switch from a chain-driven camshaft on the wartime vehicles to a more reliable gear-driven one for civilian production.

320 One of the most critical improvements to the postwar Jeeps was the decision to offer optional power takeoff units at the front, rear, and side of the vehicle. This allowed a wide range of farm equipment to be powered in the field by the Jeep engine. Equipment that included saws, water pumps, threshers, post-hole diggers, and other implements (many of them sold through Willys dealers) could now be powered anywhere they were needed on the farm, in the oilfield, or at a construction site.

321 One problem noted in wartime Jeeps as well as early civilian models was the driveline "drag" created by the constantly engaged front drive gears. It tended to make the steering heavier and to reduce fuel economy and accelerate front-end wear. Arthur Warn developed the first "free-wheeling" front hubs to eliminate the problem and went on to found Warn Industries to manufacture them. For years, the Warn hubs were a popular option on Jeeps.

322 Arthur Warn originally became interested in the idea of free-wheeling hubs because he was a Willys-Jeep dealer in Seattle, Washington. Today, Warn Industries produces winches for Jeep and other vehicles. It still makes free-wheeling hubs as well.

323 The new Willys Jeep Hurricane 134.2-ci 4-cylinder engine debuted in the new "high-hood" CJ-3B with a 6.9:1 compression ratio and developing 70 hp. This veteran engine continued to be offered in US Jeep models through the 1971 model year, and in overseas market for many years afterward. It had some faults, but overall it was sturdy, reliable, and inexpensive to make.

Designed for the senior Jeep line as well as the CJ-3B "high-hood" Jeep, the Jeep F-head four-banger was a modification of the Go-Devil four.

324 As one of the last companies still building 4-cylinder engines in America during the 1950s, Willys-Overland was an easy choice for Kaiser-Frazer Corporation to supply the base engine for its new Henry J compact car that debuted in 1951. As used in the Henry J, the little engine was called the Supersonic 4 and was optimistically rated at 68 hp. Willys-Overland also supplied the new Henry J with its 6-cylinder engine, which it called, naturally enough, the Supersonic 6, and which was officially rated at 80 hp. It's very likely that these business transactions between the two independent car companies led to the decision by Henry J. Kaiser to acquire the operating assets of Willys-Overland.

325 During the 1961 model year, Jeep expanded its powertrain offerings in the CJ line to include a Perkins 4-cylinder diesel engine. This rugged engine was offered at least through 1964. The Perkins diesel displaced 192.2 ci and was rated at 62 hp, just above the Hurricane four.

Torque, on the other hand, was a whopping 143 ft-lbs coming on at a mere 1,350 rpm, meaning that it was superb for use in an off-road vehicle where low speeds and steep hills meant that you really needed good torque at low engine speeds. Fuel economy for the Perkins was excellent, and of course, being a diesel, the thing ran just about forever. It appears that most vehicles sold overseas were the Perkins-powered Jeeps.

326 How do you convert a Go-Devil 4-cylinder engine into a Lightning Four? One easy way is to change the name. In 1963, Jeep called the engine in the Dispatcher vehicles the "Lightning Four" even though for all intents and purposes it was the same Go-Devil as pictured in the 1956 DJ-3A sales brochures.

327 The 4-cylinder Jeep CJ-5 and CJ-6 were considerably under-powered by the standards of the early 1960s, and it was holding back sales. Jeep produced its own 6-cylinder engines, but they were too long to fit under the hood of the CJ. In August 1965, Jeep solved the problem by borrowing a trick that hot rodders had been using for a while: Engineers stuffed the potent 225-ci Buick V-6 engine under the CJ hood. This newly optional mill, which Jeep dubbed the Dauntless V-6, produced a robust 155 hp, more than double the Hurricane four's 75-hp rating. Owners bragged of being able to do four-wheel burnouts!

328 Initially, Kaiser Jeep purchased V-6 engines from Buick, but in time the company made the decision to purchase the tooling from Buick, which by the end of 1967 was no longer using the engine in any of its cars.

329 Once the Buick V-6 became available, sales of Jeeps equipped with the four-banger dropped like a stone. After all, the four

could barely keep up with traffic, while the V-6 went like a rocket and was pretty economical with gas. By 1966, Jeep was heavily advertising the new V-6 with ads that spoke about its power. One headline stated, "Go Jeep V6; it's really fun."

330 One Jeep model used a Chevrolet 4-cylinder engine: the original DJ-5 Dispatcher postal vehicle of 1969 and 1970. It featured a permanent steel roof, unit-body construction with sliding doors, a 4-cylinder Chevy Nova engine, and a GM Hydramatic transmission. This specialty vehicle, sold only to the US Post Office, was considered a Jeep model until 1971 when Jeep Corporation's government vehicles' business was spun off into a new separate company called AM General. By that point, Jeep had switched to using the AMC six in the Dispatchers. AM General is still an active company in the tactical vehicle industry.

AMC stylists considered changing the front end styling of the CJ-5 but in the end decided the existing vehicle had a classic "look" they couldn't improve upon. On the left is one idea for a new front end style; on the right is a circa-1973 CJ-5 Renegade.

331 Many old-time Jeep enthusiasts used to insist that when American Motors took over Jeep ". . . they ruined the vehicle." But I, for one, can't see why anyone would say that. For 1972, AMC replaced the tired old Hurricane 4-cylinder engine with its own excellent 232-ci inline-6 as the standard engine. The 232 six

had more horsepower and more torque, was a good deal quieter and smoother, and proved to be a much more robust and long-lived engine. Also updated and improved were the Jeep's suspension, axles, transmission, steering gear, brakes, and heater, which especially needed improvement.

Sure, the Jeep wasn't as quaint or simple as before, but it was tougher, longer lasting, and overall a better vehicle for use as a full-time driver.

By 1973, sales of Jeep vehicles were beginning to climb rapidly, helped by the improvements that AMC introduced to the brand, as well as AMC's larger and more experienced dealer network.

332 The American Motors 232 six was a seven-main-bearing engine with a counterweighted crankshaft, and it developed 145 hp. Introduced in AMC cars for 1964, by the time it was fitted in the CJs, it had been improved to the point that it was the most robust 6-cylinder engine made in America. An optional 258-ci version was soon offered with a bit more horsepower and torque. By 1987, that engine had evolved into the awesome Jeep 4.0-liter engine, which was used in production through the 2006 model year. The AMC inline-6 was thus in production for more than 40 years, and is one of the most admired engines of all time.

This 1973 CJ-5 is equipped as a garage service vehicle, with a half cab, rooftop light, heavy-duty push bumper, tailgate, and side-mounted spare tire. Note the lock-out front hubs and dual mirrors.

333 The Jeep Renegade received some real guts in the 1972 model year when Jeep engineers discontinued the rough-idling V-6 in favor of the smoother American Motors 304-ci V-8 engine as standard equipment. The 304 V-8 could also be ordered as an option on any CJ-5.

334 Jeep Corporation never offered a V-8 engine larger than 304 ci in the CJ series, but because the later AMC V-8 blocks are all the same size, a 360 ci or even a 401-ci V-8 will fit right in. For a while, a dealer out West offered a 401-V-8-powered CJ-6, which must have been a terror to drive.

335 Around 1974, demand for Jeep CJs was red-hot, while at the same time AMC was selling every car it could build, placing a strain on component production capacity. One item in particular shortage was the 232-ci 6-cylinder engine used in both the

car and Jeep lines. Internal memos show that AMC management investigated restarting production of the old Buick V-6 engines for use in CJs in an effort to keep up with soaring demand. In the end, however, the company chose to invest in expanding 232 six production, concluding that adding the V-6 would make its production lines even more complicated. Besides, the 232 six was overall a much better engine than the V-6.

336 Have you ever wondered whatever became of the Buick V-6 engine tooling once Jeep no longer needed it? American Motors put it in mothballs for several years just in case it might be needed again. Then, after the fuel crisis, Buick approached AMC with an offer to buy back the production tooling. Buick needed a good small six for use in its car lines. The GM division kept the engine in production for decades afterward, and it became one of the better-known engines in the GM portfolio.

337 All Jeep CJs were given an all-new electronic ignition system for 1975 to improve starting, drivability, fuel economy, and reliability. A quieter muffler was also installed, along with an improved electrical system and a stronger frame. All of this was American Motors' on-going efforts (led by Chief Engineer Roy Lunn) to improve Jeep technology.

338 For several years, people had been asking for an automatic transmission on the Jeep CJ-5, but the problem was that its 83.5-inch wheelbase was simply too short to fit an automatic transmission. In August 1975, Jeep introduced the new CJ-7 model, which boasted a 10-inch longer (93.5 inches) wheelbase and an optional automatic transmission. However, the automatic came only with the Quadra-Trac four-wheel-drive system which, although superior to the part-time systems, proved to be a gas hog. That didn't matter in 1976, but a few years later when a gas crisis hit it did.

339 In March 1977, Jeep displayed a prototype CJ-7 fitted with a new 2.7-liter Perkins diesel. The company announced that

the new engine would be available in Jeep CJ-5, CJ-6, and CJ-7 models, and issued a slick press release and photos. However, although the vehicles were produced in the Toledo, Ohio, main plant, the new diesel engine was offered for overseas markets only.

340 Effective with the 1978 model year, the CJ's optional 258-ci six was fitted with a 2-barrel carburetor and was now rated at 110 hp net and 195 ft-lbs of torque. The following model year, 1979, that engine became the standard mill for the CJ, and the 232-ci was phased out. Testing showed that the 258-ci engine attained better fuel economy than the smaller mill.

341 For 1980, in response to rising gasoline prices and worries about availability, Jeep introduced a 4-cylinder engine for the Jeep CJs (the company had ceased offering the old Hurricane engine in US models in 1972, although it continued for overseas markets). The new 4-cylinder was the GM 151-ci Iron Duke, an exceptionally sturdy unit good for 82 hp. Jeep named the new engine the Hurricane in honor of the earlier Jeep 4-cylinder. The big news was its city mileage rating of 21, making the Jeep CJ the first domestic four-wheel-drive vehicle to break the 20-mpg barrier. The highway rating for the little Jeep was an impressive 25 mpg.

Offered only with a 4-speed transmission (it lacked enough power for the automatic transmission), the new Hurricane four required a lot of gearbox shifting to get any kind of performance out of it, but its fuel economy was considered exceptional for the era.

342 In addition to the new 4-cylinder engine during 1980, the Jeep CJ-7 also offered a new part-time four-wheel-drive system in conjunction with an automatic transmission, which replaced the gas-guzzling former Quadra-Trac system used on the CJs. The automatic transmission and part-time four-wheel-drive setup could only be ordered with the 6-cylinder or V-8 engine. This drivetrain change was made purely for fuel economy improvement and was meant to address customer complaints about the Quadra-Trac's heavy fuel consumption.

343 The new transfer case for the 1980 Jeep CJ models was the Dana 300, which was an upgraded version of the prior year's transfer case. It was used on all CJs regardless of the engine transmission combination.

344 All Jeep CJs also received a slick new 4-speed transmission as standard equipment for 1980. Unlike previous Jeep 4-speeds, the new gearbox was a full "road-going" unit, meaning that first gear wasn't a "granny gear" reserved for tough off-roading; it was a regular drive gear. A smooth-operating, self-adjusting hydraulic clutch was also included.

345 In yet another sign of the times, the formerly optional free-wheeling front hubs became standard equipment on all Jeep CJs for the 1980 model year. It was a move to boost real-world fuel economy and improve the Jeep's handling while reducing front-end component wear.

346 For 1980, the Jeep CJ's new optional Chrysler TorqueFlite automatic transmission was both lighter in weight and more fuel efficient than before. Weight reduction was achieved through greater use of aluminum in the case and internal parts. The new transmission was available only with part-time four-wheel drive.

347 In 1981, Jeep dropped the optional V-8 from the CJ line because of low demand caused by an ongoing fuel crisis and extremely high gasoline prices. Engineers continued to massage fuel economy of the Hurricane four, and it rose to 22 mpg city and 27 mpg highway for 1981.

348 Effective with 1984 model year production, the GM Iron Duke 4-cylinder was replaced by the all-new American Motors 150-ci 2.5-liter four. The new engine was engineered to be a true truck engine and designed to surpass ordinary passenger car durability standards by a wide margin. It was a much more durable engine than the Iron Duke four.

349 Here's a little nugget for you to consider: In 1986, the Jeep CJ-7 with the 5-speed manual transmission was rated by the Environmental Protection Agency (EPA) at 1 mpg worse gas mileage than the 4-speed, both city and highway. How could that be?

350 Right to the end of CJ production the company never offered any of the CJ models with a fuel-injected engine. It was a shame because the new Jeep Cherokee XJ's fuel-injected 4-cylinder was essentially the same engine as in the CJ but offered more power and better fuel economy.

Suspension and Brakes

351 It's perhaps not all that surprising that when Willys-Overland engineers began to redesign the MB for the post-war civilian market one of the first things they did was install softer springs for the suspension.

352 The brake system used for the initial postwar Jeeps consisted of four-wheel drum brakes with 9.0x1.75-inch linings; they were adequate but not exactly high-performance brakes. The parking brake was a drum-type unit that worked on the transfer case.

353 Postwar Jeep CJs were fitted with tall and narrow 16x4.50-inch wheels, on which were fitted 6.00x16-inch tires.

354 In 1946, the civilian Jeep's semi-floating axle was replaced by a full-floating axle, beginning with serial number 13453. This move was made to improve ride and handling.

355 All the Jeep CJs and DJs were fitted with conventional, unassisted (non-power assisted) brake systems with drum brakes at all four wheels from 1945 to 1971. In 1972, the drum brakes continued, but power assist was finally available as an option. Front disc brakes weren't offered on the CJs until the 1977 model year.

356 The Jeep CJ series was one of the last road-use vehicles in America to use a four-wheel leaf-spring suspension and a solid front axle. These rather old-fashioned components were used to provide the Jeep with maximum strength in severe off-road situations, and they worked fine at that, although they gave a stiff ride on-road.

357 The 1976 CJ-7 weighed only about 40 pounds more than the CJ-5, despite its 10-inch-longer wheelbase, and their suspension systems were essentially the same. A wider, splayed side-rail frame debuted for the 1976 models to provide a wider foundation at the rear of the vehicle. The new frame featured improved bending strength and significantly greater torsional rigidity, which improved on-road ride as well as off-road durability.

358 One added benefit of the CJ-7's longer wheelbase was a greatly improved ride and more secure handling. This was especially noticeable on the highway, where the CJ-5 had a tendency to bounce and wander. The CJ-7 proved to be much better in that regard, and the optional plastic hardtop made it quieter than the CJ-5's steel cab. These product improvements helped to fuel demand for the Jeep. By April 1977, the Jeep plant in Toledo was working overtime trying to handle the flood of orders for new Jeeps.

359 For 1977, Jeep switched to using Goodyear Tracker A/T tires as standard equipment on the Renegade package rather than the less-aggressive Suburbanite tires used previously. The new tires came fitted on white spoke wheels rather than the more expensive (and less durable) alloy wheels used on prior Renegades.

360 The 1981 Scrambler pickup added an even longer-wheelbase model to the CJ line: 103.5 inches. Front springs were of four-leaf design with a rating of 170 pounds per inch. The rear springs were also four-leafs but rated at 185 pounds per inch. The gross vehicle weight (GVW) rating for the new Scrambler was 4,150 pounds.

New for 1981 was the Jeep Scrambler (aka the CJ-8). Designed primarily to be sold as a pickup truck, for some reason Jeep made the base vehicle an open roadster just like the CJ-5. This Scrambler SR has the optional hardtop and wood side rails. These trucks are highly collectible today.

Numbers Crunching and Press Commentary

361 Ever wonder what the numbers and letters in a Jeep's name mean? To illustrate, take the Jeep CJ-2A as an example. The letters CJ stand for Civilian Jeep (or Commercial Jeep, as some people insist). The 2 stands for the second series; all the CJ-1 and CJ-2 vehicles were preproduction jobs. The letter A stands for first alteration. In this case, the CJ-2 preproduction model was the first iteration, so the second version was the CJ-2A.

A rarely seen option for the Jeep Surrey are the side curtains in this vintage press photo. To date, I've never seen a Surrey that still had them.

362 In 1944, the management at Willys-Overland made an informed guess at how many civilian Jeep CJs could be sold in the United States after the close of the war. They quickly decided the company would have to add a line of trucks and station wagons to the mix or the firm would probably go out of business within a few years. During 1945, the company produced less than 2,000 civilian Jeeps, but for 1946 that number soared to a whopping 71,554. For 1947, the company built 65,078 civilian Jeep CJs and then another 74,122 units for 1948.

So, had they guessed wrong? Nope, the first year's sales were simply the result of pent-up demand; by 1949, production of the CJ-3A was fewer than 30,000 units. Thankfully, by that time Willys had a full roster of senior vehicles to sell.

363 In all, Willys-Overland produced more than 113,000 vehicles for 1947. Demand for new Jeeps was so robust that the company reopened its West Coast factory in Los Angeles, California, that year to build new Jeeps for the western states.

364 The company kept an eye on the future even as postwar demand was at its highest. Willys-Overland management realized that in the future overseas sales might prove to be vitally important, so even at the height of Jeep demand in America they allocated 15 percent of Jeep production to overseas markets. This was done in order to maintain and grow its export business for what they knew would be the inevitable day when US demand would slacken.

Because of this far-sighted decision, Willys had a healthy and highly profitable export business in built-up vehicles as well as completely knocked down (CKD) units for assembly overseas. In many of the later years, the company earned more profits from its overseas business than from its US sales.

This busy Jeep assembly line circa-1954 contains a variety of Jeep vehicles in various stages of assembly.

365 In 1948, Willys-Overland ranked 5th overall in export sales of American vehicles out of the 12 domestic producers in business at the time. For a rather small company building only a limited range of truck-type vehicles (most of them four-wheel drive), this was a surprising success and added greatly to its profitability.

366 The Jeep CJ-2A model was in production for five years (from 1945 to 1949), and its successor, the similar-looking Jeep CJ-3A was likewise in production for five years (from 1949 to 1953). And yes, production of the two series of CJs actually overlapped during 1949.

367 Surprisingly, the Jeep CJ-3B, known as the last of the so-called "flat-fender Jeeps," was produced from 1953 to 1968, a period of 16 years, which was a great deal longer than its predecessors. One reason is that it was kept in the line to provide a lower-priced alternative to the CJ-5. It was also produced for overseas markets, where it was very popular.

368 Less well-known than the CJ Jeep vehicles is the DJ series, which first debuted for 1956. The original models were two-wheel-drive versions of the CJ-3A. Also known as the Dispatcher, the DJ-3As were engineered on the cheap to provide dealers with another product to sell (and without Willys incurring much development cost). Three models were offered initially: roadster, roadster with soft top, and steel cab hardtop fitted with a fiberglass roof panel.

The main purpose of the DJs was to serve as a low-cost delivery vehicle. A base roadster was priced at a mere $1,205. With a soft top added to the vehicle, the price rose to $1,261. Even when the hardtop was ordered, the vehicle price was just $1,397. That was ultra-cheap even for 1956.

369 By 1965, the Jeep DJ-3A was replaced by the DJ-5, which was basically a two-wheel-drive version of the CJ-5 vehicle. The DJ-5A was offered in three distinct models: roadster with a soft top, hardtop, and Special trim. The Special was actually a Surrey-

type vehicle, although much less ornate than the earlier Surrey. These models are extremely rare today, although probably not very valuable.

370 There was also a two-wheel-drive DJ-6 on the 101-inch wheelbase. Introduced for 1965, it came only as an open-roadster model with optional soft tops from the factory. Meyer steel cabs could also be ordered for dealer installation.

371 Jeep offered a special Prairie Gold model CJ-5 during 1966, although so far, I've been able to locate only a single dealer ad that mentions it. A photo of it appears in the late Arch Brown's book *Jeep: The Unstoppable Legend* (published in 1994), and that is the only reference to it that I've ever seen anywhere.

372 One special-edition model that I can verify is the 1969 Jeep 462, which was a CJ-5 fitted with a factory-installed roll bar, a V-6 engine, two front bucket seats, underbody skid plates, ammeter and oil gauges, big Polyglas tubeless tires, and stylish full-wheel covers. The Jeep 462 was considered a factory performance vehicle, and believe it or not, in the off-road market that's what passed for high-performance in that era. No one seems to know how many were built or how many have survived. Probably not many in either case.

373 *Off-Road Fun Cars* magazine (yes, that was really the name of the magazine) tested the new Jeep 462 for 1969 and called it ". . . the factory muscle car of the off-road world." It was the dawn of the customizing era for Jeep.

374 After noticing that many owners were modifying their Jeep vehicles to make them look sportier, Jeep designers decided to create a special sport model for 1970 that they dubbed the Renegade I. It was offered in two wild colors: Mint Green and Wild Plum, although one source claims that red was a third choice.

The Renegade I was equipped with the Dauntless V-6 engine, two front bucket seats, big 8-inch-wide steel wheels painted white,

hood stripe, roll bar, swing-out spare tire carrier, Trac-Lok rear axle, and more. Big G70x15 Polyglas tires were standard. It's estimated that somewhere between 350 and 500 Renegade Is were produced. When they sold out immediately, company marketing executives were astounded.

375 The 1970 Renegade I had only one option for wheels. If you wanted something other than the plain white steel wheels, you could order factory full-disc wheel covers similar to those used on the Wagoneer and the earlier 462 model. That was it. If you felt the need for further dressing up, you could order whitewall tires or go to one of the many aftermarket shops to see what they offered.

376 The regular Jeep CJ models could be ordered with hood side stripes in 1970, in an attempt to give them a sportier look at a low cost. Full-wheel covers, bucket seats, and a spare tire cover were other dress-up options.

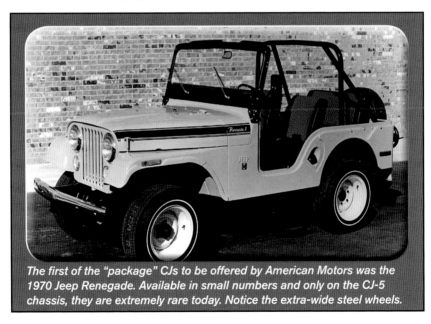

The first of the "package" CJs to be offered by American Motors was the 1970 Jeep Renegade. Available in small numbers and only on the CJ-5 chassis, they are extremely rare today. Notice the extra-wide steel wheels.

377 Following up on the 1970 Renegade I's success was the 1971 Renegade II, which now featured beautiful alloy wheels in

addition to the other standard goodies and was offered in four color choices. According to American Motors, of the 600 Renegade IIs built for 1971, 200 of them were painted Baja Yellow, 200 were painted Mint Green, 150 were painted Big Bad orange, and 50 were painted Riverside Red. All of these vehicles were quickly snapped up by buyers, once again surprising Jeep management.

378 The 1971 Renegade II has a hood-top center stripe that the 1970 Renegade I lacks. The side stripes are nearly identical, but of course, the series number is different. Other differences between the two: The 1971 model came with roll bar padding and a black-painted front bumper; the 1970 model has no roll bar padding and has a chrome front bumper.

379 There was supposed to be a Renegade III introduced for 1972, and photos of styling mockups exist to prove that, but in the end company officials decided to just call it the Jeep Renegade, although it was still produced in limited quantities because of a shortage of the alloy wheels. Jeep Corporation was able to produce more Renegades for 1973, albeit still on a limited basis. Finally, for 1974 the component supply problems were solved, and the CJ-5 Renegade became a regular-production option. It was sold as an optional package instead of as a distinct model.

380 The Jeep Renegade package proved to be so popular that when the factory ran short of alloy wheels during the 1973 run, the company rushed an alternative package into production. Dubbed the Super Jeep, it was a CJ-5 with a wild triple-stripe job that ran from the hood to the body sides, along with custom interior trim and white-painted steel wheels like those seen on the 1970 Renegade models.

381 Talk about a bargain! The retail price of the Super Jeep package for 1973 was a mere $159.95. It included Mod stripes in Red and Blue or Orange and White, special seat trim, dual sun visors, instrument panel pad, fender lip extensions, big L78x15 whitewall Polyglas Suburbanite tires and white-painted wheels, and a chrome

front bumper. There was a catch, however: It required the purchase of the 258-ci six, passenger seat, rear seat, seat belts, roll bar, draw bar, fixed tailgate with rear spare tire mount, and quite a few other extra-cost items, all of which, although desirable, drove up the total price.

382 Here's some fuel for a bit of controversary: Legend has it that the Super Jeep CJ-5 supposedly was reintroduced for 1976. I've never seen one, nor have I seen any printed materials to confirm their existence. Most photos of reputed 1976 Super Jeeps have been 1973 models, which are easy to spot because the windshield frames on the 1973 CJs were painted black, in contrast to 1976 models that had the windshield frames painted body color.

383 I have seen pictures of a supposedly "authentic" 1976 Super Jeep still in existence. However, I remain skeptical about it. In my opinion, that particular vehicle was either created as an aftermarket product by the local Jeep Zone Office or, more likely, was produced as a dealer modification. I don't believe the Super Jeep package was installed at the factory. I'm willing to be convinced if anyone can show me supporting documents.

384 Here's a bit of nostalgia that will bring a tear to your eyes: In 1971, the base price of a Jeep CJ-5 was $2,886. If you were looking for an even lower price, a two-wheel-drive Jeep DJ-5 could be bought for just $2,382. Now, both of those vehicles would have needed the addition of several options to bring them to the point where you'd want to actually drive them, but still, those were good, low prices.

385 Jeep stopped referring to the CJ models as the Jeep Universal starting in 1972. From that time on, the smallest Jeeps were referred to as the Jeep CJ-5, Jeep CJ-6, or Jeep DJ-5 Dispatcher. The point of this was to emphasize the Jeep name rather than the Universal name. In the same manner, Jeep Gladiators became known simply as Jeep trucks with a model number as the suffix.

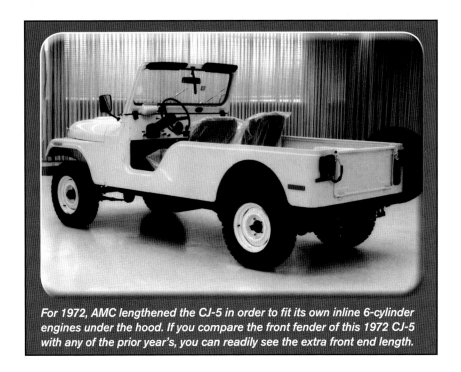

For 1972, AMC lengthened the CJ-5 in order to fit its own inline 6-cylinder engines under the hood. If you compare the front fender of this 1972 CJ-5 with any of the prior year's, you can readily see the extra front end length.

386 Here's one road tester's summary of driving the newly "improved" Jeep 1972 CJ-5: "It's hard to get into and even harder to get out of. Vision is restricted with the top up, the steering isn't quick, and the gearbox is short of stalk. The spare tire hangs over the side, cargo room is sparse, and the highway ride is hard. The cloth top flaps and rumbles, and the horn sounds ridiculous. But forget all that. When you buy a CJ-5 this is what you get, and you might as well accept the vehicle for what it is." Obviously, Jeep's new engineering team still had a lot more work to do.

387 The August 1972 issue of *Four-Wheeler* magazine road tested the new Jeep Renegade powered by the new standard V-8 engine and said this: "If a few custom touches are your bag, the Renegade will surely make your little heart go pit-pat. With the 'Renegade' hood stripe, the black-out hood, and the wild paint jobs, it is a mean-looking machine. We saw quite a few heads turn as we drove around Los Angeles, and especially off-road."

388 For 1973, Jeep switched to two-digit model numbers for the CJ and DJ series. The new model numbers were: Model 83 for the CJ-5, Model 84 for the CJ-6, and Model 85 for the DJ-5.

389 For 1973, an unusual Jeep Model DJ-5C was available. It was the Dispatcher full-cab vehicle similar to those sold to the US Post Office by AM General, and it could be ordered with either left- or right-hand steering. The AMC 6-cylinder engine and 3-speed automatic transmission were standard equipment. The base price was $3,057, and they were marketed toward security firms and other commercial users.

390 *Pickup, Van and Four-Wheel-Drive* magazine named the new Jeep CJ-7 its 1976 Four-Wheel-Drive of the Year. It was the beginning of a string of awards and recognition for the Jeep vehicles that continues to this day.

391 In 1977, an auto industry magazine writer visited the Jeep plant in Toledo, Ohio, and noted that 25 percent of all CJ models were being ordered with the optional Renegade package (a very profitable option for Jeep). He also concluded that nearly 20 percent of the Jeep J-series trucks were being ordered with the optional Honcho package.

392 Despite Jeep enjoying so much success with the Renegade and Super Jeep, it was a few years before company designers began to create other special "package models" for the CJ line. The next one to debut was the limited-production Golden Eagle, which was released in January 1977 as an option for both the Jeep CJ-5 and CJ-7.

The only body color offered for the Golden Eagle that year was Oakleaf Brown, although in succeeding years other colors became available. A large gold, black, and white Eagle decal covered the hood, and its gold-painted wheels were shod with 9-15 Goodyear Wrangler white-letter tires. A tan Levi's interior trim was included.

The Golden Eagle package was offered from 1977 to 1980. Unfortunately, it wasn't as popular as the Renegade package, probably because it was quite a bit more expensive.

393 For 1980, Jeep introduced the stylish new Laredo package, which provided a good deal of luxury along with a solid measure of sportiness. The package included special body striping, decals with the Laredo name on the hood sides, a beautiful chromed grille, chrome wheels, and a chrome front bumper, dual rear bumperettes, special high-back bucket seats with special trim, and much more.

The Renegade and Golden Eagle packages continued to be offered as well. The new Laredo package became the top of the CJ line.

394 A very special model was the Jeep Golden Hawk, which arrived in mid-1980 and was a one-year-only trim package. Appearance-wise it was extremely nice, with a large stylized golden hawk decal on the hood, a chrome grille, brown denim seats, and more. It was offered in both CJ-5 and CJ-7 versions and is rarely seen today.

395 One of the most collectible "package Jeeps" is the 1982 Jeep CJ-7 Jamboree Edition, which was produced to commemorate the 30th anniversary of the Jeepers Jamboree in Georgetown, California. Painted a special Topaz Gold metallic, with a unique Jamboree decal on the hood sides, equipment included chrome wheels, chrome bumpers, a special numbered plaque for the instrument panel, a roll bar with saddle bags, big Goodyear Wrangler tires, and gold accents on the seats. The base vehicle included the 258-ci six, 5-speed manual transmission, power steering, power brakes, and a 20-gallon fuel tank.

396 In the New York marketing area, which included southern Connecticut, a special CJ-7 Superstar package was offered for 1982. It came with the usual interior and road-wheel upgrades and can be identified by its special "starburst" hood decal that was quite attractive.

I was told by a Jeep sales representative that the CJ Superstar was created as a tribute to baseball player Reggie Jackson, although to date I've seen no literature to verify that nor does any information on the Superstar package appear in the Jeep ordering guide. Reportedly only 100 were produced. The dealership where I worked received one to sell.

397 With the four-wheel-drive market suffering from a severe drop in sales for 1981, Jeep introduced a new Limited package for the CJ-7 for 1982. The most luxurious CJ ever built (even to this day), the CJ-7 Limited came equipped with extra-quiet insulation, power steering, power brakes, AM-FM two-speaker radio, monochromatic paint scheme with color-keyed hardtop and wheel lip extensions, special striping, special interior trim with leather seats available, color-keyed spoke wheels with bright trim rings, Goodyear Arriva tires, improved ride suspension, and a heck of a lot more standard equipment. It was very pricey, so not many were sold, and only a few of them seem to be around today. I'm proud to say that I sold the first one that arrived at the dealership where I worked.

398 The Jeep Sahara model was originally supposed to be called the Jeep Banana Republic, using the name of the well-known clothing maker. A prototype vehicle with a custom interior and an attractive logo was created and approved by AMC management, but then the retailer demanded a higher royalty fee than what was originally discussed. After fruitless negotiations, Jeep canceled the Banana Republic project and designer Vince Geraci and his team went on to create the Sahara package. It soon became one of the most popular Jeep dress-up packages of all time.

399 When AMC bought Jeep in 1970, the factory was producing about 35,000 civilian Jeep vehicles for the US market per year. Under American Motors' leadership, by early 1977, Jeep was producing 165 CJ-5s each day, plus 135 CJ-7s, 130 Cherokees, 90 pickups, and 80 Wagoneers. That totaled 600 vehicles each day (or more than 150,000 units per year), and that wasn't even counting overseas production. In truth, American Motors probably saved Jeep from going out of business, at least as a civilian vehicle producer. The company may have been able to hang on as a tactical truck builder because that business was very profitable, but American Motors was its real savior.

400 Sergio Marchionne, the CEO of Fiat Chrysler Automobiles (FCA), was on record as saying that Jeep Wranglers should never be built anywhere but in the United States. However, in 1978,

American Motors began switching its Canadian automobile factory to the production of the Jeep CJ because the Toledo plant couldn't keep up with demand. The new plant produced an additional 50,000 CJs per year to help meet growing worldwide demand. The truth is, the Jeep CJs were produced in many countries around the world. So why not do the same with the Wrangler?

401 After nine years of continuously increasing production at Toledo to keep up with ever-growing demand for Jeep vehicles, the company announced a major expansion in March 1979 with the goal of doubling Jeep output within three years. It was a long overdue idea but, unfortunately, in the middle of the expansion a major recession hit the world economy and Jeep's plans had to be halted. The Canadian CJ plant was reconverted to passenger car production.

402 For 1980, Jeep introduced the Laredo package available on the CJ-5 and CJ-7, in both hardtop and soft top versions. Standard on Laredo were Wrangler 9Rx15 radial tires on chrome-plated styled

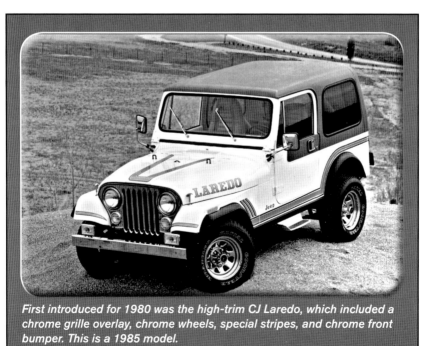

First introduced for 1980 was the high-trim CJ Laredo, which included a chrome grille overlay, chrome wheels, special stripes, and chrome front bumper. This is a 1985 model.

wheels, unique vinyl high-back bucket seats and door trim, leather-wrapped steering wheel, luxury carpeting, and special styling accents and stripes. Believe it or not, this marked the first time that high-back bucket seats were offered on a CJ vehicle from the factory.

403 As the decade of the 1980s opened, Jeep CJ base prices were $6,095 for the CJ-5 and $6,295 for the CJ-7. The optional Renegade Package was an additional $875, the Golden Eagle soft top package was $1,425, and the Golden eagle hardtop cost $1,845. The top-of-the line CJ Laredo hardtop package cost $2,400, but you received an awful lot of nice features for that price.

404 In my opinion, the 1982 Jeep CJ-7 Limited CJ was the most unusual of the "Package Jeeps." It certainly created outrage among longtime Jeep enthusiasts who still hadn't gotten used to the idea of the CJ-7's optional automatic transmission and now were confronted with an all-out luxury CJ. The CJ-7 Limited came about after the marketing staff at American Motors decided that many of the people who were downsizing from a Blazer or Bronco in search of better fuel economy might want to still have the same level of luxury and comfort in a CJ vehicle.

To that end they had engineering design a softer suspension, widen the track, add more sound insulation, and design a quieter hardtop. Stylists added two interior choices (cloth or leather), along with every luxury touch they could fit including plush carpeting, leather-wrapped steering wheel, padded roll bar, color-keyed styled wheels, body-color wheel lip extensions, AM/FM two-speaker stereo, and more. Power steering and brakes were standard as well.

Although the CJ Limited wasn't very popular, the people who bought them generally were very pleased with the vehicles.

405 If you're really lucky, you may come across a used 1984 CJ-7 fitted with unusual argent-painted styled-steel wheels with chrome trim rings and hub covers, plus chrome side mirrors, and black denim high-back bucket seats. It also included fog lamps, center console, 5-speed transmission, and a full-size spare. You may notice that the Jeep is painted a shade of dark charcoal clear coat metallic that

you haven't seen on other Jeeps. If you happen to spot such a vehicle, you're looking at the one-year-only Jeep CJ-7 Special Value Package, which was offered for only a very short time during the 1984 model year and was priced at $8,813.

1984 JEEP CJ-7 SPECIAL VALUE PACKAGE

Rarely seen today, the 1984 CJ-7 Special Value Package was a base CJ-7 equipped with special wheels, special paint, black or white soft top, black denim high-back bucket seats, and more.

406 The Jeep Scrambler pickup truck was discontinued at the end of the 1985 model run. Its replacement, the Comanche XJ long-bed pickup (and later short bed as well), was considered a much more competitive offering in the compact truck market, so the company focused its attention on that.

407 For 1986, the CJ-7 was offered in only three trim series: base, Renegade, and Laredo. The reason? Jeep was preparing to phase out the CJ series in advance of the upcoming new Wrangler and wanted to limit inventory of any possible leftovers to just the best-selling models.

The nice thing about a Jeep CJ is that it can be made more beautiful with just one or two added items, such as the chrome wheels seen on this 1986 model.

408 The final CJs produced in 1986 were dubbed the Collector's Edition, and Jeep produced a small brochure touting their appeal. The brochure (which can often be found for sale on eBay) talks about Jeep's history and heritage and even shows what appears to be a body decal proclaiming "Last of a Great Breed" but gives no information as to what, if anything, was special about them, equipment-wise. The CJ's replacement, the Jeep Wrangler, looked very similar but was a vastly improved vehicle in all respects except for its styling.

These final production CJ-5 models are ready to be shipped to waiting dealers.

J-Series Jeep Wagoneers, Gladiators, Cherokees, and Panel Trucks

Legend and Lore

409 The Jeep Wagoneer is one of the most iconic Jeep vehicles of all time because it was the vehicle that really ignited the SUV market. Introduced in late 1962 as a 1963 model, the Wagoneer was the first sport utility designed from the ground up as a four-wheel-drive station wagon for families.

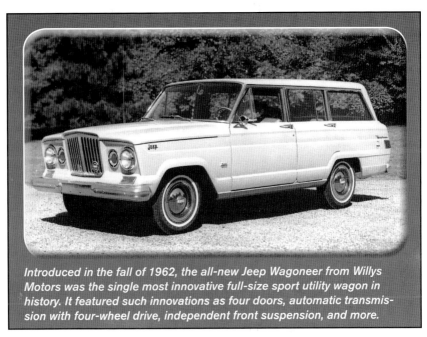

Introduced in the fall of 1962, the all-new Jeep Wagoneer from Willys Motors was the single most innovative full-size sport utility wagon in history. It featured such innovations as four doors, automatic transmission with four-wheel drive, independent front suspension, and more.

410 The main reason why the Wagoneer was so successful in the marketplace was that it was so innovative. Rather than copying and rehashing old Jeep styling themes from the past, it created an entirely new look that set the pace for senior Jeep styling for the next 20 years and beyond.

411 Prior to the introduction of the J-series Wagoneer and Gladiator, Jeep station wagons had simply been known as Willys Jeep wagons with no names except for a few subseries such as the Parkway conversions or the Traveler wagons. Jeep trucks were known simply as Jeep Trucks. The full-size Jeep Wagoneer and

Gladiator introduced actual model names, thereby better serving to implant their name and image in the minds of car shoppers.

Based on the Jeep Wagoneer two-door body, the Jeep Panel Delivery offered two rear doors for easier access to cargo. This is a 1964 model.

412 During 1964, a Jeep Wagoneer played a prominent role in the Rock Hudson comedy film *Man's Favorite Sport*, in which the handsome Hudson plays an "expert" outdoorsman who had never actually gone camping or fishing. Although a bit dated, it's still a pretty good film.

413 Not surprisingly, the first true all-out luxury SUV was introduced for 1966 by Kaiser Jeep Corporation. Called the Super Wagoneer, it was a Custom Wagoneer that was loaded with every luxury feature imaginable at the time. The standard equipment included a special high-compression 270-hp version of the AMC-sourced 327-ci Vigilante V-8, a 3-speed Hydramatic fully automatic transmission, power steering, power brakes (drums all around), a power tailgate window, air-conditioning, AM radio, tinted glass in all windows, a tilt steering wheel, and much more.

Another huge innovation for Jeep was the Super Wagoneer introduced for 1966. It was an all-out luxury wagon loaded with just about every option available and wearing a vinyl top and anodized side trim. These rare vehicles are highly collectible today.

414 In 1966, legendary auto writer Tom McCahill wrote, "My front yard usually resembles a clearing house for a hot car ring. At present, better than $50,000 worth of new autos stand there baking in the Florida sun. Of the whole kit and caboodle, my first choice would be the Jeep Wagoneer. . . . It rides like the best Detroit has to offer, but it'll go places you just wouldn't dream of going in an ordinary car."

415 In 1967, Henry J. Kaiser, the founder of Kaiser Industries, which was the parent company of Kaiser Jeep Corporation, passed away in Hawaii. His son Edgar Kaiser took over the giant company and remained at its helm. Edgar Kaiser ended up selling Kaiser Jeep to American Motors in late 1969. His father had been trying for several years to sell the Jeep company but could find no buyers.

416 The Jeep Wagoneer (along with its successors the Wagoneer Limited and the Grand Wagoneer) had one of the longest production runs of any American vehicle in the industry. It was introduced in late 1962 as a 1963 model, and it continued in production through the 1991 model year. That's 29 consecutive model years without a significant change in the bodystyle. In fact, if you remove the grille from one of the late-model Grand Wagoneers with the rectangular headlamps, you can see the original Willys sheet metal stampings where the round headlamps were fitted.

417 Here's a special senior Jeep model you may not be familiar with: During 1974, Jeep Corporation offered its dealers a very special red, white, and blue version of the long-wheelbase Jeep J-10 and J-20 pickup trucks. Meant to be used as a dealer parts and service truck, the vehicles featured a two-tone blue and white body paint scheme with bright red accent stripes.

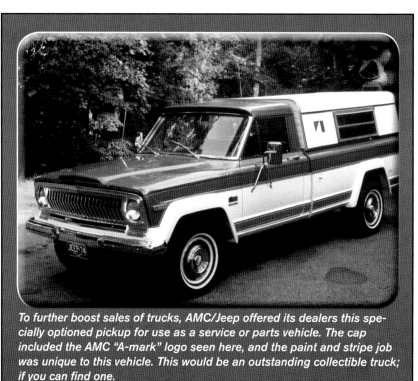

To further boost sales of trucks, AMC/Jeep offered its dealers this specially optioned pickup for use as a service or parts vehicle. The cap included the AMC "A-mark" logo seen here, and the paint and stripe job was unique to this vehicle. This would be an outstanding collectible truck; if you can find one.

It came only with the Townside body, and also included a stylish pickup bed cap with jalousie windows, a large American Motors "A-Mark" decal (which was the corporate ID) placed on both sides of the cap, a white-painted rear step bumper, Custom interior and exterior trim, the potent 360-ci 2-barrel V-8, standard power steering and power disc brakes, along with dual low-profile mirrors.

This sharp-looking truck offered such work options as V-8s up to a 401-ci version, a factory-approved snowplow, various winches, the Quadra-Trac full-time four-wheel-drive system with the automatic transmission, and an approved trailer hitch.

Although the company claimed that these trucks would be offered to dealers every six months, it appears that they were a one-time offering, as I have found no follow-up offerings from AMC. These specials are extremely rare today, but they do come up for sale now and then at very reasonable prices.

418 It's not known exactly who came up with the Cherokee name for Jeep's new sport utility vehicle for 1974, but it probably was influenced by the success of the Renegade name earlier. The president and chairman of American Motors, William Luneburg and Roy D Chapin Jr., respectively, met with the leaders of the Cherokee Nation to reach an agreement on the company's use of the Cherokee name on the Jeep line. Chapin in particular was sensitive to the Native Americans' feelings because he had spent a great deal of time out West when he was younger and felt a real affinity for their culture.

419 At the Detroit Auto Show in January 1975, Jeep Corporation unveiled an exciting new sports model called the Cherokee Chief. This name went on to become one of the most legendary nameplates in automotive history. Based on the Cherokee wide-wheel platform, it boasted wider axles and wheels along with big Goodyear Tracker A/T tires as standard equipment.

420 For 1976, Jeep added to its growing catalog of specialty sport packages when it unveiled the new Jeep J-10 Honcho pickup. It a great-looking and popular sport appearance package that

included big Tracker A/T tires, white-painted spoke wheels, jazzy exterior appearance upgrades, and the attractive Levi's interior trim. It proved to be a smash hit with Jeep enthusiasts.

421 American Motors and Jeep introduced the first American sport utility vehicle to offer a genuine leather interior when it debuted the Jeep Wagoneer Limited in early 1978. It offered a level of luxury features and standard equipment that was simply unheard of in the four-wheel-drive market at that time.

Standard features included air-conditioning, an AM/FM/CB radio, cruise control, plush floor carpeting, leather seat upholstery, and a leather-wrapped sports steering wheel. Extra insulation helped bring the interior to a new level of quietness.

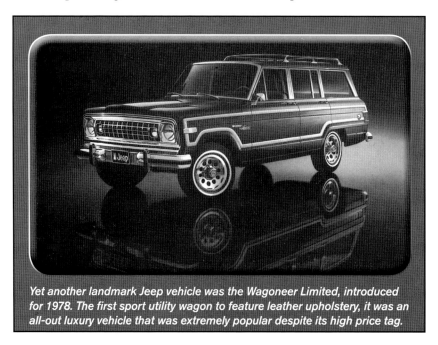

Yet another landmark Jeep vehicle was the Wagoneer Limited, introduced for 1978. The first sport utility wagon to feature leather upholstery, it was an all-out luxury vehicle that was extremely popular despite its high price tag.

422 Jeep maintained its image as an expert on snow removal for many years. In 1979, it offered a factory-installed option called the Snow Boss package. Included were a factory-approved snowplow with all brackets and hardware, a lift unit, two plow lights, plus "Snow Boss" hood side decals. Available on the Jeep

J-10 and J-20 trucks, as well as on the Jeep Cherokee and Wagoneer models, required equipment that also had to be ordered included a heavy-duty alternator, battery, and cooling system, plus power steering, extra-duty suspension, and specific tires.

423 For 1980, Jeep introduced the Laredo trim package, which was available on the Cherokee wide-wheel two-door model and the J-10 pickup. Standard equipment with the Laredo package included Wrangler 10Rx15 radial ply tires mounted on chrome-plated styled wheels. Inside were unique vinyl bucket seats and fancy door trim, a leather-wrapped steering wheel, and luxury floor carpeting. On the exterior were special styling accents and body stripes.

424 Probably the rarest of the package Jeep Cherokees is the 1980 Golden Hawk. Available for a short time only, and only on the Cherokee two-door wide-wheel model, the Golden Hawk included a stylized Hawk hood graphic that flowed from the hood onto the body sides, plus gold-painted wheels, a brush guard, sport steering wheel, halogen fog lights, sweet-looking denim interior trim, and a host of other features. The Golden Hawk package price was $1,049.

Two rare and desirable Jeep vehicles are the 1980 Cherokee Golden Hawk and the 1980 CJ-7 Golden Hawk; each was produced just that one model year.

425 Here's one to try on your friends: In the 1980s when Venezuela was prosperous (before the dictators took over), Jeep de Venezuela was such a large company it manufactured Jeep vehicles in its own factories rather than import them. In the early 1980s, Jeep de Venezuela offered a short-bed pickup truck that looked like the J-10 but was produced on the shorter Jeep Wagoneer wheelbase. For the local market, Jeep de Venezuela named it the Wagoneer Pickup.

426 Another little-known fact about the rarely seen Venezuelan Jeep vehicles is that for certain model years the Wagoneer used the Jeep truck grille, which in my opinion was better looking than the US version.

427 Remember the 1991 comedy film *What About Bob?* In the movie, therapist Leo Marvin (played by Richard Dreyfuss) is tormented by a mental patient named Bob Wiley (played by Bill Murray). To drive home the point that Dr. Marvin is a rich yuppie, he drives a gorgeous Jeep Grand Wagoneer, and it has a prominent role in the film. If you haven't seen it, do so; I think that it's one of the all-time funniest movies.

428 Once the XJ series Cherokee and Wagoneer (including the Wagoneer Limited XJ) debuted, the J-series Wagoneer Limited was renamed the Grand Wagoneer and continued in production. However, there was some concern that the company might lose a few customers who still wanted a full-size sport utility vehicle but didn't want to shell out the big bucks demanded for the Grand Wagoneer, so engineers cobbled together a vehicle that they named the Custom Wagoneer for 1984.

The Custom Wagoneer used the same J-series body as the Grand Wagoneer but was substantially de-contented and de-trimmed to lower the base price as far as possible. With an automatic transmission, part-time four-wheel-drive system, air-conditioning, and stereo radio, the Custom Wagoneer was priced at $15,995 compared to $19,306 for a Grand Wagoneer.

Jeep covered its bets for 1984 by also offering this rare Jeep Wagoneer Custom model. Essentially a de-contented Grand Wagoneer, it wasn't popular.

Body and Interior

429 The J-series Jeep Wagoneer was the first sport utility vehicle with four doors that was ever offered to the public. It ended up creating a minor sensation when it debuted because for the first time a sport utility wagon could offer a reasonable alternative to the traditional family four-door station wagon.

430 Although everyone remembers the four-door Wagoneer, Jeep actually offered a two-door version of the Wagoneer as well, at least for the first few years of production. From the start, however, the four-door Wagoneer was the most popular seller by far.

431 Here's an interesting fact: The Wagoneer's front doors are the same for two-doors and four-doors. This was done to save money on tooling, and it worked surprisingly well. The later Cherokee two- and four-door models shared the same doors, as did the pickup trucks.

432 Exterior paint color choices for the 1963 Jeep Wagoneer included Parkway Green, President Red, White Cap, Tree Bark Brown, Spruce Tip Green, Sierra Blue, Nordic Blue, Jet Line Grey, Parade Blue, and Amber Metallic.

433 Interior color choices for the all-new 1963 Wagoneer included Sylvan Green, Nordic Blue, Black, and Amber.

434 Despite its compact overall size, the Wagoneer had a lot of room, especially cargo space. With the tailgate open, the Wagoneer offered a cargo length of 111 inches, along with a floor width of 55 inches. The unobstructed rear opening was a full 39.5 inches in height.

435 So exactly who styled the new Jeep Wagoneer? Brooks Stevens always said he did, although I haven't seen any drawing by him that looks anything like the Wagoneer. One highly placed Willys Jeep executive told me that the design was created entirely by Jeep stylist Jim Anger. However, two years later, this same executive reversed himself and told me that it really was Brooks Stevens who did it. Confused? Me too. In the end, I believe that it was Jeep design chief Jim Angers who did it. Perhaps Brooks Stevens had some input on the design.

436 Take a look at the body lines of the Jeep Wagoneer and notice the thin roof pillars. This was an idea that helped to create the Wagoneer's feeling of spacious interior room by letting in more light.

437 The first Wagoneers came with a few surprising extra features. For example, standard equipment on all 1963 Wagoneer four-wheel-drive models was a dash-mounted compass in the center of the instrument panel.

438 Although boasting compact exterior dimensions, the new Wagoneer rode a sturdy 110-inch wheelbase, which was a full 6 inches longer than the old Willys wagon and helped to provide exceptional interior room.

439 The array of Jeep Gladiator models introduced in 1963 and 1964 is dizzying. To begin, two series were offered: One was the J-200 series, which included GVW ratings that ranged from 4,000 to 8,600 pounds and rode on a generous 120-inch wheelbase chassis. The other was the J-300, which offered GVWs that ranged from 5,000 to 8,600 pounds, on a longer 126-inch wheelbase.

440 The Gladiator offered two pickup box options. The standard pickup box was an old-fashioned-style step-side model that Jeep called the Thriftside, which is rarely seen today. The optional full-width flat-sided Townside body offered extra carrying room along with more modern styling.

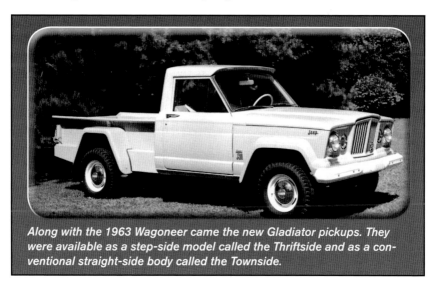

Along with the 1963 Wagoneer came the new Gladiator pickups. They were available as a step-side model called the Thriftside and as a conventional straight-side body called the Townside.

441 The Gladiator J-200 and J-300 series both offered a stake-body model, which could be ordered with single rear wheels or with dual rear wheels for extra carrying capacity. The Gladiator trucks were also offered in stripped cab and chassis units with either single rear wheels or as a "dually." These models were created to make it easier for installation of specialty work bodies, many of which could be ordered from the local Jeep dealer.

The Gladiator also offered cab and chassis models and the stake-side body seen here. This is a 1964 model.

442 The Jeep Wagoneer established yet another first in the four-wheel-drive market during the 1964 model year when the company introduced factory-installed air-conditioning as an option in a sport utility vehicle. The Jeep Gladiator trucks, which used the same dashboard as the Wagoneer, also offered air-conditioning that year.

443 The Jeep Gladiators came in a standard "work" model and could be ordered with an extra-cost Custom Cab trim option. This package included a color-keyed instrument panel and door panels, a full headliner, a cigar lighter, dual sun visors, right and left armrests, a foam seat cushion, stainless steel rear cab trim, bright side window and windshield moldings, a chrome grille (a body-color grille was standard initially), plus a chrome front bumper, chrome hub caps, and stainless steel vent window trim.

444 In 1964, Kaiser Jeep introduced an optional camper-type soft top that covered the entire bed of the Gladiator pickup and included plastic side windows. The idea was that it was a simple and relatively inexpensive way to provide hunters and outdoorsmen with

a sleeping platform that was off the ground and also free from mosquitos. Unlike a conventional camper cap or camper shell, this soft top could be removed and stored away easily whenever the truck was needed to haul things.

445 The original Jeep Wagoneer had a keystone-style grille theme that was a bit like the Studebaker Lark automobiles of the time. But in mid-1965, the Wagoneer's front end was restyled with a broad horizontal theme that was much more modern and attractive. The company called it the Action Look, and it not only improved the styling, it also tended to make the Wagoneer look wider and more substantial than before. This new look continued into the 1970s.

In mid-1965, Kaiser Jeep unveiled new frontal styling for the Wagoneer. The Gladiator truck series continued to use the original keystone grille theme for several more years. This is a 1967 model.

446 During the 1960s, camper shells became popular with families wanting to enjoy the great outdoors. Jeep engineered factory-installed camper packages specially designed to handle the extra weight of a camper shell. Jeep also introduced a side-mounted spare tire for the Gladiator trucks, so that when a large camper body was installed the spare tire wouldn't have to be left behind. You had to be extra careful when driving in tight spots, however, because the spare tire stuck out so far you might accidently graze a tree or another vehicle and rip the tire right off the side of the truck.

With the introduction of the V-8 engine, the Gladiators could carry heavier loads, such as this slide-in camper unit. Note the side-mounted spare tire.

447 The Jeep Super Wagoneer, introduced for 1966, featured its own custom interior trim with handsome bucket seats, full carpeting, a floor console with shifter, and much more. On the exterior, special anodized side and rear trim panels, along with gorgeous wheel covers, mimicked the look of styled alloy wheels.

Fewer than 4,000 Super Wagoneers were produced in a four-year model run that ended in mid-1969. The reason it didn't sell

better than that is that the thinking behind it was just a little too advanced for the time. Years later, buyers began to insist on ever-more luxury in their four-wheel-drive vehicles.

448 The 1966–1969 Super Wagoneer also boasted a full vinyl top as standard equipment, which was a first for a Jeep vehicle and may have been a first for the sport utility market. Can you think of another SUV that offered a vinyl top before the Super Wagoneer?

449 The Wagoneer basic two-door model continued in production through 1967 (although some references say a two-wheel-drive two-door was still offered in 1968). The two-door Wagoneers were never very popular with buyers and are rarely seen today.

450 The Jeep Wagoneers received their second styling update during 1970, when a new eggcrate grille was adopted, along with some minor exterior trim changes including a tailgate trim panel

As this 1965 Gladiator illustrates, the Jeep J-series trucks were handsome vehicles. This one is a V-8 model, as identified by the front fender emblem.

similar in style to the new grille, and revised side-marker lamps. The change came midway through the model year; early brochures show the older style and later brochures feature the new look.

451 The Gladiator line of trucks retained the original keystone grille and front-end treatment through mid-1970, when they were finally restyled. However, this must have been the lowest-cost facelift in history because the new look was created when Jeep stylists simply took the old "buck-tooth" grille of the 1965–1969 Wagoneer and fitted it to the Gladiator. It meant that it cost the factory nothing in tooling or engineering expense.

By 1971, Jeep had also given new grilles to both the Wagoneer and the pickups. The trucks received the grille formerly used on the Wagoneer. Two-tone paint was a nice option.

452 For 1970, Jeep also introduced an electric sliding sunroof for the Wagoneer. This was yet another important SUV innovation by Jeep. It required a vinyl top (probably to hide the cutting and sanding marks), but the vinyl top added even more to the Wagoneer's good looks.

In 1971, Jeep Corporation debuted a new electrically powered sliding-steel sunroof option for the Wagoneer, demonstrated here by this young woman.

453 By 1974, Jeep had pushed the Wagoneer even further upmarket by making the revolutionary Quadra-Trac four-wheel-drive system standard equipment, along with a big 360-ci V-8 engine, automatic transmission (with column shift), power steering, and power disc brakes.

A 1974 Jeep Wagoneer Custom sits in the foreground, and the base Wagoneer rests in the background. Wagoneer sales were strong this year and the factory struggled to keep up with demand.

454 The biggest news for Jeep's 1974 model year was the introduction of a Jeep designed to compete with Chevy's top-selling Blazer. The Cherokee was probably the most successful new vehicle designed for next to nothing that the auto industry has ever seen. Basically, it was the old Wagoneer two-door body shell updated with a sportier side-window treatment along with a raft of new dress-up options.

Unfortunately, the Jeep marketing people badly miscalculated how popular the Cherokee was going to be: It just about set the market on fire. It remained in a sold-out condition for many months after introduction. It became one of the most profitable Jeep vehicles in the company's history.

455 The Jeep Wagoneer was given a full bodyside woodgrain option for the 1975 model year, and it was very attractive, much like the later Wagoneer Limited was. The Wagoneer retained this look for one year only; the 1976 models reverted to a much narrower woodgrain body side decal.

For 1975, Jeep introduced a new woodgrain side decal for the Wagoneer Custom that is particularly stylish, and quite similar to what later debuted on the Wagoneer Limited model.

456 In one of the most audacious marketing moves of the 1970s, Jeep management introduced the four-door Jeep Cherokee for 1977. Why call it audacious? Because it was nothing but a Jeep Wagoneer with different exterior and interior trim and fewer standard features. It was very well-received; buyers saw it as more youthful and sportier compared to the essentially similar Wagoneer. At the same time, sales of the Wagoneer continued to climb ever upward, as these vehicles appealed to a whole different crowd. They were older and more affluent than the Cherokee crowd, and they were looking for the utmost luxury they could find in a sport utility wagon.

457 The new Cherokee Wide-Wheel model debuted for 1977. Available in the two-door bodystyle only, it used the same wider axles and fender flares as the Cherokee Chief but was offered in a stripped-down base version or could be ordered as a sportier Cherokee S model.

This is a new Cherokee Chief for 1976; it was one of the hottest-selling Jeep wagons of all time.

458 The Cherokee added the Golden Eagle package for 1979, and it was available on the wide-wheel chassis only. Despite a rather high price tag, it was soon in a sold-out position. No wonder; it included beige denim bucket seats, a sports steering wheel, big Eagle decal on the hood, special stripes, bronze-tone tinted glass for the rear side windows, front brush guard, gold-painted wheels, and a whole lot more.

459 The 1979 model year was the first year that the new rectangular headlamps were featured on the J-series, so all three models

Here are the 1979 Cherokee S four-door model and the 1979 Cherokee Chief two-door model. The S package emphasized stylish trim, while the Chief had a more aggressive demeanor. This year, square headlamps debuted.

(trucks, Cherokee, and Wagoneer) were also given new grilles to accommodate the new lamps. It was a relatively inexpensive way to update the vehicles' styling and keep their looks contemporary.

460 American Motors had a Mexico affiliate, Vehiculos Automores Mexicanos (VAM). In 1980, that company built a short-bed version of the J-10 pickup truck that was even shorter than the US model because VAM decided to build it on the same 109-inch wheelbase chassis as the Wagoneer as a way to save the cost of new tooling. Most people don't notice the difference in length until they are told about it.

461 After nine years of almost uninterrupted growth, the US sport utility market turned abruptly downward in 1980 due to high fuel prices, growing unemployment, and rampant inflation. In the Jeep model lineup, sales of the Cherokee were affected the most, mainly because they were expensive, fuel-thirsty vehicles that were usually purchased by families. Sales of the Wagoneer (especially the Limited models) were much less affected because they tended to be purchased by affluent people who were unaffected by the economic downturn. Sales of the CJ vehicles turned down for a while but soon began to climb back because Jeep marketing people ran special promotions that offered lower prices.

462 Jeep added a really great-looking sport model to the truck line for 1980: the J-10 Sportside, which was available in both Custom and Honcho trim. Offered only on the shorter wheelbase J-10, the Sportside boasted wide step-side rear fenders, which were made of fiberglass due to high tooling costs for steel fenders.

Because of their Custom trim and special beds, the J-10 Sportside pickups were fairly expensive, and they didn't sell all that well because the economy was in such poor shape. However, that makes them rare and highly collectible today. They are probably the most collectible of the J-series pickups, but they are rather difficult to find.

463 To try to revive sales of its senior line (the J-series vehicles), Jeep introduced additional new models for 1981. They included a

four-door version of the Cherokee Chief and Laredo wagons along with a Wagoneer Brougham that, price-wise, was between the basic Wagoneer Custom and the topline Wagoneer Limited. The Wagoneer Brougham sales volume proved to be pretty good.

464 Look underneath the front bumper of any 1981 or newer J-series vehicle and you notice a small rubber air dam. This was introduced that model year in an effort to improve "real world" fuel economy for customers. The air dam didn't affect the actual EPA fuel economy numbers because that entity tests vehicles in an indoor lab.

465 For 1981, the Jeep trucks lost their trademark roof front lip in an effort to provide a little appearance change while also improving aerodynamics, again to improve "real world" fuel economy. Although the new roof looked good at the time, it modernized the Jeep's appearance. The classic overhanging roof lip has since become an iconic style mark for Jeep and has been used on many of its modern concept vehicles.

466 One drawback to the Wagoneer Limited and Grand Wagoneer was that in most years their individual front seats didn't allow for three-across seating. The center armrest was deliberately fixed in place to prevent it from being folded up, which would have created room for a third front-seat passenger, which in turn would have required Jeep to fit another seat belt for that passenger.

Due to customer demand, the 1985 Jeep was put through an engineering change to allow the center armrest to fold up so a third passenger could occupy the front seat. As required by law, a third seat belt was installed as well. The big Grand Wagoneer thus became a six-passenger vehicle once again, just as the original Wagoneer had been.

467 For the 1988 model year, Jeep introduced a new electric powered sunroof with an integral air deflector as an option for the Grand Wagoneer. Also new this year was an AM/FM/MPX electronically tuned stereo system with cassette and four Jensen speakers, which was fitted as standard equipment on the Grand Wagoneer.

Engine and Drivetrain

468 During the 1960s, Wagoneer was the only sport utility with an OHC engine, other than the carryover Willys Jeep wagons, which were mainly sold to overseas markets once the Wagoneer was introduced.

469 To give you an idea of what driving the new Jeep Wagoneer was like, consider the performance results from a road test by *Motor Trend* magazine. As reported in the March 1963 issue: Acceleration 0–30 mph took 4.6 seconds, to go 0–45 mph took 8.8 seconds. To travel 0–60 mph (the benchmark test at the time) took 16.1 seconds. A quarter-mile run took 20.5 seconds. Top speed was a true 90 mph. The vehicle tested was equipped with the standard 230-ci OHC six (the only engine offered that year) fitted with the GM automatic transmission.

470 The new Wagoneer (and trucks) came standard with an alternator and all-transistor voltage regulator; two advanced items that many passenger cars had not yet adopted. They helped to keep the battery fully charged even when the engine was idling.

471 The Jeep Wagoneer revolutionized the four-wheel-drive market in 1963 because it was the first four-wheel-drive sport utility vehicle to offer an optional automatic transmission. This opened the market to family-car buyers and made the idea of an all-wheel-drive wagon much more appealing to women drivers, not to mention male drives who either never learned to drive a manual transmission or preferred an automatic.

472 Early Wagoneers used an optional BorgWarner AS-8F 3-speed automatic transmission, which was a solid, reliable unit. However, when the company switched to using American Motors' engines beginning in mid-1964, it also switched to using the GM Hydramatic, which was a much better transmission overall, with smoother shifts and bulletproof reliability.

473 Initially, a single-range four-wheel-drive transfer case was the only offering on the Jeep J-series Wagoneer and Gladiator four-wheel-drive models when fitted with an automatic transmission. Versions of the Wagoneer and Gladiator models ordered with the standard 3-speed manual transmission were equipped with a 2-speed transfer case.

474 Jeep said that its new four-wheel drive was so smooth that the company decided it had to include indicator lights, so that drivers could tell at a glance whether or not they were in four-wheel drive. These handy indicator lights appeared as standard equipment on the 1963–1964 models equipped with four-wheel drive only.

475 The introduction of the new Gladiator trucks marked Jeep's return to the two-wheel-drive pickup market, which it had left after 1951. Jeep eventually decided to exit the two-wheel-drive truck market once again (after the 1968 model year) and never again offered a two-wheel-drive J-series pickup truck in the US market.

476 Buyers of 1963 and early 1964 Jeep Wagoneers and Gladiators had to be content with the Tornado-OHC six engine

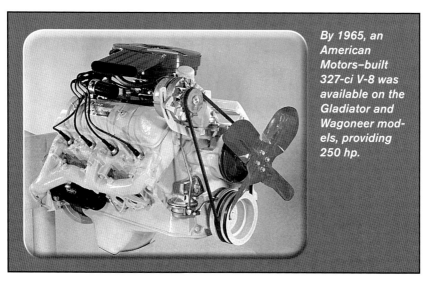

By 1965, an American Motors–built 327-ci V-8 was available on the Gladiator and Wagoneer models, providing 250 hp.

because that was the only mill offered. But Jeep management realized that customers would eventually demand V-8 engines for their trucks, so in mid-1964 Jeep introduced the Vigilante V-8, with 327 ci, 250 hp, and a thumping 340 ft-lbs of torque. With an eye toward saving money, this new engine ran on regular fuel.

477 Contrary to popular belief, the Jeep Vigilante 327-ci V-8 was not a Chevy engine, nor was it related in any way to Chevrolet. The engine was produced by American Motors at its plant in Kenosha, Wisconsin. The AMC 327 V-8 actually debuted in the 1957 Rambler Rebel, Nash Ambassador, and Hudson Hornet models, which was years before Chevy introduced its own 327 V-8.

478 The Vigilante V-8 was designed by AMC engineer Ralph Isbrandt, who'd begun investigating V-8 designs while employed at Kaiser-Frazer Corporation. Kaiser-Frazer needed a V-8 to power its big cars, but management staff felt that the company couldn't afford the cost of tooling, so it never built one.

After Ralph Isbrandt left Kaiser-Frazer to join AMC, he designed the 327 V-8 for its car lines. It was later used in the senior Rambler models, and (in a case of serendipity) it eventually ended up being used in Kaiser vehicles after all: the Jeep Wagoneer and Gladiator.

479 As mentioned above, the 1964–1967 Jeep Vigilante V-8 was manufactured by American Motors, which also produced the engine in a 275-hp high-compression version that Jeep eventually offered in a special version of the Wagoneer. The Vigilante was the first AMC engine used in a Jeep, but it was soon joined by other AMC engines.

480 Not long after the Vigilante V-8 debuted, Kaiser Jeep introduced the Hi-Torque 6, which was also sourced from American Motors. The Hi-Torque 6 was essentially the 232-ci Rambler inline-6, a sturdy, economical inline-6 good for 145 hp and 215 ft-lbs of torque. Initially, Jeep used the engine in the J-series vehicles only. These seven-main-bearing OHV engines are amazingly long lived and exceptionally smooth running.

481 Some Jeep enthusiasts might bemoan the discontinuance of the OHC six, but in practice it received a lot of customer complaints for being noisy and prone to oil leaks. By comparison, the AMC six was nearly silent and didn't suffer any oil leak problems until 1982, when the company switched to the notorious plastic valve cover that was often prone to leaking.

482 So, you might wonder, why didn't Kaiser Jeep use its own V-6 engine (the former Buick mill) in the Wagoneer, rather than source it from another company? After all, the V-6 had more horsepower and torque than the Rambler six. The reason for the choice was engine smoothness. The AMC six had seven main bearings and twice as many counterweights as other American-made sixes. It idled as smooth as a V-8 while the V-6 had kind of a rather lumpy idle due to its inherently unbalanced design.

The rough idle was considered acceptable in the CJ series but not for the J-series vehicles. The reason Jeep didn't switch to using the AMC six in the CJ-series was that it wouldn't fit; it was too long for the underhood area. American Motors addressed that problem in 1972 by redesigning the CJ's front end structure and lengthening the wheelbase ahead of the cowl.

483 The Vigilante V-8 and Hi-Torque 6 were produced by American Motors and are essentially identical to the AMC version with only minor exceptions. The block color was gold for the Jeep versions and red or green (depending on the model year) when fitted to an American Motors car.

484 Like the earlier Willys Jeep trucks, the Gladiator offered an optional power takeoff unit to run various accessories such as saws, pumps, winches, and wrecker equipment. Jeep Wagoneer also offered the power takeoff unit as an option.

485 Here's yet another Jeep first: The 1963 Jeep Gladiator was the first four-wheel-drive pickup in the world to offer an optional automatic transmission. In late 1964, it also offered the optional Vigilante V-8.

486 To illustrate how badly Jeep needed to offer a V-8 in its J-series vehicle: When the Vigilante V-8 debuted, Jeep customers immediately turned away from the Tornado-OHC six in favor of the V-8 engines, leaving dealers stuck with a large stock of the now slow-selling older 6-cylinder models. It proved to be a very large problem for months. In the auto industry, dealers can't return a vehicle once it's in stock, so eventually all the 6-cylinder models were sold, usually at bargain prices.

487 Jeep Wagoneer buyers in 1963 could order a 3-speed manual transmission with overdrive if they wanted to but only on two-wheel-drive models. It came only with a column shifter for the gearbox. The overdrive unit provided reduced engine speeds on the highway, which made for a much quieter ride while also reducing engine wear and oil consumption. At the same time, the overdrive also provided greatly increased fuel economy because the engine didn't have to work so hard.

488 Here's yet another Jeep first: For the 1966–1969 model years, Jeep offered an ultra-high-line trim luxury wagon called the Super Wagoneer. It was the first SUV to offer both automatic transmission and V-8 power as standard equipment.

489 The last year you could buy a two-wheel-drive Gladiator was during the 1967 model year. Retail sales of the Gladiator two-wheelers was never very strong, so Jeep decided to drop them from the lineup to help simplify the factory's operations. Although some reference guides claim that the two-wheel-drive Wagoneer was still offered in 1968, that model doesn't appear in the company's Data Book for that year. There is a chance it was offered for a short time that year before being dropped.

In any event, today both the Gladiator and Wagoneer two-wheel-drive models are extremely rare. Their collectability, on the other hand, is hard to estimate because they appeal only to people looking for rare Jeep models. Traditional four-wheel-drive enthusiasts either don't want them or do something stupid like convert them to four-wheel drive.

490 The 1967 model year was also the last time that the Jeep Panel Truck and the two-door Wagoneer were offered. As mentioned earlier, the two-door Wagoneer was resurrected in 1974 as the Jeep Cherokee, albeit with a bunch of styling updates. The panel truck was never revived, probably because there were so many cargo van models available at other companies.

491 For 1968, in the Wagoneer and Gladiator, Kaiser Jeep Corporation made yet another engine change when it began installing Buick 350-ci V-8s as replacements for the AMC 327 engines. This wasn't really an improvement, however, because the Buick offered only 230 hp versus the AMC's 250 hp. By that point, the AMC 327 V-8 was out of production, having been replaced by the new, lighter, and more modern AMC 343 V-8 that was rated at 235 hp.

The decision to begin using the Buick engine may well have been something as simple as pricing; in all probability the Buick engine cost less. In any case, the fact is that the Buick 350 V-8 is an outstanding engine: powerful, quiet, and long lasting.

492 Some reference guides claim that the AMC 327 V-8 continued to be used in the 1969–1970 Wagoneer Super models, but that's incorrect because there were no 1969 or 1970 Super Wagoneers produced. Anyway, as mentioned above, the AMC 327 engine was already out of production by then.

If by chance you happen to come across a Super Wagoneer that is titled as a 1969–1970 model, it's most likely a leftover 1967 that had sat on a dealer's lot and was retitled until it was finally sold.

493 The 1971 model year was the last one for the Gladiator name. Beginning with the 1972 J-series truck models, they were simply named the Jeep Truck and they came in two series: J-10 and J-20. The J-10 was rated as a 1/2-ton model and could be ordered with beefed-up suspension to carry heavier loads. The J-20 was rated as a 3/4-ton truck and likewise could be ordered beefed-up for heavier loads. The J-10 could be ordered in regular-bed and long-bed versions, while the J-20 truck came only as a long bed.

494 Here comes another first for Jeep vehicles: In August 1972, Jeep Corporation forever changed the four-wheel-drive market when it introduced the Quadra-Trac full-time four-wheel-drive system for the 1973 model year J-series Wagoneer and pickup trucks. Backed by the most extensive testing of any major engineering advance developed by Jeep in the previous three decades, it was available on the 1973 Jeep Wagoneer and in four 1973 Truck models.

The Quadra-Trac system made it possible for a four-wheel-drive vehicle to be driven on hard, dry surfaces without damage by allowing each wheel to operate at its own speed. This prevented the stresses that build up in the driveline as a result of the vehicles' four wheels attempting to travel at the same speeds in places such as in turns and corners.

Quadra-Trac also eliminated the need for lockout hubs and for shifting in and out of four-wheel drive because it was a full-time system. It was at first available in conjunction with the 360-ci V-8 only.

495 AMC's vice president of Jeep product development at the time was the capable Marv Stuckey. He called Quadra-Trac ". . . as significant to the four-wheel-drive vehicle as the automatic transmission was to the automobile," and that was no overstatement. Today most of the four-wheel-drive vehicles use a full-time system, and experts agree that the SUV market growth of the past 30 years would have been impossible without full-time four-wheel drive.

496 So exactly how was Quadra-Trac different from other so-called full-time four-wheel-drive systems? The Jeep system incorporated a third controlled-slip differential in the transfer case that automatically delivered power to the axle that had the most traction.

497 For 1973, Jeep added a potent 4-barrel version of the AMC 360-ci V-8 as an option on both the Wagoneer and the Jeep trucks. The standard engine on the Wagoneer and J-10 trucks was the 258-ci AMC six, which was a larger version of the 232-ci unit.

498 If you have the chance to look through an old product catalog of Graymarine boat engines from the 1970s, you notice some familiar engine sizes: 232, 304, and 360 ci. Yep, those are Jeep engines that Graymarine converted to marine-type. American Motors had a special Component Sales office charged with selling engines and other parts and components to outside firms, and Graymarine happened to be one of its larger customers. Sports car builder Bricklin was another engine buyer, for just one year. International Harvester was a major customer and used the Jeep sixes and V-8s in its lines of light trucks.

499 The big news for the 1974 model year was the availability of the AMC-designed and -built 401-ci V-8 good for 235 hp net and a thumping 320 ft-lbs of torque, which provided towing capacity of up to 7,000 pounds! This rugged, potent engine was offered as an option in all of the J-series models.

500 Senior Jeep models (aka the J-series or full-size Jeeps) were treated to a completely new electronic ignition system for 1975 in an effort to improve drivability and fuel economy while reducing service requirements. The electronic ignition eliminated the separate points and condenser used in prior years.

501 When the Cherokee Chief was introduced in January 1975, it pioneered a wide-wheel stance previously unseen in the big wagons, with much wider front and rear axles, special slotted alloy wheels, and the popular 10-15 wide-tread Goodyear Tracker tires. Large front and rear wheel openings were capped with steel fender extensions that covered the extra width to prevent stones from flying out, and they greatly improved the Cherokee's styling, making them look much more aggressive. In time, a "wide-wheel" Cherokee model also debuted in base form, without the Chief package but available with the stylish Cherokee S trim.

502 After the new full-time four-wheel-drive systems debuted on other vehicles during the mid-1970s, off-road enthusiasts began arguing about which one was best. In 1978, Jeep settled the

matter by having an independent company conduct traction tests on Fords, Chevys, Dodges, and Jeeps equipped with their respective full-time four-wheel-drive systems. Not surprisingly, the Jeep Quadra-Trac system proved to be superior by a large margin over all the others.

This J-series chassis is fitted with the AMC 6-cylinder engine.

503 The Jeep J-series vehicles for 1980 also offered a new part-time four-wheel-drive system in conjunction with an automatic transmission, planned to serve as an alternative to the more fuel-hungry Quadra-Trac system. The automatic/part-time four-wheel-drive setup included a New Process Gear Model NP208 transfer case (same as on the manual transmission models) and could be ordered with the full range of 6-cylinder and V-8 engines. Marking the first time in seven years that Jeep had offered part-time four-wheel-drive with an automatic transmission, the new drive-train option was made purely for its fuel economy improvement, and that was because the Quadra-Trac system was known as a bit of a gas hog.

504 The Jeep engineers had a lot of faith in the superior performance of Quadra-Trac but needed to improve its fuel efficiency. So, for 1980 the Quadra-Trac system was completely redesigned with an all-new viscous-drive configuration that provided greatly improved fuel efficiency, and in operation it was smoother and quieter as well. The new version offered two four-wheel-drive ranges rather than one. The new transfer case was the NP 219, built by New Process Gear.

505 The Jeep Cherokee and truck models were given a slick new 4-speed transmission as standard equipment for 1980. The new gearbox was a full "road-going" unit, meaning that first gear wasn't a "granny gear" reserved for tough off-roading, but was instead a regular-drive gear. The Jeep Wagoneers came standard with an automatic transmission but could be ordered with the 4-speed manual gearbox if the customer desired.

506 Although the 1980 J-10 and J-20 both came with a standard 4-speed transmission, there's a big difference between them. The J-10 has the ordinary road-use gearbox used on the Cherokee and Wagoneer, and first gear on the J-20's transmission is a low "granny gear" to provide maximum pulling power at low speeds.

507 Also for 1980, the automatic transmission for the Cherokee, Wagoneer, and truck models was redesigned to be lighter and more fuel efficient than in previous years. The weight loss was mostly courtesy of a new aluminum transmission case.

508 Effective with the 1979 model year, the 401-ci V-8 and the 360 4-barrel V-8 were both dropped from the Jeep line. The only V-8 engine for the J-series vehicles was AMC's 360-ci 2-barrel, which was rated at 175 hp and 285 ft-lbs of torque. This engine was standard on the Wagoneer and J-20 models and optional on the Jeep Cherokee and J-10. The reduced engine lineup was due to the high expense of certifying them with the EPA and due to concerns about fuel economy.

509 With fuel economy a continuing concern in 1981, Jeep decided to make the 258-ci six standard equipment on the Wagoneer. The J-20 trucks continued to use the 360 V-8 as standard equipment, but even they could be ordered with the six if desired. I don't know if anyone actually ordered a 6-cylinder J-20; I've never seen one. The J-20 was always a slow-selling truck anyway.

510 Good news arrived for the 1982 model year when the J-series Jeep vehicles equipped with the standard 6-cylinder engine could be ordered with an optional 5-speed manual transmission, with which they earned an EPA fuel economy rating of 18 mpg city and a whopping 25 mpg highway.

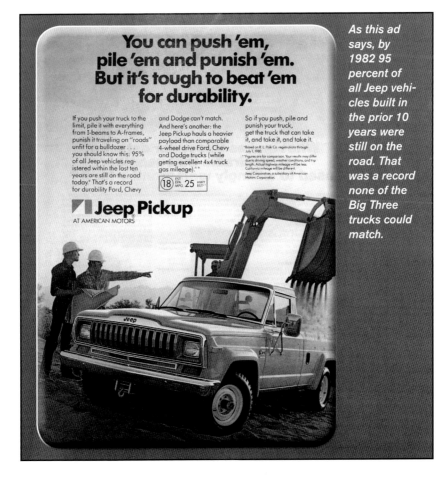

As this ad says, by 1982 95 percent of all Jeep vehicles built in the prior 10 years were still on the road. That was a record none of the Big Three trucks could match.

511 Another neat feature for 1982 Jeep J-series models was the new Selec-Trac system, which combined the convenience of a full-time four-wheel-drive system with the ability to switch to two-wheel drive for maximum fuel economy. The Selec-Trac, which came with a standard low-range feature, replaced Quadra-Trac and was a much better system overall because it was smoother, quieter, provided better traction, and enabled better fuel economy.

In an interview, Jeep's vice president of product engineering called the Selec-Trac a ". . . step forward in the evolution of sophisticated four-wheel-drive systems." If you think about it, a full-time four-wheel-drive system that can disengage and run in two-wheel-drive is actually more advanced than the systems used on most of today's SUVs.

512 In 1982, Jeep was the *only* manufacturer to offer full-time four-wheel drive; the Big Three had dropped their systems for fuel economy reasons. Jeep was thus the only company offering both full-time and part-time four-wheel drive. At this point, the Selec-Trac did require that the driver come to a full stop to engage four-wheel drive; an improved shift-on-the-fly version debuted later.

513 For the 1985 model year, the Jeep Grand Wagoneer finally received a shift-on-the-fly version for its standard full-time four-wheel-drive setup as standard equipment. The 6-cylinder models of the Grand Wagoneer used the New Process Gear NP229 transfer case; 8-cylinder models received the NP208 box.

Suspension and Brakes

514 In the beginning, the four-wheel-drive Wagoneers came standard with a solid axle and leaf-spring front suspension, while the two-wheel-drive Wagoneers came standard with an independent front suspension. This meant that the new Jeep actually offered two completely different front suspensions on the same vehicle. The independent front suspension could be ordered as optional equipment on the four-wheel-drive Wagoneers.

515 The Jeep Gladiator trucks came with a four-wheel leaf-spring suspension as standard equipment, but they also offered the independent front suspension, which could be specified on both the two-wheel-drive and four-wheel-drive models.

516 The two-wheel-drive J-series standard leaf-spring front suspension is very similar to that of the four-wheel-drive models. The two-wheel-drive models use a sturdy tubular front axle.

517 Jeep boasted that the four-wheel-drive Wagoneers step-in height was as much as 7 inches lower than competitors' vehicles. That was because both the Wagoneer and the Gladiator were designed from the beginning to be four-wheel-drive vehicles, so every major driveline component was integrated into the design. Other four-wheel-drive vehicles suffered from a "jacked-up" look as a result of trying to squeeze the four-wheel-drive componentry into the chassis. The tall height of those vehicles made it difficult to get in and out of them.

518 The standard front axles on the 1963 Wagoneer were rated at 2,500 pounds; the rear axles were rated at 3,000 pounds. A 4.09:1 rear axle ratio was standard equipment, and it was necessary because the only engine offered during 1963 was the Willys OHC six.

519 When they were introduced for 1963, the Jeep Wagoneer and the Gladiator came with cam-and-lever steering, a system that Willys engineers seemed to prefer. Power-assisted steering was optional, and it reduced steering effort to just 5.6 turns lock to lock. The Wagoneer's turning circle was a trim 41.2 feet.

520 Jeep Wagoneer's service brakes for 1963 were four-wheeldrums, which were 11x2 inches wide and had an effective lining area of 161.16 square inches. Power assist for the brakes was optional at extra cost.

521 The 1966 Super Wagoneer was the first SUV to provide power steering and power brakes as standard equipment, along with an automatic transmission and a host of luxury interior and exterior trim features.

522 The Wagoneer, Cherokee, and truck lines were given improved shock absorbers for 1975, along with a new power steering gear and new leaf springs to improve ride and handling.

523 By 1985, the Grand Wagoneer had become a luxury car costing more than $20,000. Most buyers expected it to offer a decent ride, so that model year the Grand Wagoneer was given a new suspension system that included new front and rear track bars, lower-friction leaf springs, premium gas-filled shock absorbers all around, a longer sway bar, and improved suspension bushings. Jeep Grand Wagoneers were rated to tow up to 5,000 pounds.

Numbers Crunching and Press Commentary

524 The curb weight of the 1963 Wagoneer four-wheel-drive model was 3,701 pounds, and the curb weight of the two-wheel-drive model was 3,546 pounds. The four-wheel-drive version offered a standard GVW of 4,500 pounds, and the two-wheel-drive version offered 4,200 pounds. The J-series Panel Delivery truck had the same GVW ratings.

525 Kaiser Industries changed the name of its vehicle-making subsidiary to Kaiser Jeep Corporation midway through the 1963 model year, dropping the Willys Motors name forever, at least for the US market. The early 1963 Jeep brochures that I have in my files are marked "Willys Motors" on the back; the later 1963 brochures say "Kaiser Jeep." The Willys name lived on for many years in Jeep's foreign subsidiaries, however. And Jeep sometimes offers special "Willys" versions of the popular Wrangler.

526 One 1963 road test report by *Motor Trend* magazine revealed that the Wagoneer equipped with the OHC six and

automatic transmission could accelerate 0–60 mph in 16.1 seconds, which was not bad for a six, although rather sedate for lead-foot drivers. Other testers reported longer times in acceleration runs.

527 When the Jeep Wagoneer debuted in the fall of 1962, sales demand was far beyond Willys' highest hopes, and the factory was unable to keep up with demand. At the same time, demand for the older Willys wagons dropped like a stone. Luckily, the factory had used incentive money to help dealers clear out most of their older stock before the new Wagoneers arrived.

528 One of the happiest days in the life of Edgar Kaiser, the president of Kaiser Industries, was December 2, 1969. That's the day he signed an agreement to sell Kaiser Jeep Corporation to American Motors Corporation. The truth is, after the first blush of success had worn off, the Kaiser family never really enjoyed the automotive business and had been trying to sell Jeep since 1959. The company had approached AMC that year as well as in 1963, but neither time could AMC management be convinced to purchase Jeep. When Jeep was finally sold, the complex deal was agreed to in December 1969, consummated in January 1970, and backdated to 1969. The purchase price was approximately $70 million, which included Jeep's extensive overseas network as well.

This is a Wagoneer Custom for 1969, the final year that Jeep was part of Kaiser Industries Corporation.

529 Early 1970 Jeep sales catalogs list the manufacturer as Kaiser Jeep Corporation. As the catalogs ran out, they were replaced with new ones that did not list a maker because Kaiser Jeep wasn't sure what name AMC was going to assign to its new subsidiary; AMC-Jeep, Jeep, or maybe something else. Perhaps even AMC wasn't sure.

530 For 1973, Jeep switched to two-digit model numbers. For the J-series vehicles the numbers are:
- Model 14 Standard Wagoneer
- Model 15 Custom Wagoneer
- Model 25 J-2500 Truck (5,000 GVW)
- Model 26 J-2600 Truck (6,000 GVW)
- Model 45 J-4500 Truck (5,000 GVW)
- Model 46 J-4600 Truck (6,000 GVW)
- Model 47 J-4700 Truck (7,000 GVW)
- Model 48 J-4800 Truck (8,000 GVW)

531 How's this for a steal of a deal? During the 1973 model year, Jeep offered to its dealers the Truck Cap Special, which was an aluminum pickup bed cap equipped with jalousie windows on the sides and a lockable liftgate with a safety glass rear window, for no charge! All that a dealer had to do to get this special offer

The Jeep trucks were never strong sellers, but American Motors was able to boost their sales during 1973 when it offered this free cargo cap as an incentive to buy.

was order a J-4500 or J-4600 132-inch-wheelbase truck with certain minimum equipment that included the Townside box, Custom Cab trim, a unique two-tone paint treatment, a woodgrain side stripe, Custom wheel covers, an AM pushbutton radio, a 360 2-barrel V-8 engine, power steering, power brakes, and dual low-profile mirrors.

Thus equipped, the J-4500 price was $4,502.85; the J-4600 was $4,638.90. This special offer was an effort to entice dealers to order more trucks and to load them up with more appearance goodies.

532 The 1975 Jeep price book illustrates how Jeep was able to market four nearly identical vehicles. The stripped Cherokee was base priced at $4,851, and the much better trimmed Cherokee S was $5,339. The standard Wagoneer was priced at $6,013, and the more popular and better trimmed Wagoneer Custom carried a price tag of $6,246.

One difference between the two Cherokee models and the Wagoneer models was that the Wagoneer included a lot of standard features that cost extra on the Cherokee. Also, the Wagoneer was a four-door model while Cherokee only came in a two-door model at the time.

533 However, when it comes to describing the differences between Jeep Cherokee and Wagoneer, you need to also talk about image. In buyers' eyes, the Cherokee was viewed as youthful and sporty, while the Wagoneer was seen as mature and luxurious. It didn't come about by accident; Jeep's marketeers did an outstanding job creating those images in the public's mind.

534 For 1977, the Jeep Wagoneer line was shrunk to a single model, priced at $6,966 plus the cost of options. This was nearly $1,000 more than the least expensive 1976 Wagoneer but included much more standard equipment, including upgraded interior trim, 360-2V V-8 engine, automatic transmission, and full-time four-wheel drive. As usual, Jeep sold every Wagoneer it could build.

The 1977 Jeep Wagoneer Custom and the J-10 Honcho pickup were two of the most popular of the J-series offerings that year. By this point, the J-series vehicles were in their 15th model year and selling better than ever.

535 Beginning in 1980, all Jeep vehicles received a much better paint job than ever before, along with improved rust protection, both courtesy of a costly all-new paint line installed at the Toledo factory. Each Jeep body was given a negative electrical charge as it moved through a dip tank filled with primer that was given a positive charge, which attracted the primer into every nook and cranny of the body.

536 In an attempt to rationalize its product range, Jeep consolidated its J-series range for 1983 to the following models:
- Two-door Cherokee base model
- Two-door Cherokee Pioneer
- Two-door Cherokee Chief (wide-wheel)
- Two-door Cherokee Laredo (wide-wheel)
- Four-door Cherokee Pioneer
- Wagoneer Brougham
- Wagoneer Limited
- J-10 Custom

- J-10 Pioneer
- J-10 Laredo (119-inch wheelbase only)
- J-10 Honcho Sportside (119-inch wheelbase only)
- J-20 Custom
- J-20 Pioneer

537 When the new XJ Jeeps appeared in late 1983 as 1984 models, the line included both Wagoneer and Wagoneer Limited models, so the former Wagoneer Limited was renamed the Grand Wagoneer. It remained in production essentially unchanged for another eight years due to its popularity. A little-known tidbit is that as soon as Chrysler bought AMC, most top-level Chrysler executives demanded Grand Wagoneers as company cars.

With the introduction of the XJ series Jeep wagons for 1984, the Wagoneer Limited became the Grand Wagoneer, and its popularity continued to grow.

538 Once Chrysler bought Jeep in 1987, the J-series Jeep trucks were deemed superfluous and were dropped from the lineup a few months into the 1988 model year. Sales by then were running at fewer than 2,000 units per year, and the only reason they'd been continued was because they shared an assembly line with the Grand Wagoneer and were thus easy to build. The 1988 J-10 and J-20 are the rarest Jeep trucks.

The final model year for the J-series trucks was 1988, when this one was built. Not many were produced before Chrysler pulled the plug on them.

539 The Grand Wagoneer was discontinued at the end of the 1991 model year, which was a decision that the company later regretted. Sales had fallen off, but the vehicles were still tremendously popular with wealthy buyers and still very profitable. In fact, the Grand Wagoneer had the richest owner demographics of all Chrysler vehicles by a large margin.

540 I'll end this section with this: There's a rumor that approximately 300 1992 Grand Wagoneers were produced, but thus far I've seen no evidence to convince me that it's true.

The most luxurious of all SUVs was the Grand Wagoneer. This is a 1985 model.

Willys Jeepster, Kaiser Jeepster, and Jeepster Commando

Legend and Lore

541 Although Willys-Overland had described its new station wagon as a family car, when the all-new Jeepster was introduced for 1948, management said that it considered the Jeepster to be "... the company's return to the passenger car market." Company president Ward Canaday was desperate to get Willys back to building passenger cars because that was where the big volume and profits were.

The new Willys Jeepster for 1948 was a sports phaeton with room for four or five passengers, a 4-cylinder engine, and two-wheel drive.

542 Some people still refer to the Willys Jeepster as the last phaeton (i.e., a four-passenger soft top without roll-up windows) from an American manufacturer, but it wasn't. The Excalibur neo-classic car was the last true phaeton from an American company, although they were built in very small numbers. Jeepster was the last phaeton from a major American firm.

543 Legend has it that Willys produced a coupe version of the Jeepster, and that's true. In fact, the company built two of them around 1951. They were fitted with aluminum body panels riding on shortened wheelbases and boasting a Studebaker-style wraparound rear window. Although extremely attractive, the

projected selling price for the Jeepster coupe was deemed too high, so the project was dropped after just two prototypes were built. At least one of those cars still survives.

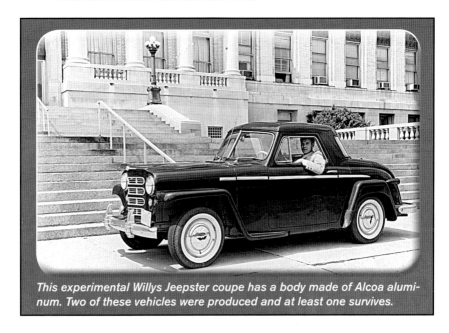

This experimental Willys Jeepster coupe has a body made of Alcoa aluminum. Two of these vehicles were produced and at least one survives.

544 Although the company introduced a line of Jeepsters for 1951, they were apparently leftover 1950 models that were retitled, with the possible exception of a handful of "true" 1951s. Their existence is not entirely certain because Willys production records have not survived intact.

545 When Kaiser Jeep decided to reintroduce the Jeepster to the line, the original plan was to build it on a heavily modified Wagoneer two-door body shell with a shorter wheelbase. Although it looked okay in the rough drawings that were produced, once a full-size mockup was built, management felt that it wasn't sporty enough, and accounting said it would cost too much. So they switched to building it on a CJ platform.

546 One enduring legend is that in order to create the 1967 Jeepster, the company rounded up all the tooling for the 1948–

1951 series and used them in production. That's so not true! None of the body parts interchange because they're completely different vehicles. Few of the driveline parts are the same either.

The most popular model in the Jeepster Commando line was the station wagon, which featured a removable top painted white.

547 The Jeep XJ-002 (a concept vehicle that is almost unknown today) was a Jeep sports car prototype equipped with an AMC inline 6-cylinder engine, four-wheel drive, and a fiberglass body. It was built under contract around 1971 on a brand-new Jeep Commando chassis. Amazingly, this vehicle still exists in the hands of a private owner.

Body and Interior

548 When the original Willys Jeepster debuted, it offered just two exterior paint color choices: yellow with a black soft top or bright red with a gray soft top. There was also a black-painted band around the base of the windshield and going down along the sides on most models, but not all. In some cases, the colored band was white, and I've also seen press photos in which the vehicle has no paint band at all.

THE **Jeepster**
AN EXCITING NEW SPORTS PHAETON

Think of it! A distinctly personal car delightfully different, for people of every age. Smart continental styling . . . brilliant performance, combined with amazing economy . . . for you who expect the particular and select in a motor car . . .
Come in and try it

COMPANION FOR CAREFREE HOUR

Being a phaeton, the Willys Jeepster had a snug soft top but lacked roll-up windows. Instead, plastic side curtains could be put in place to provide fairly good weather protection.

549 The Jeepster's standard fabric soft top was designed as a four-bow type for a tight fit. There were no roll-up windows; instead, the car was equipped with plastic side-curtain-type windows that slid into place. The left door curtain even had a zippered flap to allow the driver to perform hand signals or pay tolls.

550 Although the Jeepster's narrow front seat only holds two people, it is possible for three passengers to sit together in the rear seat, provided they're good friends. It is a little difficult getting back there, however.

551 The Willys Jeepster had a sort of trunk, but not the usual type with a lift-up lid. Instead, the rear seat folded forward so that luggage could be placed in the area behind the rear seat. Once the seat was folded back, the luggage was secure. The spare tire was outside, bolted to the rear of the vehicle for easy access, as well as to lend the Jeepster the sporty "Continental" look that stylists wanted.

552 The layout of controls on the Willys Jeepster was simplicity itself, with the handbrake and the overdrive lever both on the left side of the Jeepster's dash, while the ignition key and instruments were in the center of the dash area. The ample glove box occupied the far right of the dash.

553 The windshield wiper system on the Willys Jeepster was a vacuum type, and the fuel pump included a power booster to provide enough vacuum so that the wipers didn't quit on hills. They still did sometimes, but the cure for that was to back off the gas pedal for a second to allow the wipers one quick sweep of the windshield. Yes, it was as crappy as it sounds, but that's what most cars were equipped with back then.

554 There was no cheap "standard" interior trim for the original Willys Jeepster; it was meant to be a premium vehicle, so it came standard with high-quality vinyl upholstery complete with luxury pipe trimming. Dual sun visors were standard equipment in an era when the passenger-side visor was often extra cost. A locking glove box was also standard equipment.

555 On the first-year Jeepsters, the chrome T-shaped grille overlay was standard equipment, as were the full wheel discs, whitewall tires, and lots of other small extras. Once the

As this ad illustrates, in its second year on the market the Willys Jeepster was stripped of its standard grille bar, full wheel covers, chrome side steps, and more to enable Willys to reduce the price.

public balked at the Jeepster's high price, however, those items were taken off the standard equipment list and moved onto the options list to allow for a major reduction in the vehicle's base price.

556 Dealer training materials for the Willys Jeepster taught salesmen to talk about "all-weather protection" rather than "side-curtains," which had a negative connotation with buyers because everyone knew they tended to leak. By the time the Jeepster debuted, it was almost the last American car with plastic side curtains.

557 The factory model numbers for Willys Jeepster are as follows:

- 1948 Model VJ-2
- 1949 Model 4-63 VJ-2 (4-cylinder) and Model 6-63 VJ (6-cylinder)
- 1950 First Series: Model 4-63 VJ (4-cylinder) and Model 6-63 VJ (6-cylinder)
- 1950 Second Series: Model 4-73 VJ (4-cylinder) and Model 6-73 VJ (6-cylinder)
- 1951 Model 4-73 VJ (4-cylinder) and Model 6-73 VJ (6-cylinder)

The final year for the Willys Jeepster was 1951, when it sported new front end styling introduced in mid-1950.

558 The Jeepster name returned for the 1967 model year in response to the very successful International Scout, which was stealing sales from Jeep, as was the red-hot Ford Bronco. To save money on tooling, Jeep based the new Kaiser Jeepster on a lengthened CJ platform.

559 The Jeepster's body panels are mostly unique to that vehicle, but the front fenders do interchange with the CJ-5 and CJ-6. Some enthusiasts have modified their Jeepsters by replacing the wide grille with a standard CJ grille, and some also have fitted a standard CJ hood. It's an interesting look.

560 When the Jeepster was being developed by the styling and engineering departments at Kaiser Jeep Corporation, several prototypes were painted in monotone colors (i.e., the roof was painted the same color as the body). They were attractive in most cases. However, for some reason this scheme was never offered by the factory; the top was always painted white instead.

561 The 1967-and-later Kaiser Jeepster series names always tend to confuse people, so here's the story of how they work: The Jeepster was the top-line model and it came in only one version: a well-equipped convertible. The Jeepster Commando was the lower-priced series, and it comprised several body styles.

562 To further aid in identifying the various Jeepster models, the factory model numbers for the 1967 Kaiser Jeep Jeepster are:
- Model 8701 Jeepster Convertible (the highline model)
- Model 8705 Commando Open Roadster
- Model 8705F Commando Station Wagon
- Model 8705H Commando Pickup

For 1967, Kaiser Jeep revived the Jeepster name with the Jeepster and Jeepster Commando series. This is a preproduction Jeepster Commando roadster fitted with a pull-off soft top similar to the type used on the Jeep CJs.

563 The 1967 Jeepster Model 8701 was a really nice vehicle with plush interior trim (at least by Jeep standards) and even a small trunk with a top-mounted lid. It featured a painted band

around the base of the windshield and along the sides, as did the original Willys Jeepster. The Continental spare-tire mount and two-tone paint are styling touches that helped to set it apart from the much more common Commandos and also helped to give it the feel of the classic Willys Jeepster. Standard equipment on the Jeepster included attractive full-wheel covers.

Probably the rarest body style is the Commando roadster pickup with a pull-off type of soft top.

The star of the Jeepster/Jeepster Commando series was the Jeepster convertible, which was a high-trim version with nice interior trim, full-wheel covers, two-tone paint that mimicked the original Willys Jeepster, a trunk, and a true convertible top, available as a manually folding top or as a powered top.

564 For 1968, Kaiser Jeep added a new model to the Commando lineup: the budget-priced Commando convertible. It bore the designation Model 8702 Commando. This was a true convertible, unlike the roadster with its pull-off soft top. The Model 8702 Commando convertible had a full fold-down convertible top mechanism allowing you to fold the top either manually or automatically with the optional electrically controlled soft top. The Commando convertible's top also reached all the way to the rear of the vehicle, unlike the Model 8701. It had no separate trunk, but there was a bit of storage space behind the rear seat.

For 1968, Kaiser Jeep added a true convertible to the Commando lineup, and it was completely different from the Jeepster convertible. With bare-bones trim and no trunk, buyers needed to add options if they wanted to dress it up.

565 For both the Model 8701 Jeepster convertible and the 8702 Jeepster Commando convertible, a manual soft top was standard equipment with an optional power soft top available at extra cost. However, as noted before, the tops were different in size and shape.

566 So what's the difference between a Jeepster/Commando convertible and a roadster? The roadster came without a standard top; it was a completely open car and people living in warm climates sometimes bought them in that form. A pull-off soft top was available for extra cost, either from the factory, from the dealer, or from one of the many aftermarket companies that sold Jeep accessories.

567 Here's a little FYI: The paint codes for the 1967–1970 Jeepster are: Empire Blue 385, Glacier White 406, Gold Beige 393, President Red 226, and Spruce Tip Green 393.

568 Further, the paint codes for 1971 Jeepster are: Avocado Mist metallic 431, Burnished Bronze metallic 435, Candlelight Yellow 478, Champagne White 432, Island Blue metallic 477, President Red 226, Spring Green 433, Spruce Tip Green metallic 225, and Vintage Gold metallic 434.

Here's a Jeepster Commando for 1970. As can be seen, there were no substantive changes this year.

569 Here is still more paint code information. Paint codes for 1972 Jeepster are: Avocado Mist metallic 431, Butterscotch Gold 490, Champagne White 432, Copper Tan 517, Daisy Yellow 513, Fawn Beige 514, Fairway Green metallic 512, and Trans Am Red 515.

570 And finally, paint codes for 1973 Jeep Commando are: Avocado Mist metallic 431, Butterscotch Gold 490, Canary Yellow 495, Champagne White 432, Jetset Blue metallic 492, Julip Green 491, President Red 226, and Yuca Tan metallic 493.

571 For 1972, American Motors introduced a restyled Jeepster Commando and simultaneously changed the name to "Jeep Commando," a subtle but important distinction meant to highlight the Jeep brand name. At the same time, the Commando model range was shrunk to just three: roadster, pickup, and station wagon. The station wagon was by far the most popular model.

572 For some reason, Jeep Corporation chose to issue new model numbers for the 1973 Jeep Commando, which was its final year of production. Model 87 was the base roadster, Model 88 was the pickup, and Model 89 was the station wagon.

573 The rarest bodystyle of the Kaiser Jeepster series is the Model 8702, which was the Commando convertible that was introduced for the 1968 model year. Despite a price tag much lower than the upscale Jeepster convertible, only 1,772 of the budget-priced convertibles were built in four years of production.

574 Not surprisingly, the second-rarest Kaiser Jeepster is the Model 8701, which is the high-line Jeepster convertible. From 1967 to 1969, a total of 2,885 units were produced. These are much more desirable as collector cars and fetch the highest prices of any Jeepster/Commando examples.

575 So what happened to the body tooling for the Jeepster Commando once it was replaced by the Jeep Cherokee? It appears that it was sold to Jeep's Spanish affiliate Viasa because that firm began offering a locally built Jeepster right after production ended in the United States.

Jeep had a longtime habit of selling old tooling to its overseas affiliates, including Industrias Kaiser Argentina, Willys-Overland

Brazil, Mahindra & Mahindra in India, and Mitsubishi of Japan. That's why so many older Jeep models survived in production long after ending their run in the United States.

Engine and Drivetrain

576 The 1948 Jeepster, designated the model VJ-2, came with only one drivetrain: the Willys Go-Devil 4-cylinder engine, rated at a modest 63 hp and mated to a 3-speed manual transmission with column shifter and overdrive as standard equipment. Why was a column shifter specified instead of the more conventional floor shifter? Because it was considered more modern compared to the old-fashioned floor shifter.

577 The Go-Devil engine used in the Willys Jeepster had a $3^1/8$-inch bore, $4^3/8$-inch stroke, and 6.48:1 compression ratio. Producing 106 ft-lbs of torque, it was made for low-speed pulling power. It was very similar to the wartime engine, although with several modifications to make it more suitable for civilian use.

578 Even with just 63 hp on tap, the Jeepster could move smartly from a traffic light because of its excellent torque, and the low rear axle ratio actually came with 4.88:1 gears. But those gears meant that at 50 mph or 60 mph in third gear, the engine would be screaming for mercy. To enable relatively quiet high-speed cruising, the overdrive unit was made standard equipment, but only for the first year of production.

579 Because they were considered passenger cars, all 1948–1951 Jeepsters were two-wheel-drive models. If you find one with four-wheel drive, it's a conversion, and a pretty stupid waste of a perfectly good Jeep. On the other hand, all the 1967–1973 Jeepsters were four-wheel drive, and that makes sense because they were designed from the ground up for four-wheel drive. Plus, it's authentic; not some knucklehead's backyard mash-up.

580 Willys-Overland claimed that the Jeepster could achieve 29 mpg at a steady speed of 35 mph, and that was most likely if the driver was using overdrive. However, who really drives at a steady 35 mph for any length of time?

581 After realizing that buyers expected more than a 4-cylinder engine in a pricey, full-size convertible (er, I mean phaeton), Willys management introduced the 148-ci 72-hp Lightning Six L-head 6-cylinder engine in 1949 for the Model 6-63. The new engine (the smallest 6-cylinder engine offered by an American manufacturer at the time) was much smoother and quieter than the Go-Devil and produced somewhat better performance.

582 When the 1967 Jeepster was introduced by Kaiser Jeep, it used the F-head four-banger as its standard engine, with the ex-Buick V-6 as an option. By that point, Kaiser Jeep had purchased the tooling for the Buick V-6 engine from General Motors and was assembling it in its plant in Toledo. Despite a somewhat uneven idle (a result of being an odd-firing engine), the V-6 proved to be far more popular than the standard engine.

583 By 1971 standards, the Jeepster 4-cylinder was hopelessly underpowered, so for 1972 American Motors decided to install its 232-ci 6-cylinder engine as standard equipment. With seven main bearings, it was velvety smooth and nearly indestructible, and it put out 100 hp, which was a solid 33-percent increase from the four's 75 hp. An American Motors–built 258-ci six with 110 hp was optional that year.

The AMC engines were inline units, however, and they didn't fit under the Jeepster's hood. In order to have enough room for the new standard six (along with some optional engines), the company redesigned the front end for the 1972 model year, lengthening the chassis wheelbase as well. Apparently, the company decided that if it was going to have to pay for all-new body tooling it might as well restyle the Jeep's front end at the same time.

584 With the extra underhood space provided by the redesign of the front end, the Commando was able to also offer the AMC 304-ci V-8 as an option. This engine was fitted with a 2-barrel carburetor and produced 150 net hp and 245 ft-lbs of torque. I should also mention that the AMC V-8s of this era used the same basic blocks, which means you can fit a 360 or even a 401-ci AMC V-8 under the Commando's hood. That is, if you're up for it.

585 Another performance note: The 4-barrel carburetor and manifold from the AMC 360 fits on the 304 V 8 engine if you're looking for a fast and easy horsepower boost. So does a dual-exhaust setup to a certain extent, and it's easy to have a muffler shop fabricate the exhaust pipes and mufflers to fit.

586 Along the same lines, the later Jeep 4.0-liter inline-6 is essentially the same size as the 232 six, so swapping the later engine into a 1972–1973 Jeep Commando is relatively easy and, with up to 190 hp on tap, it gives the Jeepster tremendous performance. Because the 4.0-liter could be purchased with factory fuel injection and anti-knock sensors, you could have a vehicle that's powerful, reliable, fuel efficient, and smooth. It's a win all the way around.

Suspension and Brakes

587 The first Jeepster used Willys' unusual independent planar type of front suspension, which used upper A-arms and a multi-leaf transverse spring acting as the axle (remember, the first Jeepster was a two-wheel-drive vehicle). Designed by Willys chief engineer Barney Roos, this novel suspension system was rugged, provided a reasonably smooth ride, and was inexpensive to make.

588 The later Kaiser Jeepster used a more conventional multi-leaf front suspension with a stabilizer bar. Rear suspension on the Kaiser Jeepster was by single-leaf spring rather than a multi-leaf.

589 What's it like to drive the two Jeepsters? The Willys Jeepster feels really vintage, with a soft ride, slow shifting, and leisurely acceleration. The Kaiser Jeepster feels more like a CJ-5 or CJ-6 with a larger body, which is what it is essentially. In the Willys Jeepster you sit up tall, and in the Kaiser Jeepster you sit low to the floor.

590 The Willys Jeepsters came standard with what were considered excellent tires for that period: 5.90x15 4-ply Super Cushion bias-ply with wide whitewalls. The wide white tires were standard only for the first year of production. After that, they were put on the optional equipment list.

591 The Willys Jeepster frame was a sturdy box-section type with X-bracing for reinforcement. It was heavily based on the prewar Willys passenger car frame, although with improvements and modifications.

592 I sure hope that you like drum brakes because both the Willys Jeepsters and the Kaiser Jeepsters use them front and rear. The Willys featured 133 square inches of brake surface. When driving either vehicle on the highway, you have to adjust your speed to allow more room between you and the car in front because chances are it can stop a whole lot quicker than you can.

593 Despite being built for on-road use only, the Willys Jeepster still offered surprisingly good ground clearance: $8^5/_{16}$ inches at the rear axle. Many SUVs of today don't offer that much clearance.

594 The Willys Jeepster roadster's chassis had a 104-inch wheelbase and is basically the same as the Willys wagons. This was a cost-saving measure. Willys-Overland management was highly averse to spending money on new tooling and avoided it whenever possible.

595 The Kaiser Jeep Jeepster (aka Model 101) rode on a 101-inch wheelbase, basically the same as the Jeep CJ-6. This too was a cost-saving measure for the same reason: to save money on tooling and to simplify production.

The Commando station wagon continued to be the best seller in the Commando line, but sales were drooping due to heavy competition from Chevy, Ford, and International.

596 When it was introduced, the Kaiser Jeepster came with a full-floating hypoid front axle rated at 2,000 pounds and a semi-floating rear axle rated at 2,500 pounds standard with a 3,000-pound-rated rear axle optional.

597 In 1972, when American Motors had the Jeep Commando restyled and the front end lengthened in order to accommodate the AMC inline 6-cylinder engine and optional V-8, the wheelbase was also stretched to 104 inches, which was the same as the newly lengthened CJ-6. The newer-style Jeepsters (the 1972 and 1973 models) are today popularly known as the Jeepster 104.

Numbers Crunching and Press Commentary

598 Built on the same 104-inch wheelbase as the wagons and panel trucks, the Willys Jeepster weighed about 2,500 pounds. Overall length was a trim 174 inches, while the overall width was a svelte 69 inches. The Willys Jeepster was fairly tall, standing a full 62 inches high with the top up.

599 Although Willys-Overland management expected that the Jeepster would sell in substantial volume, it didn't. Part of the problem was pricing. At $1,765, it cost more than a new Ford convertible, which came equipped with a V-8 engine, roll-up windows, better trim, and a better ride. When it was figuring out the price of the new Jeepster, Willys had counted on the postwar seller's market continuing into 1948. By then, however, the pent-up demand had been nearly sated, competition was heating up, and prices were being reduced to meet the new selling conditions.

600 Despite the high prices, Willys managed to convince its dealers to load up on stock of the new Jeepster, and thus the company was able to produce 10,326 Jeepsters for the 1948 model year. However, the high prices turned off many buyers (as did the plastic side curtains), so many of the 1948 Jeepsters remained sitting on dealer lots, unsold, at year end. Most of them were retitled as 1949 models, which led to a big drop in production of the "true" 1949 Jeepster line.

601 Willys included a lot of normally optional equipment in the new Jeepster for 1948: overdrive, T-shaped chrome grille overlay, whitewall tires, Continental-style spare-tire mount, and custom interior trim. To reduce the price for 1949, most of that equipment was moved from the standard equipment list onto the optional equipment list. The Jeepster's base price then dropped to $1,495, which was probably right where it should have been all along.

But Willys dealers still had a lot of the $1,765 Jeepsters on the lot, so sales remained slow. As noted, most of the leftover Jeepsters were retitled as 1949 models and many were sold at "fire sale" prices.

602 Because of the huge load of unsold 1948 Jeepsters, production of the 1949 models didn't commence until May 3, 1949, for the 4-cylinder VJ-3. The 6-cylinder VJ3-6 production didn't start until June 30, 1949! Many companies begin to change production to the next model year in July or August, so to introduce a new model in later June was unusual.

603 As noted, the Jeepster's original price, $1,765, went down to $1,495 for 1949 via stripping off many of its formerly standard features. By the time the second-series 1950 Jeepster debuted, the price had been lowered even further to $1,390 for the 4-cylinder model and $1,490 for the 6-cylinder version.

604 To the uninitiated, the Jeepster nomenclature can sometimes become confusing. It was called the Willys Jeepster from 1948 to 1951, then the Jeepster and Jeepster Commando from 1967 to 1971. From 1972 to 1973, it was called the Jeep Commando.

605 As proof or confirmation that many of the leftover 1948 Jeepsters were retitled as 1949s, in later years, Kaiser Jeep Corporation noted in an official memo that many Jeepster serial numbers for 1948 were mixed in with 1949 models, which means the same thing.

606 Jeepster model designations for 1950 are the 4-73 (aka 473VJ) for the four-banger and 6-73 (aka 673VJ) for the six. With inventories finally beginning to align with retail demand, the Jeepster production was begun on November 1, 1949, for both models.

607 Although there was a 1951 model-year Jeepster, most or all of them were actually leftover 1950 models that were reserialized as 1951s. One source claims that a small number of "real" 1951 Jeepsters were built (maybe 20 in all) but I've never seen any corroborating evidence.

608 Willys Jeepster production figures are as follows:

- 1948 4-cylinder 10,326 units
- 1949 4-cylinder 2,698
- 1949 6-cylinder 654 units
- 1950 4-cylinder 4,066 units
- 1950 6-cylinder 1,779 units
- 1951 Perhaps 20 units were built in all, but as previously mentioned, that's not entirely certain. Most 1951s that you find today are leftover 1950 models.

609 The later Jeepster model list can be confusing too. In 1967, the model range included a roadster, a soft-top roadster, and a pickup; a hardtop pickup in the Commando series; plus the single Jeepster topline model. Then in 1968 a true convertible model was added to the Commando series, although with a completely different

Kaiser Jeep had high hopes for decent sales of the topline Jeepster, although sales were fairly modest due to its high price tag. Unlike the Willys Jeepster, all the Kaiser models were four-wheel drives.

soft top from the Jeepster model and without the Jeepster's "trunk." By 1970, the range was reduced to three models: Commando roadster, pickup, and station wagon. It remained that way through 1972, although two limited-edition models were briefly offered in 1971 and one in 1972.

610 American Motors introduced two limited-edition Jeepster station wagons for 1971. The most collectible is the Hurst Jeepster, which featured upgrades designed by Hurst Performance Products including a hood-mounted tachometer, racing stripes, and a Hurst shifter for either the standard 3-speed manual gearbox or the optional Hydramatic transmission. All were white with red and blue stripes and came with the V-6 engine. The best estimate I've seen for the number of Hurst Jeepsters produced is 102 units, making it among the rarest and most desirable of the collectible Jeeps.

611 The second limited-edition Jeepster produced by American Motors for 1971 is the Jeepster SC-1, which came in a single color (Butterscotch Gold) and was equipped with the V-6 engine

In an effort to spur sales of the Jeep Commando, American Motors introduced the Commando SC-1 wagon for 1971. A special trim and option package, these are very rare and desirable collector cars today.

custom interior trim, radio, full-wheel covers, roof rack, rally side stripe with SC-1 identification, and more. I haven't found an estimate on how many were produced, but they're rarely seen today.

612 One Jeepster you may never have seen (and probably never will) is the ultra-rare 1972 Jeepster SC-2, which was designed as a follow-up to the SC-1. I've been looking for years for any factory info on the SC-2, and all I've been able to find thus far is a couple of pretty good press photos and a junked SC-2 at a local Jeep shop. The SC-2's main identifying feature is an odd-looking woodgrain side-spear decal.

For 1972, the Jeepster Commando was restyled and received a name change to Jeep Commando. A special SC-2 package was offered and is even rarer than the SC-1 but not as desirable.

613 For 1972, Jeep Corporation restyled the front end of the Jeepster and renamed it the Jeep Commando. The new front end was squared off to give it a more modern look; it somewhat resembled the top-selling Ford Bronco. It's perhaps the strangest restyling in Jeep history because it doesn't share a family look with any other Jeep product.

614 So who was responsible for styling the 1972 Commando? It's not completely certain, but Jim Angers, who had been Kaiser Jeep's head of design for years, had stayed on board with American Motors after the merger, and the Commando restyling is very similar to some of his concepts in the 1960s. My opinion is that Jim Angers was responsible for the 1972–1973 Jeepster restyle.

615 Oddly enough, in the collector car market the 1972–1973 Jeep Commandos usually fetch higher prices than the more traditional-looking 1967–1971 Jeepster Commandos. But as mentioned, the most valuable Jeepster is the Hurst Jeepster followed by the 1971 SC-1 and the 1967–1969 Jeepster Convertible topline model. I'm not sure what a Jeepster SC-2 would fetch because I've never seen one for sale.

616 The late Jim Alexander, a Jeep designer and product planner during the AMC era and a friend of mine, told me that the team he worked on actually designed the CJ-7 to replace the Jeepster. He pointed out the CJ-7's available hardtop, which was much nicer than the CJ-5's steel cab, along with the CJ-7's optional automatic transmission and extra passenger and cargo room were all features that owners said they appreciated in their Jeepsters, and which potential buyers looked for in a small SUV.

Jeep Wrangler YJ and TJ

Legend and Lore

617 In development for more than five years, the all-new 1987 Jeep Wrangler was introduced in May 1986 as a replacement for the venerable Jeep CJ series. Customer tastes were changing, with more people using their Jeeps for daily commutes, and that was spurring calls for a better ride and a better-trimmed interior. In addition, the company needed to improve the small Jeep's handling, due to rollover concerns, along with on-road ride quality. Customers were also demanding better fit and finish, a quieter cabin, and better fuel economy, all while retaining or improving Jeep's legendary capability.

The name change was mostly to place a "wall" between the CJ and the new vehicle. By that point, there were numerous lawsuits filed against American Motors for injuries and deaths resulting from Jeep rollover accidents.

The all-new Wrangler debuted as a 1987 model, replacing the CJ series. Although similar in styling, the new Wrangler had more in common with the Cherokee XJ than the CJ.

618 The Wrangler was developed under the direction of the legendary Bob Nixon, director of exterior design for American Motors. The exterior styling team was led by Chuck "Mash" Mashigan, who had designed the original American Motors Javelin and AMX cars. Mash was a longtime Jeep enthusiast who kept a vintage 1944 military Jeep MB parked inside the styling department to remind all of his designers of the Jeep's heritage. When stumped for styling ideas, he used to sit for a while behind the wheel of that Jeep MB; his designers even referred to the MB as "Mashigan's office."

Shown here in the lobby of American Motors headquarters in Southfield, Michigan, the new Wrangler was an exciting new vehicle with tremendous potential.

619 Wrangler's interior styling was created by a design team led by the incomparable Vince Geraci, who noted, "We've gotten away from the 'no frills' approach because our consumer research told us people wanted more creature comforts. But we were careful not to abandon the rugged, functional look." Especially under American Motors ownership, Jeep styling kept a close eye on heritage even while redefining what a Jeep SUV should look like.

620 Prior to authorizing production of the new Wrangler, Jeep engineers made certain that it was engineered to be a true Jeep vehicle, and that meant it had to be able to pass the ultimate off-road test: traversing the legendary Rubicon Trail, which is a nearly impassable off-road route in Northern California. Many four-wheel-drive vehicles from other companies have been left by the side of the trail when trying to negotiate the treacherous Rubicon. Wrangler, of course, could traverse the Rubicon with relative ease.

621 When investigating using the Wrangler name in export markets, it turned out that the name was already trademarked for another product in Canada. So for the Canadian market, the Wrangler was known as the Jeep YJ, which was also its in-house model designation (replacing the CJ designation). The YJ codename is also used by Jeep enthusiasts to identify the first generation of US-model Wranglers.

622 For 1988, Jeep introduced a new high-trim Wrangler model called the Sahara. It was designed prior to the merger with Chrysler by a team led by AMC design chief Vince Geraci. Geraci is an old movie buff and the Wrangler Sahara name was probably influenced by the Humphrey Bogart movie *Sahara*; it's one of his favorite old films and he has a poster of that movie hanging on a wall in his family room at home. Stylist Phil Payne came up with the logo design used on the Sahara. The Sahara became perhaps the most popular package of Wranglers and is still produced today.

623 Another name that was almost chosen by Jeep management for what became the Sahara was the Wrangler Ivory Coast. A photo of a proposed logo by Phil Payne still exists, and the styling team says that program was almost given the green light.

624 The new Jeep Wrangler was offered in Base, Sport Décor, and Laredo trim, and in a big move for Jeep, they came with a standard soft top and steel half-doors or an optional removable hardtop. The Wrangler Laredo came with the hardtop as standard equipment.

625 Suzuki had been stealing sales from Jeep with its low-priced Sidekick four-wheel-drive models. In response, American Motors (and later Chrysler) tried to develop a smaller Jeep, which was code named the JJ, for Junior Jeep. It was meant to compete directly with the Suzuki. However, development program costs eventually went out of control, so the project was dropped. Instead, Jeep introduced the new 1988½ Wrangler S model priced at a budget-friendly $8,995. That was still higher than the Suzuki, but the Wrangler S's value message was much better than that of the competition, and it helped win back sales for Jeep.

To reduce manufacturing costs, the Wrangler S exterior color choices were limited to Olympic White, Classic Black, Sand Dune Yellow, Coffee, and Red. The vehicle offered only the base 4-cylinder engine and 5-speed transmission with no upgrading of the driveline.

For the 1988 model year, Jeep brought out a new Wrangler S model designed to compete with the annoying Japanese Suzuki Samurai. Priced at a rock bottom $8,995, it was an altogether better vehicle and better value than any other four-wheel-drive vehicle in the marketplace.

626 One omission in the new Wrangler series that I don't understand was the absence of the Renegade package that had been so popular in the CJ series. It wasn't until 1991 that Jeep finally offered a Wrangler Renegade model, and then it was a sort of high-priced limited-edition thing. Powered by the new Wrangler 4.0-liter 6-cylinder engine, it was offered in red, white, or black, with big color-keyed wheel flares, integrated body side steps, aluminum wheels with all-terrain tires, red interior, and even an optional red hardtop.

Jeep revived the Renegade name during 1991 with the Wrangler Renegade model. Loaded with features, powered by the new 180-hp 4.0-liter six, and priced rather high, not very many were produced during the three-year run.

627 Here's a fun fact to fool your friends: Tell them you're willing to give them a million bucks if they can find you a nice, clean 1996 Wrangler. Your ace in the hole is that there never was a 1996 Wrangler. Jeep had the all-new 1997 Wrangler TJ series ready for a March 1996 introduction, so the company decided to skip the 1996 model year for Wrangler.

In fact, the Wrangler pictured in the 1996 Jeep full-line brochure is the 1997 Wrangler TJ, surely one of the few times in history when a company showed vehicles from two model years in one catalog. The factory produced extra 1995 Wranglers to keep dealers supplied with products until the new vehicle was ready.

628 The hand of history rests heavily on those who design Jeep vehicles. When the all-new Wrangler TJ was introduced, Jeep platform manager Craig Winn said, "Our goal for the new Wrangler was pretty straightforward: to make an acceptable road vehicle and an *exceptional* off-road vehicle." That sounds simple enough, but to actually accomplish it in a vehicle that people can actually afford to buy is difficult.

This is a base model Wrangler for 1991. Roll bar padding was standard equipment on Wranglers that year, but the base model had padding only on the side bars. The other Wrangler had full padding on all the roll bars.

629 As much as the Wrangler YJ was a bold advancement in Jeep design, the new Wrangler TJ for 1997 was even more so. In stock form, it was the best-performing small Jeep to that point, both on- and off-road. Engineering-wise it was a universe ahead of the Jeep YJ. The TJ was an example of Jeep engineering really showing off its skills.

630 Since 1942, Jeep has been a worldwide vehicle in both sales and production. During 1997, Jeep vehicles were produced through major joint ventures in Venezuela, Mexico, China, and Egypt. Other overseas operations included Australia and India. Besides those, Jeeps were being sold in more than 100 countries around the globe.

631 Jeep management has stated recently that Wrangler models will only be produced in America. Although that sounds patriotic, it means the company will probably miss out on a lot of overseas sales because of the higher cost of building the vehicles in America rather than in local markets. Besides, over the years the Jeep CJ series was built in more than a dozen countries around the world, so why not do the same with Wrangler?

The 2001 Wrangler Sport was a popular value-priced model powered by the potent 4.0-liter six.

632 X marks the spot. The 2002 Jeep Wrangler lineup included a new budget-priced model called the Wrangler X. Positioned as a high-value model slotted in the price structure between the base Wrangler SE and the Wrangler Sport, the X model was essentially an SE with a standard 4.0-liter engine and some decals.

633 One special Jeep that you have probably never heard of is the Wrangler Apex. A mid-year limited-run model, the Apex came with the 4.0-liter engine, AM/FM/CD player, and a full center console as standard equipment. Exclusive features on the Apex included Bright Silver paint (regular-production options dark blue and black were also available), a unique "strobe" hood graphic, earth-toned Cognac ultrahide seats, and really gorgeous chrome full-face wheels. The vehicle MSRP was $20,385.

634 The big news that was being bandied about during 2003 was that Jeep was planning to reintroduce the Scrambler pickup for 2004. In fact, the company even displayed a Scrambler concept model at the 2003 National Automobile Dealers Association (NADA) convention. It was a beauty; much nicer than the overgrown tank that finally debuted as a 2020 model. A two-door model, the concept Scrambler was based on a lengthened Wrangler chassis. Well, as you know, the 2004 Scrambler somehow became lost along the trail and came out 15 years later as an almost full-size (and expensive) four-door truck.

635 The 2003 model year was a big one for Wrangler. During the year, Jeep unveiled a new Freedom Edition limited-production model with body-color wheel flares, special badges, a soft top with full metal doors, front-mounted fog lamps, and tow hooks. Outline White Letter (OWL) P225/75/R15 Goodyear all-terrain tires were mounted on 15-inch chrome wheels. Standard equipment included air-conditioning, Sentry-Key anti-theft system, a Fold-and-Tumble rear seat, and a choice of Dark Slate cloth or vinyl seat upholstery. The 4.0-liter six was also standard equipment.

636 Talk about legends in their own time! For 2003, Jeep released the new Wrangler Rubicon model, declaring that it was engineered to take on the most demanding trails, including those previously reserved for highly modified vehicles only. Craig Love, vice president of the Jeep Product Team, said, "The 2003 Jeep Wrangler Rubicon features an off-road performance package, as only Jeep can engineer, allowing serious off-road enthusiasts the opportunity to drive over some of the most extreme trails in the country, and then drive it home."

637 Tough? The new Rubicon was the toughest, most-capable small Jeep ever sold to the public, and it has become even tougher over the years. Rumor has it that the Rubicon was originally developed as a military project that wasn't approved.

638 Have you ever seen a Wrangler Tomb Raider edition? Don't feel bad if you haven't; with just over 1,000 produced, they're pretty rare. Jeep introduced the Tomb Raider edition in July 2003 to coincide with the release of the movie *Lara Croft: Tomb Raider: The Cradle of Life*. The Wrangler Tomb Raider was a Rubicon model that included Bright Silver exterior paint with special badging, an overhead light bar, special Alcoa aluminum wheels, a tubular grille guard, diamond-plate bumper guards, graphite-colored fender flares, fog-lamp guards, and sturdy rock rails.

639 For 2004, Jeep kept the pot boiling when it introduced the Columbia Edition, a Wrangler "value-model" with equipment that came near the level of the Wrangler Sahara but at a value-price of just $20,980. Columbia Editions (they are named for the sportswear company) included graphite-color body accents along with graphite-color spoke wheels and fender flares. Fog lamps and "Columbia Edition" badges helped complete the exterior identifiers.

640 Jeep introduced the Wrangler Unlimited for 2004. Its base price was $24,995. Although that sounds like a bargain in today's context, I should note that other Wranglers were base priced between $16,940 and $25,755, so the Unlimited was marketed as a premium model.

641 The middle of 2004 brought another new Wrangler model: the Jeep Wrangler Willys. It boasted special Moss Green paint, diamond-plate sill guards painted Dark Green, body-color fenders flares, flat-green-painted wheels, and a dark green soft top. The interior boasted water-resistant camouflage seat upholstery.

642 In photos, you usually see the Wrangler Willys model with a military star decal on the hood along with the numbers 41MB-04TJ on the hood sides (the hood numbers translate to 1941 military Jeep MB model and 2004 Jeep Wrangler TJ model). Those decals didn't automatically come with the vehicle; they were part of an extra-cost dealer-installed graphics package that also included a military-style "Fuel" decal above the filler cap. Mesh fog-lamp covers were also included in the dealer-installed package.

643 One of the best off-road parties in existence is the factory-sponsored event known as Camp Jeep. Designed to bring Jeep enthusiasts together in a group celebration, it features off-road training courses, live music, and plenty of good food. On July 15, 2004, Camp Jeep celebrated its 10th year in existence. By that point, it had become one of the best-attended owner events in the country.

644 For 2005, Jeep finally offered a Wrangler Unlimited Rubicon model, thus combining the extra-long wheelbase and expanded carrying capacity of the four-door Unlimited model with the Best-in-Class off-road capability of the Rubicon.

Body and Interior

645 The first Wrangler was a polarizing vehicle for Jeep enthusiasts, because it was the first (and only) small Jeep to have rectangular headlamps. These were used to give the Jeep a more modern look and also to help separate it in the public's mind from the recently departed CJs. Many Jeep enthusiasts revolted, however, wearing T-shirts that read "Real Jeeps Have Round Headlamps."

646 The other polarizing feature of the 1987 Wrangler was its bent grille, which was actually a whole lot less pronounced than it might have been. In my Jeep archive are surviving photos from the Jeep styling department showing mockups that had a much sharper bend, with the grille center actually jutting

forward several inches. Longtime Jeep enthusiasts hated the production Wrangler's grille, and I'm sure they would have hated the other proposed grilles even more.

Longtime Jeep enthusiasts bemoaned the Wrangler's bent grille, but it could have been much worse, as this photo of one proposal illustrates.

647 All Wrangler YJ models included flexible wheel flares as standard equipment. The soft-top models also now included steel half-doors as standard equipment, which were much safer than the soft doors used on CJs. Both the standard soft top and optional hardtop were all-new designs and were engineered to provide greatly improved sealing and noise reduction.

648 It was in the interior details where the Wrangler was really different from the Jeep CJ. A car-like instrument panel featured integrated controls and vents, including the optional air-conditioning system, providing a much cleaner, more civilized appearance. The fit and finish of floor carpeting was likewise greatly improved. The seats were comfier as well. However, engi-

neers made sure to retain the ability to wash out the Wrangler's interior with a garden hose by including drain plugs in the floor.

649 Speaking of floor drain plugs, when I was a Jeep salesman selling the CJ models in the 1970s, I always assumed that the floor drains had been installed by the factory because the CJ's doors let in so much rain that if the water didn't have a place to drain out it would rot the floors. I still wonder if that was the case. In any event, the weather sealing on the Wrangler was far superior to the outgoing CJ, and the floor drains were only needed for washing the interior.

650 The Wrangler YJ also introduced a novel dashboard "central stack" idea, in which the instrument panel's main components (the heating, ventilating, air-conditioning controls, and main vents) are placed in a centrally located stack rather than spread out over various sections of the instrument panel. The central stack made it easier to produce a vehicle in both left- and right-hand-drive versions, thus making it easier to sell in right-hand drive markets. There's actually something like 26 countries around the globe are right-hand-steering markets.

651 Wrangler YJ models also introduced steering column–mounted controls for the windshield washer along with the high and low headlamp beams.

652 Wrangler YJ benefited from greatly improved rust protection (always a weak point in the CJ models) along with a better paint finish than ever before due to better welding techniques and greatly increased usage of galvanized steel in critical areas. Factory painting processes were also improved.

653 Another new feature of Wrangler body was the fully integrated running lights and side-marker lights. Jeep had clearly come a long way from the 1969–1970 model years when it tacked on those big side-marker lights to the CJ's fenders.

654 The 1987 Wrangler Laredo also boasted a new buffalo-grain vinyl-seat upholstery and carpeting on the lower door panels. This was part of Jeep's ongoing upgrading of the product to meet new-customer expectations. Interior features in particular were becoming more stylish and, you might even say, luxurious. The days of the stripped-down utility truck were heading to a close.

655 Other standard equipment on the YJ included comfortable high-back bucket seats, a new Fold-and-Tumble rear seat, a swing-away rear tailgate (which replaced the bulky, former swing-out spare tire carrier), and a tinted windshield.

656 The Jeep Wrangler Sahara model for 1988 came in two exterior colors (Coffee or Khaki) along with khaki-painted wheels, unique khaki interior trim, foglights with mesh protector screens, and special body stripes.

657 The Wrangler's model range for 1988 was expanded to include the Base, Sport Décor, Sahara, and Laredo models. Then the value-priced Wrangler S model was added midway through the

The Wrangler Laredo hardtop for 1988 was the top of the Wrangler line and extremely popular with buyers.

model run. This was one of the largest ranges of models in the history of the smallest Jeeps.

658 In 1988, Jeep offered a special Olympic Team Edition of the Wrangler, featuring a special 1988 US Olympic Team decal, special striping, power steering, five-spoke alloy wheels, an AM-FM-ET radio, Trailcloth seat trim, floor carpeting, a center console, and color-keyed wheel flares (black when Colorado Red exterior color was chosen), and floor mats. A value-priced model, it reflected a savings of $400 in contrast to purchasing those options separately.

659 In 1989, the Wrangler Islander replaced the previous Sport Décor model in the lineup. The Islander offered a bold side and colorful graphic decal and tropical paint colors for the body that included Malibu Yellow, Bright Red, Pacific Blue, and Pearl White. Also included were silver-painted styled-steel wheels with white-letter tires.

Adding spice to the 1990 Wrangler lineup was the Islander model, equipped and priced to offer good value for the dollar.

660 For the 1992 model year, the Wrangler Sahara offered new low-gloss exterior paint choices in Sand or Sage Green for a more "elemental" look. The Wrangler Sahara also now offered a dark green interior option.

661 Beginning late in the 1994 model year, Wrangler offered an easy-operating soft top with full steel doors as an option on soft-top Wranglers. Engineers had spent years working on a long-hoped-for improvement in the Jeep's soft top.

662 Also appearing late in the 1994 model year was an optional Add-a-Trunk for Wranglers, designed to provide a lockable storage space for Wrangler owners. Also new and appearing mid-year was the optional sound bar, which was now available even on the S model.

663 In an effort to maintain interest in the YJ Jeep introduced for 1995, a new Rio Grande package was made available on

This is a 1995 Wrangler Rio Grande with styled-steel wheels, standard steel half-doors, slide-in side curtains, and a tan denim top.

the entry-level S model. This move was quite out of the ordinary for Jeep because it traditionally reserved special editions for the upscale models.

The Rio Grande included sportier interior trim, new exterior color choices, a standard AM/FM stereo radio with cassette player, a sound bar, full-face styled-steel wheels with P215 all-terrain tires, standard rear bumperettes, full floor carpeting, and reclining front seats. Decals on the body served to identify the Rio Grande models.

This is the same 1995 Rio Grande, this time top down. Note the full roll bar padding. If you've ever banged your head against an unpadded roll bar, you can really appreciate the padding used on later models.

664 The all-new Wrangler TJ series introduced for 1997 reintroduced round headlamps for the Wrangler, which were greeted with tremendous enthusiasm by Jeep traditionalists. Designers also wisely ditched the controversial bent grille, once again endowing the small Jeep with classic good looks.

665 The 1997 Wrangler TJ also introduced park and turn signal lamps that were located in the front fenders. The hood hinges were now flush-mounted for a more integrated look. The gas cap, previously located behind the license plate, was relocated to the left side of the body for easier access. It was also recessed for a neater look.

The all-new Wrangler TJ series, introduced as a 1997 model, was vastly improved in just about every area. Enthusiasts especially appreciated the return to round headlamps.

666 The base of the windshield on the 1997 TJ was pulled forward a full 4 inches to improve the Jeep's aerodynamics, which in turn served to reduce wind noise. The change also provided space to allow for operation of the new airbags. The cowl was also made 1 inch higher to provide room for the airbags; heating, ventilation, and air-conditioning (HVAC) unit; and the wiper motor. The change to a slanted windshield was styled so subtly that most Jeep enthusiasts never notice it.

667 The 1997 Wrangler TJ was given dual airbags as standard equipment, along with an integrated heating, ventilating, and air-conditioning system. All-new seats provided an extra 1.6 inches of travel up front.

668 The 1997 TJ also boasted larger wheelhouse dimensions, both front and rear, along with larger and wider fender flares. Both of these improvements were undertaken to allow for bigger tires than what came standard and were a result of feedback from Jeep owners.

669 The front bucket seats of the 1997 Wrangler TJ featured new lateral support "wings" to help keep passengers in place; the rear seat was wider and much more comfortable than before. The stylish seats were in sharp contrast to the flat-style bench or bucket seats used on the old CJ models during the 1960s and early 1970s. The improvement in rear seat width was made possible by an increase in the TJ's overall width.

670 The Wrangler TJ's all-new hardtop included quick-release header latches up front to help ensure a tight fit and to

Notice the gorgeous spoke wheel on this 1997 Wrangler Sahara. The bumper end caps, body side steps, and fog lamps all help give this vehicle a classic Jeep look.

make removal of the top much easier. The redesigned hardtop was also 15 pounds lighter, making it easier to remove.

671 Pardon the pun, but I have to note that Jeep really "topped" itself for 1998 when it introduced a new dual-top option. For the first time, you could order a Wrangler from the factory with both a hardtop and a soft top. Cruise control was also available this year.

672 So whad'ya do with your Wrangler's hardtop in the summer? Store it in the shed? Nope! Today, many Jeep dealers offer to store the top for a slight monthly fee. They'll even take it off and remount it for you.

673 For 1999, the Wrangler TJ was given a 19-gallon fuel tank as standard equipment, along with an improved air-conditioning system. The larger 19-gallon fuel tank was something off-roaders had been asking for because a smaller tank limited their range in the wild unless they brought along extra fuel cans.

674 The Wrangler TJ series also boasted a major upgrade to the interior with richer-looking seating materials and a new instrument panel. As stylish as they now looked, the new seats were still waterproof, the floor carpeting was removable, and floor drains were still included so the interior could be hosed out for a fast cleanup.

675 For 1999, a new Dark Tan soft-top color debuted for the Wrangler, along with new Camel and Agate interior trim colors. Sahara models also received Dark Green seat trim. New exterior colors included Medium Fern, Forest Green, Blue, and Desert Sand.

676 The Wrangler interior improvements for 2000 included an all-new and better-integrated HVAC system plus new front tweeters for the optional Premium Audio System.

677 QUIET! For the 2001 model year, Jeep introduced a new 4-ply soft top that provided Wrangler with a much quieter cabin and greater top durability. The new soft top reduced "drumming" at highway speeds to a minimum and also greatly reduced wind noise along with air and rainwater intrusion.

678 The 2003 Wrangler Rubicon featured several unique styling touches. Reminiscent of legendary Jeep vehicles, a new "Rubicon" graphic was prominent on each side of the hood. New heavy-gauge diamond-plate sill guards, bolted to the body side, protected the rocker panels from damage in off-road situations. Stylish new 16-inch, five-spoke aluminum wheels boasted a dished face to protect the wheel from damage in off-road situations.

679 For the 2004 model year, Jeep introduced a new long-wheelbase Wrangler known as the Wrangler Unlimited. Similar in concept to the earlier CJ-6 and CJ-8, it came as a two-door-only model, with the extra body length used to provide more rear seat and rear storage room. Officially a 2004½ model, the 103-inch wheelbase Wrangler Unlimiteds of 2004–2006 are also known unofficially as the Wrangler LJ (Long Jeep).

680 The Unlimited introduced a new soft top known as the Sunrider. In addition to the usual full top-down capability, it could also be folded over just above the front seat passengers, providing a 45x23-inch sunroof opening. The Sunrider top also included larger, deep-tinted side windows.

681 Also new for 2004 was a right-hand-drive Wrangler model, aimed at postal route delivery and parking meter patrol. The Wrangler already offered steering on the right for certain export markets, so it was easy to offer the same thing for the US market.

682 The big news for 2006 was that the new Sirius Satellite Radio was now available as an extra-cost option on all Wrangler models except the SE. Although probably most cars have a

satellite radio these days, in 2006 it was still unusual, especially in a vehicle such as the Wrangler. Leave it to Jeep to innovate.

Engine and Drivetrain

683 Standard equipment on the new Wrangler for 1987 was the AMC/Jeep 2.5-liter 4-cylinder engine, which this year was upgraded to 112 hp and included throttle body fuel injection for the first time on the smallest Jeep. For 1991, this engine was further upgraded via multiport fuel injection, raising output to 122 hp.

684 Initially, the only optional engine for the Wrangler was AMC's tried-and-true 258-ci inline-6, a carbureted mill that was smooth running and could easily go a couple hundred thousand miles with no sweat. Although somewhat old in design, it was the largest engine in the Wrangler's class.

685 The new Wranglers were given a 5-speed transmission with hydraulic clutch actuation as standard equipment and could be ordered with an optional Chrysler TorqueFlite Model 999 3-speed automatic transmission, which was available only with the six. The manual transmission on the 4-cylinder models was a pretty good Aisin-Seki manual gearbox; the 6-cylinders received a Peugeot-supplied 5-speed that many consider the worst transmission ever put in a Jeep. Why Jeep chose a French gearbox is unknown, but more than likely Renault insisted.

686 For the 1991 model year, the old 4.2-liter carbureted six was replaced by Jeep's new 4.0-liter HO 6-cylinder engine producing 180 hp. The 4.0 was heavily based on the outgoing 4.2-liter engine and they look similar. As noted a bit earlier, this same year the base 4-cylinder engine now offered multipoint fuel injection for greater power and better drivability.

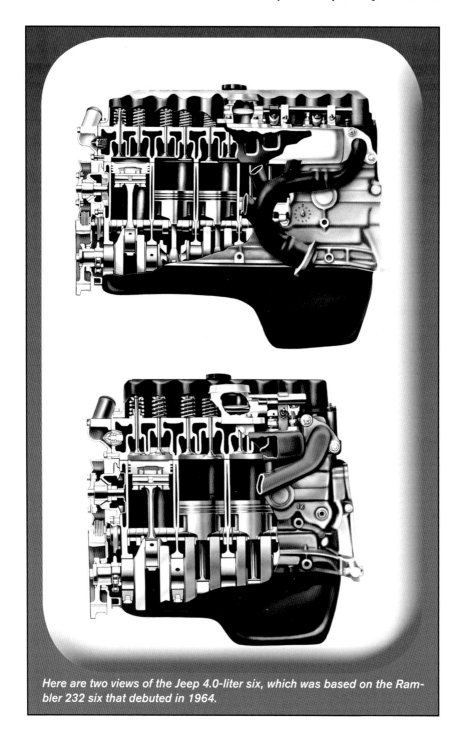

Here are two views of the Jeep 4.0-liter six, which was based on the Rambler 232 six that debuted in 1964.

687 In previous generations, engine size was always listed in cubic inches, but gradually, for reasons unknown, American automakers began to post them in metric sizes; for example, the 4.0-liter six translates to roughly 242 ci. The old 4.2-liter six was 258 ci.

688 The new Wrangler YJ came standard with shift-on-the-fly capability, which was not available on its nearest competitors, the Mitsubishi Montero or Isuzu Trooper. It was offered as an extra-cost item on the Ford Bronco II.

689 Effective with the 1992 models, all Wrangler Islander and Sahara models came with the 4.0-liter 6-cylinder engine as standard equipment. The S- and Base-model Wranglers received the 123-hp four-banger as standard equipment.

The 1992 Wrangler Sahara received new styled wheels for the 1992 model year.

690 The 4-cylinder Wrangler wasn't offered with an optional automatic gearbox until the 1994 model year, when a Chrysler-built 3-speed automatic transmission became available. In some official Jeep reference materials, you sometimes see it listed in earlier years, but to my knowledge it wasn't actually offered in production until 1994.

691 The Wrangler TJ for 1997 included a standard Dana 30 front axle and Dana 35 rear axle, both of which were carried over from the YJ. For the first time in a Wrangler, a Dana 44-3 rear axle with a 3.55:1 ratio was available as an option (although only on the Sport and Sahara models).

692 Jeep Wrangler's 4.0-liter six was redesigned for 2000. Output remained at 181 hp, but the engine showed a marked reduction in noise, vibration, and harshness as a result of engineers managing to isolate each individual noise to determine where it came from and then take steps to eliminate it.

693 Also for the 2000 model year, the Wrangler received the New Venture Gear NV3550 5-speed manual transmission with synchronized reverse as standard equipment with the 4.0-liter engine. The new 5-speed manual gearbox was more durable than the transmission it replaced, as well as being easier to shift.

694 The American Motors 2.5-liter 4-cylinder engine was finally dropped at the end of the 2002 model year. For 2003, a Chrysler-designed 2.4-liter double overhead cam (DOHC) 4-cylinder debuted that was rated at 147 hp and 165 ft-lbs of torque.

695 Also for the Wrangler during the 2003 model year was the new 42RLE 4-speed automatic transmission, which came with a skid plate and was optional with either the 2.4- and 4.0-liter engines. This smooth-shifting transmission replaced the former 3-speed automatic used and provided a quieter highway ride, improved acceleration, and much better fuel economy.

696 As part of a comprehensive drivetrain update for 2002 Wrangler models, the NV1500 and NV3550 transmissions were introduced, which replaced the former Aisin-Seki AX-5 and AX-15. New Venture Gear was a powertrain joint venture that was started in 1990 as the first between a US Big Three automaker and an independent transmission supplier. Chrysler Corporation was one of the participants.

697 For the 2003 model year, an all-new 42RLE 4-speed automatic transmission debuted on the Jeep Wrangler. Offered on all models, this smoother-shifting transmission provided better highway fuel efficiency and quieter engine operation at highway speeds compared to the previous 3-speed automatic transmission. In addition to the standard fuel tank and transfer case skid plates, a new automatic transmission skid plate provided additional off-road protection.

698 Drivetrain upgrades were a constant thing at Jeep during the earlier 2000s. For the 2005 model, the Wrangler's standard 5-speed manual transmission was replaced by a new 6-speed manual transmission.

Suspension and Brakes

699 Although the new Wrangler for 1987 didn't appear to be that much different from the CJ, almost every part in it was new. Engine, transmission, chassis, suspension, and body were all new or dramatically improved. It was the most civilized small Jeep ever offered to that point, and yet it was still an extremely capable off-roader.

700 The new Wrangler YJ came with power front disc brakes and P215/75R15 radial-ply tires as standard equipment. The Jeep CJs had come standard with non-power-assisted disc brakes, so the addition of power was welcomed by owners.

701 To improve vehicle handling and reduce the chance of a rollover accident, the new Wrangler had a lower height than the CJs and also featured a wider track: 58 inches versus 55.8 on the CJ-7. To further improved handling, the Wrangler also was given standard track bars and thicker anti-sway bars.

702 The Wrangler YJ also benefited from a revised steering system with relocated steering knuckles, a new power steering box, and new axles. By the way, the new axles were from the Jeep

Cherokee XJ series. The Wrangler's ride and handling were a vast improvement over the outgoing CJ.

703 To ensure its core off-road customers would know they weren't forgotten, the Wrangler YJ for 1987 offered an optional Off-Road Package that consisted of heavy-duty gas-filled shock absorbers front and rear plus meaty P255/75R15 Goodyear Wrangler OWL tires.

704 For the 1993 model year, the Wrangler YJ finally offered four-wheel antilock brakes, although they were optional and could be ordered only with the 4.0-liter six engine. Jeep was the foremost innovator in antilock brakes on four-wheel-drive vehicles and in time made them standard equipment across the board.

705 The all-new Wrangler TJ series introduced a suspension system that Jeep engineers dubbed Quadra-Coil, which featured coil springs on all four wheels, a notable improvement. The new suspension provided the smoothest ride yet for a Wrangler, along with superior articulation in off-road driving conditions.

706 The Wrangler TJ's axles were located by five links at each end plus upper and lower control arms and a panhard rod. Combined with the standard stabilizer bar, it helped to greatly reduce axle wrap and axle windup.

707 Here's some proof of how surprisingly good the new 1997 Wrangler TJ was: After testing one, *Car & Driver* magazine declared, "It scampers over rocks like a lizard!" The combination of the vastly improved suspension and steering components and the tighter body plus a stronger frame helped the new Wrangler surpass Jeep's design goal of creating a vehicle that was superior to the CJ in off-road capability while delivering a smoother on-road ride.

708 The Wrangler TJ for 1997 also featured a stiffer frame for greater durability and to improve suspension tuning. Torsional rigidity was a full 15 percent greater, and bending stiffness was 30 percent greater.

709 Jeep made certain that the new Wrangler also offered greatly improved safety for its occupants. In addition to the standard antilock brakes, the new Wrangler TJ came standard with driver and passenger front-seat airbags. A new collapsible steering column was also standard equipment.

710 In 2000, the Wrangler TJ offered five distinct road wheels: the Styled Steel Wheel was standard on the SE models. The Full-Face Steel Wheel was standard on the Sport and optional on the SE. The more stylish Grizzly Cast Aluminum wheel was optional on the SE and Sport (15 inches). The 16-inch Ultra Star aluminum wheel was standard on the Sahara. The 15-inch Canyon Cast aluminum wheel was available as part of the optional 30-inch tire and wheel group for both the Sport and Sahara models.

Numbers Crunching and Press Commentary

711 The Wrangler YJ and TJ series both rode on a trim 93.4-inch wheelbase, with the exception of the 2004–2006 Wrangler Unlimited (aka the Long Jeep) which rode on a 103.4-inch wheelbase. The Wrangler Unlimited's 10-inch-longer wheelbase allowed for more rear seat legroom and hip room, as well as greater cargo space.

712 Overall length for the Wrangler YJ was 151.9 inches, which was less than the Ford Bronco II and Mitsubishi Montero. Surprisingly, the new Wrangler TJ for 1997 was even more compact at just 147.7 inches nose to tail. The TJ was also 66.7 inches wide, which was 0.7 inch greater than the outgoing YJ.

713 When it was introduced for 1987, the Wrangler came with a standard 12-month/12,000-mile warranty plus an additional 12 months or 12,000 miles on the powertrain. American Motors also provided 3 years of warranty coverage for corrosion.

714 The Wrangler YJ remained in production through late 1995 when it was scheduled to be replaced by the all-new Wrangler TJ series. Because there would be a gap in production during the massive change-

over the company stockpiled extra YJ units to tide dealers over until the TJs were ready.

Here's the full line of Jeep vehicles for 1990, including a sharp Wrangler Islander (bottom).

715 In order to simplify production at the beginning of the model run, the Wrangler TJ was initially offered in just three models: SE, Sport, and Sahara. Noticeably absent were the S, Base, and Laredo models seen in prior years.

716 In addition to producing and selling vehicles, Jeep also offers licensing opportunities for sale. Product categories that have seen

licensing agreements thus far include toys, luggage, mountain bikes, stereo equipment, eyewear, and clothing. During 1995, Jeep Licensing Operations accounted for more than $200 million in worldwide sales.

717 I found some interesting "insider" marketing info regarding the 1999 Wrangler: The demographics for the average Wrangler buyer at that time were an age between 36 and 40, but Jeep

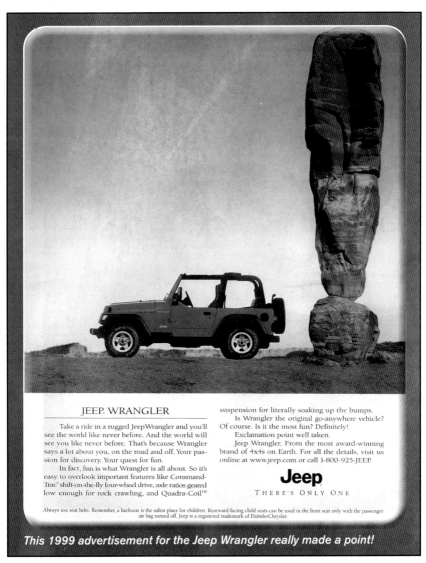

JEEP WRANGLER

Take a ride in a rugged Jeep Wrangler and you'll see the world like never before. And the world will see you like never before. That's because Wrangler says a lot about you, on the road and off. Your passion for discovery. Your quest for fun.

In fact, fun is what Wrangler is all about. So it's easy to overlook important features like Command-Trac® shift-on-the-fly four-wheel drive, axle ratios geared low enough for rock crawling, and Quadra-Coil™

suspension for literally soaking up the bumps.

Is Wrangler the original go-anywhere vehicle? Of course. Is it the most fun? Definitely! Exclamation point well taken.

Jeep Wrangler. From the most award-winning brand of 4x4s on Earth. For all the details, visit us online at www.jeep.com or call 1-800-925-JEEP.

Jeep

THERE'S ONLY ONE

Always use seat belts. Remember, a backseat is the safest place for children. Rearward-facing child seats can be used in the front seat only with the passenger air bag turned off. Jeep is a registered trademark of DaimlerChrysler.

This 1999 advertisement for the Jeep Wrangler really made a point!

officials hoped to lower that to ages 32 to 37. Income among buyers averaged $56,000 to $64,000, and Jeep expected that to rise to $58,000 to $67,000. Only about 29 percent of Wrangler buyers were female, but Jeep marketing people targeted raising that number to 35 percent.

718 A press comment that I really love about the 1999 Wrangler is this one from *Business Week* magazine: "The Wrangler took to the terrain like a third-grader hitting the playground at recess."

719 Another 1999 press remark I enjoy is this one from *Automobile* magazine: "The Wrangler can do things other SUVs can't and it goes about its task in a way the others simply wouldn't dare."

720 Jeep sold an amazing 554,000 vehicles in the United States during 1999, plus another 121,000 outside the country. The total of 675,000 (a new record for Jeep) was more than three times the unit sales for 1990!

721 New audio features available on the 2000 model year Wrangler included an amplified subwoofer optional with all radios, a new Anti-lock Brake System (ABS), plus a new long-life engine coolant that didn't need to be changed until 100,000 miles were reached, which reduced maintenance headaches considerably.

722 For 2006, the Golden Eagle Package returned to the Jeep line for the Wrangler series. The package included specific logo and script applications on the front fenders and spare tire cover, two-tone premium seats with specific logo treatment, a painted center stack bezel, Dana 44 heavy-duty rear axle, 15-inch gold aluminum wheels, and 30-inch tires.

723 So who were the buyers targeted by the 2004–2006 Wrangler Unlimited? "We are going after the male who loved the Cherokee [XJ] but didn't gravitate to the Jeep Liberty," said George Murphy, Chrysler Group senior vice president of global marketing.

Jeep Wrangler JK and JL

Legend and Lore

724 As great as the Wrangler TJ series was, Jeep engineers knew that for upcoming models they would be able to do even

This Wrangler Unlimited has some interesting optional equipment. We especially like the neat side steps, front bumper with tubular grille guard, and the headlamp protectors. (Photo Courtesy Dimitris Vetsikas from Pixabay)

The lucky owner of this red and black two-door Wrangler JK is heading for adventure in the mountains. (Photo Courtesy Scozzy from Pixabay)

better. Technology was rapidly advancing, and they knew they had the expertise and tools to dramatically improve the vehicle. In any event, it had to be done in order to maintain Jeep's premier reputation in a world awash in four-wheel-drive vehicles. After years of engineering experimentation and testing, they introduced a completely new Wrangler, known internally as the JK, for the 2007 model year.

This 2018 Wrangler Unlimited JK Sahara shows off the available body color hardtop that gives the styling a more integrated look. Note, too, the interesting round side marker lights and neat tow hooks up front. (Photo Courtesy Brett Sayles from Pexels)

725 The new and long-awaited Wrangler JK Unlimited four-door model was the first Wrangler to be rated for five passengers, which was made possible because of a substantial increase in body width as well as much greater chassis length.

Who can forget the classic scene in the action film Jurassic Park when the Tyrannosaurus Rex is chasing the Jeep Wrangler through the woods, chomping at its wheels and scaring the bejeesus out of the folks inside? To commemorate the famous, super-scary clip, Jeep created the special Jurassic Park Wrangler based on a 2018 Wrangler JK. (Photo Courtesy Claudio Schwarz | @purzlbaum on Unsplash)

726 During the 2011 model year, Jeep produced a pair of limited-edition models: the Jeep Wrangler and the Wrangler Unlimited Call of Duty Black Ops Edition. Based on the Jeep Wrangler Rubicon model and named after the popular video game, the Call of Duty featured dark Rubicon wheels, black exterior paint, and "Call of Duty: Black Ops" graphics on the roof and front quarter panels. Also featured were taillamp guards and a fuel-filler door from Mopar.

727 Debuting for the 2015 model year was the new Jeep Wrangler Rubicon Hard Rock Edition, available on either the two-door Wrangler or four-door Wrangler Unlimited models. The Hard Rock Edition was easily the most capable Wrangler in the lineup.

Based on the Rubicon model, it came equipped with a part-time four-wheel-drive system boasting electronic-locking front and rear Dana 44 axles that received power through a Rock-Trac transfer case with a "4-Low" ratio of 4:1. A 4.10:1 axle ratio, both front and rear, was also standard equipment, as were Tru-Lok locking differentials. With a 6-speed manual transmission, the Wrangler Rubicon Hard Rock edition had an impressive crawl ratio of 73.1:1, which made it possible to negotiate just about any off-road obstacle.

728 Jeep added a lower-priced special trim model for 2015: the Willys Wheeler Edition. Based on the Wrangler Sport model, the Willys Wheeler featured upgraded Dana 44 rear axle with Trac-Lok limited-slip rear differential and 3.73:1 gears, BFGoodrich KM Mud Terrain LT255/75R17 tires, rock rails, and a Jeep Trail Rated Kit that includes a D-Ring tow strap and gloves in a Jeep-branded bag.

Special exterior design cues included a gloss-black grille with black Jeep badge, gloss-black front and rear bumper appliques, a historic satin black "4 Wheel Drive" rear tailgate decal and "Willys" hood decals, plus unique high-gloss black 17-inch aluminum wheels. The Willys Wheeler Edition came with a Sunrider soft top and deep-tint sunscreen rear windows as standard equipment.

The Willys Wheeler Editions also included the Connectivity Group with SiriusXM Radio. One really nice touch was that the Jeep Wrangler's iconic half doors were available as an option.

729 Another special model for 2015 was the Jeep Wrangler Freedom Edition. Considered a tribute to US military members, it offered military-themed exterior and interior design cues. Based on the Wrangler Sport model, it was available as either a two-door or four-door and offered six exterior paint colors: Firecracker Red, Bright White, Hydro Blue, Billet Silver, Black, and Tank. The Freedom Edition's exterior features included new-for-2015 "Oscar Mike" fender badges and decals on the hood and rear quarter panels; Mineral Gray–painted 17-inch alloy wheels; Mineral Gray–painted grille and front and rear bumper inserts; body-color wheel arches; rock rails with matching black taillamp guards; a Mopar fuel-fill door; and a Sunrider soft top with deep-tint rear windows.

730 Okay, here's one even I hadn't heard of: The Jeep Wrangler Black Bear Edition. Introduced for the 2016 model year, it was available as a Wrangler or Wrangler Unlimited and was based on the Wrangler Sport. The Black Bear Edition offered nine exterior colors: Billet Silver, Black, Bright White, Firecracker Red, Granite Crystal, Hydro Blue, Hypergreen, Rhino, and Tank. Exterior features included a heritage "Wrangler" hood decal, a topographical Black Bear Pass Trail hood decal, off-road rock rails, Satin Black grille, Mineral Gray bumper, premium Sunrider soft top (a body-color hardtop was optional), 17-inch five-spoke black wheels, traction-adding Silent Armor tires, black taillamp guards, and a black fuel-fill door.

The interior of the Black Bear Edition had black cloth Sedoso seats, a leather-wrapped steering wheel with black accent stitching, Iron Gray bezels, grab handle vent rings and door handles, sport bar grab handles, all-weather slush mats, and standard air-conditioning.

If you're wondering where the name comes from, Black Bear Pass is a popular Jeep Jamboree trail in Telluride, Colorado.

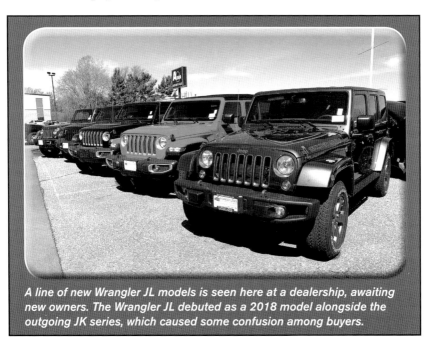

A line of new Wrangler JL models is seen here at a dealership, awaiting new owners. The Wrangler JL debuted as a 2018 model alongside the outgoing JK series, which caused some confusion among buyers.

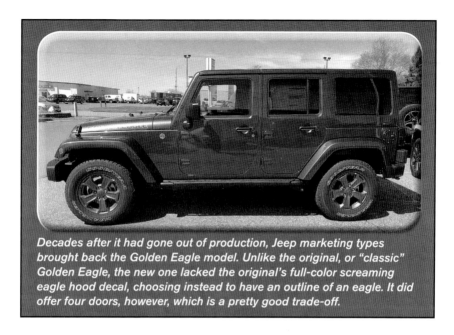

Decades after it had gone out of production, Jeep marketing types brought back the Golden Eagle model. Unlike the original, or "classic" Golden Eagle, the new one lacked the original's full-color screaming eagle hood decal, choosing instead to have an outline of an eagle. It did offer four doors, however, which is a pretty good trade-off.

731 In February 2017, Jeep unveiled yet another package: the Wrangler Rubicon Recon Edition. Based on the Wrangler Rubicon, the Rubicon Recon Edition upped the off-road ante with a front axle upgrade featuring strengthened tubes and heavy-duty end forgings, heavy-duty cast front and rear differential covers, and enhanced off-road rock rails shortened to accommodate up to 35-inch tires.

Equipment included Wrangler's part-time four-wheel-drive system plus electronic-locking front and rear Dana 44 axles with power being sent to each through a Rock-Trac transfer case with a "4-Low" ratio of 4:1. A 4.10:1 front and rear axle ratio was standard along with Tru-Lok locking differentials. With a 6-speed manual transmission, the Recon Edition boasted a crawl ratio of 73.1:1 to make climbing obstacles easy. A 5-speed automatic transmission was optional.

The Recon Edition offered seven exterior color choices: Black, Bright White, Billet Silver, Firecracker Red, Gobi, Rhino, and Granite Crystal. The Wrangler Rubicon Recon Edition also included a 1/2-inch lift, new 17-inch Low Gloss Granite Crystal-painted aluminum wheels with 32-inch BFGoodrich KM off-road tires, optional body-color fender flares, and a dual-vented Power Dome hood with

a black-silhouette "Rubicon" decal on both sides. Also featured on the exterior were a Low Gloss Black grille with Low Gloss Granite Crystal inserts and headlamp rings, Low Gloss Black off-road bumpers, and a Jeep badge with a red base, all of which help give the Recon a tougher look.

Inside, the Rubicon Recon came standard with an eight-speaker audio system, black leather heated seats with a "Rubicon" embroidered logo, and a leather-wrapped steering wheel with red accent stitching. A dashboard plaque displayed information regarding the front and rear axles, front sway bar, transfer case, and tires.

A Premium Sunrider soft top was standard, and a body-color hardtop was also available.

732 For the final year in production (the 2018 model year), the Wrangler JK models featured a new "Wrangler JK" decal on the driver-side front quarter panel. This also served to help distinguish them from the upcoming all-new Wrangler models that came onto the dealer lots before the year ended.

733 The all-new Wrangler debuted as a second-series 2018 model. This was one of the few times in history that an automaker offered two entirely different vehicles bearing the same model year (another one was the 1970 Chevy Camaro). Dubbed the JL series, the new Wrangler boasted an industry-leading, best-in-class approach angle of 44 degrees, a break-over angle of 27.8 degrees, a departure angle of 37 degrees, and a ground clearance of 10.9 inches that allowed the Wrangler to go anywhere. The new Wrangler also benefited from up to 30 inches of water fording ability and up to 3,500 pounds of towing capacity with the available towing package.

Body and Interior

734 The all-new 2007 Wrangler JK was offered in three regular trim levels: Wrangler X, Wrangler Sahara, and Wrangler Rubicon. The two-door body featured a 5.5-inch increase in overall width for more interior space and a brawnier appearance.

735 When you look at a JK hood, you notice that it slopes noticeably, which was a nod to aerodynamic efficiency that improved real-world fuel economy while also reducing wind noise.

736 How much more room did the JK-series two-door model offer? How about 4.6 inches more hip room, 5.1 inches more shoulder room, and 1 inch more rear-seat leg room. There was also 2 inches more space behind the rear seat.

737 Of course, the big news for 2007 was the introduction of the Wrangler Unlimited four-door, a model that Jeep enthusiasts had been wanting for years and that Jeep had been promising for almost as long. The Unlimited four-door was in high demand right from the beginning.

738 The wheelbase of the 2007 JK two-door was now 95.4 inches (more than a foot longer than the original Jeep CJ-5), and the four-door version rode on a 116-inch wheelbase. The wheel track on both models was 61.9 inches front and rear.

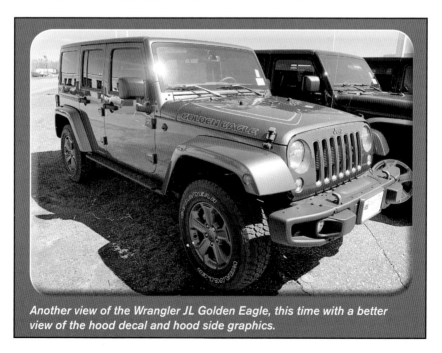

Another view of the Wrangler JL Golden Eagle, this time with a better view of the hood decal and hood side graphics.

739 The Wrangler JK series also offered multiple door, soft top, hardtop, and windshield combinations, including a new three-piece Freedom Top (a modular-type hardtop) and the innovative Sunrider soft top.

740 As far as luxury features, the Wrangler JK offered optional power windows and door locks, a Wrangler first, and one that even I found a bit disconcerting at first. In addition, buyers could order a full-screen navigation system, 368-watt Alpine® stereo with MP3 capability, and a Sirius Satellite Radio.

741 The Wrangler JK two-door model also boasted an all-new 100-percent-more-rigid frame (as rated in bending stiffness), a 2-inch-longer wheelbase, and a 3.5-inch-wider track than on the outgoing Wrangler TJ.

742 The JK Unlimited four-door models boasted an impressive 46.4 cubic feet of cargo room versus 22.3 cubic feet on the 2006 Unlimited. Jeep management was actually surprised at how popular the new model was; in the end, they realized that one of the few complaints people had about the Wrangler was its limited storage space.

743 One very appreciated new feature on the Wrangler JK was a hidden storage well that was located under the rear cargo floor area. It was a perfect place for concealing valuables, and thus safe and secure. You wonder why no one had thought of it earlier!

744 A new option for the 2008 JK was the Sahara Appearance Group, which included huge 18-inch aluminum wheels, bright steering-wheel spokes, and air-conditioning outlet rings, plus attractive front and rear bumper overlays.

745 For 2011, the Wrangler JK was given an all-new interior that featured improved ergonomics and upgraded materials. It also received an all-new body-color hardtop on the Sahara models, optional power-heated mirrors, and even heated seats!

746 Beginning with the 2012 model year, the Wrangler Rubicon also could be ordered with an attractive body-color hardtop. Featuring a smooth exterior rather than the textured exterior seen on the lower-priced models, the new top made the colors really stand out. It proved to be a very popular option and is still popular on today's models.

747 New for 2015 Wrangler models was an eight-speaker audio system with improved sound bar that was now standard equipment. In addition, the all-new nine-speaker Premium Alpine audio system with amplifier and subwoofer was available as an extra-cost option.

Here's another group of 2019 Wrangler JLs; all are in the bright color choices that are very popular today.

748 Here's a little fact that I can really appreciate: For the 2015 model year, a new standard Torx Tool Kit for removing the Wrangler's top, doors, and even the bumper end caps was included as standard equipment on all models.

749 For 2016, the Wrangler Sahara and Sahara Wrangler Unlimited were given styling updates to their exterior and interior appearance. New features included a body-color bumper applique, 18-inch wheels with Granite Crystal–painted pockets and polished surface, and a modified "Sahara" logo. Additional design touches included high-gloss, fine silver metallic seven-slot grille throats and iconic headlamp rings, Satin Chrome steering wheel bezel, and Quick Silver grab handle, bezels, and vent rings. Cool.

750 For me, at least, one of the most desirable of the JK Wrangler special package models is the 2017 Wrangler Chief Edition. Painted bright blue with a white hardtop, the four-door Wrangler Chief reminds one of a vintage 1970s J-series Jeep Cherokee Chief with its audacious paint color offset by a white sport stripe running from the hood onto the doors clear back to meet the top. Vintage-looking spoke wheels and upgraded

The all-around most capable Jeep is the Wrangler, and in the Wrangler series, the Rubicon is king. Its off-road prowess is more than most people can ever appreciate, but just knowing you have that level of ability on tap whenever you want it is very reassuring.

interior trim help to make this a really special vehicle. I especially appreciate the bright "Chief" insignia up front on the side panels. You don't see many of these around.

The projector beam–style headlamps available on the 2019 and 2020 Wrangler JL offer outstanding vision and cool looks.

751 In addition to the special-package Jeep models, for 2017 the Wrangler lineup consisted of four regular-production models: Sport, Sport S, Sahara, and Rubicon. Exterior colors for 2017 included Chief (new this year), Acid Yellow (new), Gobi (new), Xtreme Purple (this year available across the entire lineup), Billet Silver, Black, Bright White, Firecracker Red, Granite Crystal, and Rhino.

The Wrangler spare tire carrier, sans spare. The high-mounted stoplight system is simple and effective.

Although it's technically not a Wrangler, we couldn't help including the 2020 Gladiator pickup in this section. The first pickup truck from Jeep since the Comanche, it's a heavy-duty workhorse of a truck, and the only convertible pickup available today.

752 For the 2018 model year, Jeep added several new package models of the classic Wrangler JK. One of the new ones, the Wrangler Golden Eagle, included such features as a Premium tan soft top, optional tan half-doors, Golden Eagle decals on the hood center and hood sides, a body-color grille fender flares with Low Gloss Bronze throats, headlamp rings, and Jeep badging, steel front and rear bumpers with bronze tow hooks, heavy-duty rock rails with matching black taillamp guards and fuel-fill door, cool 17-inch Low Gloss Bronze wheels with meaty BFGoodrich KO2 tires, the Golden Eagle logo on both front seats, and Light Bronze accent stitching on the McKinley vinyl-wrapped front-door armrests, console lid, Black leather-wrapped steering wheel, and black cloth seats.

753 Also appearing for the 2018 JK models was the new Wrangler Altitude. Based on the Sahara model, the Wrangler JK Altitude's highlights included a body-color grille with High-Gloss Black throats, headlamp rings, front and rear bumper appliques, a Jeep badge, and 18-inch wheels wearing handsome Bridgestone Dueler tires. Other Altitude features included a body-color hardtop, power-bulge hood, black taillamp guards and fuel-fill door, black leather seats with Diesel Gray accent stitching, and a leather-wrapped steering wheel with Liquid Titanium–painted spokes and Diesel Gray stitching.

754 When the all-new Wrangler JL series appeared in mid-2018, it featured several new ideas in body construction, including the windshield's rake being optimized for improved aerodynamics, improved real-world fuel economy, and reduced wind noise. It also featured a new four-bolt design at the top of the windshield frame to allow the windshield to fold down quickly and easily. A new header bar was used to connect the A-pillars and now stayed in place even when the windshield was folded down. This smart feature allowed the rearview mirror to remain in place even when the windshield was folded.

755 Also on the all-new Wrangler JL were two-piece body-color fender flares with a black lower insert to give a raised profile. These were standard on the Sahara models and available on the Rubicons. Perhaps the biggest news were new lightweight, high-strength aluminum doors featuring the Torx bit tool size stamped directly onto the hinge to eliminate guessing which tool was needed to remove the doors. In addition, all of the Wrangler JL models featured body-colored sport bars welded to the body. The sport bars included integrated grab handles.

756 To protect critical vehicle components while on the trail (including the fuel tank, transfer case, and automatic transmission oil pan), the Wrangler JL employed four skid plates and bars. The Wrangler Rubicon models benefited

further from the use of heavy-gauge tubular-steel rock rails to limit potential body damage inflicted while out in the boonies.

Although there were persistent rumors that the new JL would have an all-aluminum body structure, it was basically made of steel. However, weight savings were achieved via the use of lightweight, high-strength aluminum closures, including the doors, door hinges, engine hood, fender flares, and windshield frame. A novel magnesium swing gate further helped to reduce vehicle weight while at the same time boost fuel economy. Other ways the Jeep engineering team was able to reduce weight included using hollow-track and stabilizer bars, new aluminum engine mounts and steering gear, and a larger, lighter master cylinder.

Engine and Drivetrain

757 For the 2007 model year, the Wrangler JK came with a new 3.8-liter V-6 engine delivering 202 hp and 237 ft-lbs of torque. The increased horsepower and torque (along with a beefier suspension) resulted in a standard towing capacity of 2,000 pounds and an available towing capacity of 3,500 pounds.

758 One drawback to the V-6 engine was that although it offered more power, peak torque came at a relatively high 4,000 rpm, so it didn't have quite the same satisfying low-end power that's so useful while lugging along in low-range.

759 As new as the JK was, its 6-speed manual and 4-speed automatic transmissions were carried over from the Wrangler TJ. However, the JK the axles are beefier with new lockers that are magnetically engaged (rather than vacuum operated) on the Rubicon version.

760 Here's a startling fact that you probably won't believe: For the 2007 model year, Jeep introduced a two-wheel-drive version of the Wrangler Unlimited four door. *No, I am not kidding!* However, it appears that right-hand steering was

no longer available in the United States, so apparently it wasn't aimed at postal route delivery. Jeep must have been targeting "four-wheel-drive posers," those people who like to be seen in Wranglers but never take them off-road. Today, Jeep officials don't like to admit that the two-wheel-drive Wrangler existed, but it did.

761 To ensure that the Wrangler JK maintained its reputation for off-road superiority, it featured enhanced Dana front and rear solid axles and new electric axle lockers, plus an innovative electronically disconnecting front sway bar for off-road use.

762 Also new for the 2007 Wrangler JK were the available next-generation Command-Trac® and Rock-Trac® transfer cases. The Rock-Trac version was desired for maximum off-road capability.

763 The 2007 JK Command-Trac Model NV241 GII transfer case was smoother, tougher, and quieter this year. Both it and the Rock-Trac NV241 OR (off-road) transfer case used 18 bolts (versus 9 bolts previously) to increase structural stiffness and to effectively double-seal them.

764 The 2008 Wrangler JK introduced a new optional Remote Start system, the first time this luxury feature was available on a Wrangler. Over the years, more and more features usually associated with luxury cars have been introduced on the Wrangler in response to customer desires.

765 For the 2012 model year, the Wrangler JK was treated to a new 3.6-liter V-6 engine that provided greatly improved fuel efficiency of up to 21 mpg, 285 hp (which was a solid 40-percent improvement), and 260 ft-lbs of torque. An interesting new option this year was a 5-speed automatic transmission shared with the Jeep Grand Cherokee.

Another view of the new Gladiator truck from Jeep. Demand for the new truck is already exceeding Jeep's sales projections.

766 With the introduction of the all-new Wrangler JK series for 2018 came a new standard engine. The all-new 2.0-liter turbocharged inline 4-cylinder engine (which included eTorque technology) was rated at a best-in-class 270 hp and 295 ft-lbs of torque and was mated to a new 8-speed automatic transmission. The 2.0-liter turbo engine's torque output surpassed that of the Wrangler's newly upgraded V-6 engine, which was rated at 260 ft-lbs.

The 2.0 liter's all-new eTorque system improved fuel economy and enhanced vehicle launch performance as well as driver comfort during start and stop operations. The eTorque system's hybrid functions included an automatic stop and start, electric power assist, extended fuel shut-off, transmission shift management, intelligent battery charging, and regenerative braking. To save fuel, both the engine and fuel flow could be turned off during stops, when coasting, or when the vehicle was decelerating.

The 2.0-liter inline 4-cylinder engine also featured a twin-scroll, low-inertia turbocharger with an electronically actuated wastegate for exceptional responsiveness and performance, even while traveling over rough terrain. The turbo was mounted directly to the cylinder head for improved durability. In addition, a dedicated cooling circuit

helped to lower the temperature of the intake air, the throttle body, and the turbocharger for improved performance and fuel efficiency. Direct injection coupled with turbocharging also worked to enable efficient combustion and increased performance.

The 2.0-liter inline 4-cylinder engine's fuel pump supplied the engine's 2,900-psi high-pressure common-rail injection system. The high pressures helped produce better fuel atomization and allow for more precise fuel delivery than the less expensive port fuel-injection systems, which in turn improved both performance and efficiency.

The 2.0-liter turbocharged engine boasted DOHCs, dual independent camshaft timing, and a cooled exhaust-gas recirculation (C-EGR) system.

767 For the all-new Wrangler JL, the 3.6-liter Pentastar V-6 engine was upgraded and improved to now deliver 285 hp and 260 ft-lbs of torque. New features included an Engine Stop-Start (ESS) system as standard equipment. It was engineered to provide a broad torque band with a particular focus on low-end torque, a trait that's needed for extreme off-roading capability.

768 The Wrangler JL also offered a new 8-speed automatic transmission, enabling the vehicle to optimize engine output while on the trail or enjoy smooth, efficient power delivery at highway speeds. The 8-speed automatic was available on all Jeep Wrangler models and offered a responsive driving experience whether commuting during the week or rock crawling on the weekend, with smooth, linear power delivery and improved fuel efficiency. A unique set of two overdrive ratios improved highway fuel economy while reducing overall noise, vibration, and harshness (NVH) levels.

769 The Wrangler JL series for 2018 also featured unmatched capability with its carryover Command-Trac and Rock-Trac four-wheel-drive systems, along with new next-generation Dana axles, Tru-Lock electric front- and rear-axle lockers, Trac-Lok limited-slip differential, and 33-inch off-road tires.

770 In addition to the Command-Trac and Rock-Trac four-wheel-drive systems, the Wrangler JL also offered a new-generation Selec-Trac full-time four-wheel-drive system that included a 2-speed transfer case. With full-time four-wheel drive it was no longer necessary to shift into two-wheel drive on hard, dry pavements, making it much easier to live with.

771 Perhaps the most anticipated engine in the Wrangler JL was the new 3.0-liter EcoDiesel V-6. This engine was available starting with the 2019 model year Wrangler four-door models. Rated at 260 hp and 442 ft-lbs of torque, and with the standard equipment ESS system, the new diesel was hooked up to a new 8-speed automatic transmission that was designed to handle the engine's greatly increased torque output.

The diesel engine (manufactured by the Fiat Chrysler Automobiles–owned VM Motori company) was modified and improved by Jeep engineers to meet the North American Free Trade Agreement (NAFTA) regulatory requirements. The EcoDiesel V-6 engine also debuted with new turbocharger technology that included a low-friction turbo bearing designed to improve low-end performance.

The upgraded EcoDiesel also featured low-friction pistons to improve fuel economy, reduce greenhouse gas emissions, and provide an enhanced combustion system including a new injector nozzle, piston bowl, and glow plugs with integrated combustion pressure sensor to optimize combustion. This new engine was the most technologically advanced engine ever offered in a Wrangler.

Suspension and Brakes

772 The Wrangler JK came with four-wheel disc ABS as standard equipment on all models, along with an innovative off-road ABS feature that enabled sustained wheel lockup for improved performance on plowable surfaces, including gravel, sand, and mud.

773 The Wrangler JK's Dana 44 solid rear axle was considered a next-generation axle because it was redesigned with a larger pinion and used wheel bearings for greater durability.

774 Although the JK's suspension looks about the same as that of the TJ, every single part of it is different, and a lot of aftermarket suspension stuff for the TJ doesn't fit the JK. Thankfully, the aftermarket companies have stepped up to the plate and created a whole new array of parts for the new vehicle. Jeep, too, offers many aftermarket parts and accessories.

775 The Wrangler JK Rubicon came with innovative new Tru-Lok electronically locking front and rear differentials equipped with the solenoids mounted within the axles to provide better protection from damage by water, by dirt, or by being struck by rocks and debris.

776 As mentioned earlier, the JK was the first Jeep to offer an optional electronic front sway bar disconnect. That new feature helped to enable the Wrangler to achieve the best-ever off-road articulation, making the King of the Off-Road an even better vehicle.

777 The Wrangler JK also boasted a modern brake-assist feature, which could actually sense a panic brake condition coming on and then automatically apply maximum braking power much faster than the driver would be able to apply.

778 The Wrangler JK's standard 32-inch BFGoodrich off-road tires have a custom-designed tread pattern that is exclusive to Jeep and provides an ideal combination of on-road ride quality and off-road capability. In addition, the Wrangler vehicle's ground clearance was increased by 1 inch for 2007. This was an important improvement because 1 inch can be the difference between getting over a hump or getting hung up on a rock.

779 The new Wrangler also included two chassis features that were important for driving safety. One was the Electronic Stability Program (ESP), which aided drivers in maintaining vehicle directional stability by automatically providing oversteer and understeer control to maintain vehicle behavior on vari-

ous road surfaces. The other was the Electronic Roll Mitigation (ERM) system, which monitors the vehicle's roll attitude and lateral forces to estimate the potential for a rollover situation. If it senses that a rollover is possible, it immediately begins to apply and release the brakes selectively as a corrective action to bring the vehicle under control.

780 With the 2007 JK, Wrangler offered factory-installed 18-inch wheels for the first time. This was possible now because of the JK's larger wheel openings, fatter fenders, and wider fender flares.

781 Additional safety features on the Wrangler JK Unlimited were advanced multistage airbags, front-seat-mounted side airbags, antilock brakes with brake assist, and sturdy side-door impact beams, making the JK the safest Wrangler yet.

782 For 2008, the Wrangler JK introduced a right-hand-drive model for the US market. The two-wheel-drive four-door version (I know, I can't believe it either!) was aimed primarily at postal route drivers.

783 Also new for the 2008 JK was the innovative Tire Pressure Monitoring (TPM) system, which monitored tire pressure on a continual basis and alerted drivers when any tire was low on air. This feature was considered so important that it was made standard equipment on all Wrangler models.

784 Adding to Wrangler's safety attitude, for 2010, Jeep made the following electronic features standard equipment on all models: Electronic Stability Control (ESC; successor to the ESP), Hill-Start Assist (HSA), and Trailer-Sway Control (TSC).

785 For the 2015 Wrangler Sport models, a new Black Steel and 31-inch Dueler Tire Package was now available. Included in the package were 16-inch Low Gloss Black Steel wheels and Bridgestone Dueler A/T Revo2 tires for extra good grip.

Numbers Crunching and Press Commentary

786 The industry trade paper *Automotive News* said of the new 2007 Wrangler JK, "It's the same, only different; way different. At first glance, the 2007 Wrangler JK looks like a natural progression of the Jeep theme; not too much has changed. But the more you know about the new Wrangler, the more you realize that everything has changed."

787 In what was now becoming a tradition, when the Wrangler JK was introduced at the 2006 Detroit Auto Show, it was driven through one of the front windows at the downtown Cobo Center as a hoard of journalists cheered it on. It then was driven out to the street and up the stairs of the nearby Hotel Pontchartrain. I was there, and it was a stunning sight to behold.

788 In addition to Camp Jeep, the company also offers JEEP 101 events in cities across the United States, where thousands of Jeep owners and prospective owners encounter steep downhill grades, log crossings, and sandbanks close to their homes, as they learn the basic skills of safe, yet adventurous off-road driving.

789 The Jeep J-8, a military derivative of the Wrangler built in Egypt, was available for a while in the United States in kit form. Offered by American Expedition Vehicles, the vehicle was sold fully assembled except for the engine, which had to be installed by the buyer. Engine choices included a Hemi V-8 and a VM Motori diesel.

790 Jeep's public relations department said that the 2012 Jeep Wrangler offered "A New Heart, the Same Soul" and the "All-new 3.6-liter V-6 powertrain provides more fuel efficiency, improved on-road driving dynamics and refinement, more power and torque; and even more legendary capability."

791 Jeep also said of the 2012 Wrangler, "The most capable production off-road vehicle in the world gets better: dramatically improved on-road performance combines with even more off-road

prowess. All-new premium powertrain will excite core Jeep follow-ers and attract new customers with improved everyday on-road performance. New 3.6-liter V-6 engine improves fuel efficiency up to 21 miles per gallon while delivering 285 hp (40 percent improve-ment) and 260 ft-lbs of torque (10 percent improvement)."

792 Like many Jeep vehicles, the new Wrangler JL continued to be built in Toledo, Ohio, but now it was manufactured in the company's Toledo North assembly plant (TNAP), which formerly produced the Jeep Cherokee models. The Cherokee production ended there on April 6, 2017, and was moved to the FCA Belvi-dere assembly plant, a huge complex that is located 60 miles west of Chicago.

The Wrangler's move from its former home in the Toledo Sup-plier Park (aka Toledo South) to the massive TNAP was the second step in a two-phased, $3.5 billion industrialization plan to realign FCA's US manufacturing operations in a bid to greatly expand production of the Jeep and Ram brands. In all, FCA invested $700 million to retool the North plant for production of the all-new Wrangler JL, which also added 700 new jobs. More than two mil-lion Wranglers have rolled off the line of Toledo's South plant.

793 Because of its impressive design, advanced engineering, and outstanding capability, the all-new Wrangler JL was named *Motor Trend* magazine's "SUV of the Year" for 2019, just another in a string of awards won by Jeep over a period of decades. As the company likes to remind people, Jeep is the most awarded SUV brand in the world.

Jeep Cherokees, Comanches, and Wagoneer XJs

Legend and Lore

794

Development of the all-new Jeep XJ series began in mid-1979 under the direction of Roy Lunn in engineering and Bob

"4X4 OF THE YEAR"

For the first time ever, all three leading off-road magazines made the same choice. Jeep.

If you're thinking about 4-wheel drive, consider this. The all-new leaner, meaner size Jeep Cherokee has just been named "4x4 of the Year" by all three leading off-road magazines: 4 Wheel & Off-Road, Four Wheeler, and Off-Road. That's never been done before.

Ride and drive is what it's all about.
The all-new Cherokee was compared to the toughest competitors available, foreign and domestic. They were driven thousands of miles through snow, soft sand, subfreezing temperatures, and high winds—on and off the road.

4 Wheel & Off-Road said: "Cherokee scored well across the board, excelling in our evaluations of mechanical, urban and off-road driving and interior comfort." Four Wheeler called the Cherokee Sportwagon: "the year's most significant advance in 4-wheeling." Off-Road said: "Jeep is a smaller, more maneuverable off-road vehicle that provides plenty of room."

Test drive it and compare for yourself.
Compared to Bronco II and S-10 Blazer 4x4, only Cherokee has four doors, room for five, and a choice of two 4-wheel drive systems. And Cherokee has higher ground clearance, higher horsepower per pound, and the highest gas mileage, (24)EPA EST MPG/33 EST HWY.*

It's nice to be named No. 1, but not unexpected. After all, Jeep wrote the book on 4-wheel drive. Buy or lease the triple award winning Cherokee, or the luxurious new Wagoneer Sportwagons. Only at your Jeep dealer.

*Use these figures for comparison. Your results may differ due to driving speed, weather conditions and trip length. Actual highway mileage and California figures will probably be less.
SAFETY BELTS SAVE LIVES.

Jeep is a registered trademark of Jeep Corporation.

Triple award winning
JEEP ◢ CHEROKEE SPORTWAGON

The all-new Cherokee XJ series, introduced for 1984, won the 4x4 of the Year award from all three leading off-road magazines, the first time any vehicle had done so.

Nixon in styling. The goal was essentially a moonshot for Jeep: to create a family of extremely rugged and durable four-wheel-drive vehicles with improved off-road capability and much better on-road ride and handling along with a weight reduction of 900 pounds or more and (among the most important features) outstanding fuel economy. To accomplish this, the company committed to employing an all-new four-wheel-drive system, developing and building its own all-new 4-cylinder engine, developing a completely unique and highly effective front suspension system, and designing, engineering, and producing an all-new body.

795 Lunn's marching orders to his engineers were simple: "Keep it Jeep, but make it better." Amazingly, every single system on the XJ was completely new or redesigned, yet vehicle quality improved in manifold ways.

796 Introduced in late 1983, the new Jeep Cherokee and Wagoneer XJ vehicles were created in response to the fuel crisis that began in late 1979. The XJ design team included Roy Lunn, vice president of engineering; Bob Nixon, American Motors styling chief for exteriors; and Vince Geraci, head of AMC interior styling. The design goal was to produce a smaller, lighter, yet highly capable four-wheel-drive vehicle that would weigh up to 1,000 pounds less than the J-series wagons while retaining at least 90 percent of their interior room. The new Jeeps would also have to be better in off-road driving and at the same time offer greatly improved on-road ride and handling.

797 The Jeep XJs were the first all-new-from-the-ground-up Jeeps in 20 years and were also the first that American Motors had designed entirely. When you consider that nearly every part and system was entirely new, the fact that they debuted on time and with a minimum of problems is nothing short of a miracle. The success of the new XJs made instant legends of people such as Bob Nixon, Roy Lunn (who was already a legend at Ford), Vince Geraci, and others.

One of the biggest reasons the compact XJs were so successful was that they offered four-door models, while Chevrolet and Ford offered only two-doors.

798 The XJs were easily the most long-awaited and prayed-for Jeeps of all time because sales of four-wheel drives had tanked, not only at Jeep but across the industry. Because it relied on Jeep for pretty much all of its profits, American Motors was on the verge of bankruptcy. The only hope for reviving Jeep as a viable brand was the new XJ; if those vehicles failed, Jeep would have failed. As it was, it came very close.

799 To ensure that the new XJs would be everything that people expected in a Jeep, they were tested for hundreds of thousands of miles in mountains, deserts, extreme northern regions, and on the rugged Rubicon Trail until Jeep engineers were completely satisfied that the Cherokee and Wagoneer were superior in every respect.

800 With a 1984 product line that included the Cherokee, Wagoneer, Wagoneer Limited, and the renamed J-series Grand Wagoneer, Jeep was able to retain its position as the only sport utility builder in America offering both standard SUVs and luxury SUVs.

801 Although the company actually considered more than 1,000 new model names for the XJ vehicles, market research with current and prospective Jeep owners showed that the buying public had a clear preference for the Cherokee and Wagoneer names. To my knowledge, Jeep has never revealed any of the unused names that it considered.

The 1984 Jeep XJ Wagoneer Limited and, in the background, the Cherokee Chief were tremendously popular vehicles right from the start. They pioneered unibody construction in SUVs, which is a design most such vehicles use today. And Jeep had it 35 years ago!

802 American Motors shelled out a whopping $250 million in plant and equipment costs in order to produce the new XJs. It was the largest product program in its history to that point; the previous record had been the AMC Pacer, which cost $60 million for tooling and equipment. Part of the enormous cost was the installation of 29 new Cybotech robots that automatically welded the body sides, undercarriage, and framing into one strong (and safe) unibody.

803 In the fall of 1985, American Motors' new joint-venture company, Beijing Jeep, began production of the Cherokee XJ in China for the local market. It was the first America–China automotive joint venture as well as the first American vehicle produced in China since before World War II. It also marked the first time the Cherokee XJ was produced outside the United States.

804 For 1986, Jeep introduced the new Comanche pickup truck. Based on a lengthened Cherokee/Wagoneer XJ chassis, it was, like them, on a rugged unibody design that Jeep calls Uniframe. Due to a shortage of capital, for the first year's production the company introduced only a single long-wheelbase Comanche model. Offered in both two- and four-wheel-drive versions, the Comanche could be ordered with any of the engines and transmissions that were offered in the other XJ models. Jeep offered the new Comanche long-bed in three trim levels: Custom, X, and XLS.

Probably the handsomest compact pickup ever made, and certainly the most capable, the Comanche was introduced for 1986.

805 In 1987, the final Jeep concept vehicle created by American Motors made the rounds of the auto shows. It was a highly styled sports truck called the Comanche Thunderchief. One look at it tells you that it's a real shame it didn't make it into production because it would probably have sold like crazy. Many of its styling features were copied by custom truck accessory makers.

The final concept Jeep from American Motors was this exciting Comanche Thunderchief pickup. It's a shame that this vehicle wasn't put into production, as it would have electrified the pickup market.

806 To further boost sales of its compact Comanche pickup, Jeep introduced the two-wheel-drive Comanche SporTruck for 1987. The SporTruck was an attractive value model priced at an amazingly low $6,495, with more standard equipment than the competition. Equipment included body stripes, slotted wheels, radial tires, power disc brakes, etc.

To juice Comanche sales, the company added this value-priced Spor-Truck two-wheel-drive model for 1987, tagged at a bargain $6,495.

807 In 1987, Chrysler Corporation, under the direction of Lee Iacocca, purchased American Motors Corporation from Renault for a reported $1.1 billion, and it did this solely to acquire Jeep Corporation. The company promptly dropped the AMC and Renault lines of passenger cars and put its product planners to

work on devising new Jeep models and trim packages in an effort
to boost Jeep sales.

808 What to do? By 1986, buyers had been loudly demanding a
luxury version of the Cherokee. So in mid-1987, Jeep introduced the full-boat Cherokee Limited four-door and fitted it with a
wide array of luxury features including full-time four-wheel drive,
air-conditioning, jazzed-up interior trim, and more. Naturally, it
priced the luxury Cherokee accordingly, making sure it didn't con-
flict with the Wagoneer models.

The Cherokee Limited could be ordered in three monochromatic colors (Black, Charcoal, and Grenadine), and it sold like
10-cent hamburgers. Within a year, it became the single most-
stolen vehicle in America. Why? Because everyone wanted one.
Before that, Corvette had held the most-stolen title.

*A new model XJ debuting for the 1987 model year was the Cherokee
Limited. It was added to the lineup because people were asking for a
more luxurious Cherokee but at a price less than the Wagoneer Limited.
This model quickly became the most-stolen vehicle in America because
everybody wanted one.*

809 Jeeps were so incredibly popular during the 1990s that film-makers who wanted to use one in a movie or a television show had to buy them. Most vehicle companies paid to have their vehicles used in films, but Jeep management didn't feel it had to.

810 For 1988, Jeep introduced the hottest performance compact truck on the market: the two-wheel-drive Jeep Comanche Eliminator. It was equipped with the hot 4.0-liter six, a 5-speed manual transmission, and a new gorgeous graphics package that was subtle yet aggressive. Testing showed that the Comanche Eliminator was the fastest accelerating compact truck by a big margin.

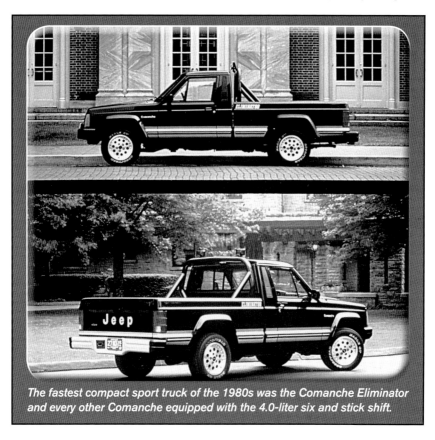

The fastest compact sport truck of the 1980s was the Comanche Eliminator and every other Comanche equipped with the 4.0-liter six and stick shift.

811 Because the Comanche Eliminator didn't offer four-wheel drive, Jeep introduced the Comanche Chief for 1988, with

stripes and trim similar to the Cherokee Chief and four-wheel drive. This truck was aimed at performance truck buyers who also wanted real four-wheel-drive capability. Seldom seen today, it's probably the rarest model of the Comanche trucks produced.

Top: The Comanche Chief was one sweet-looking short-bed truck, and not many were built. I'd love to find one today! Bottom: This is a Comanche long-bed pickup, compact but with extra room for cargo.

812 As nice a truck as it was, the Jeep Comanche was dropped after the 1992 model year due to sales that had been drifting downward for too long. It's a shame because the little-known styling concept called the Comanche Thunderchief showed how Comanche styling could have been updated to create a tough new look that would have boosted interest for very little capital invested.

813 It's interesting that the introduction of one new vehicle can affect other vehicles in a maker's lineup. When the new Grand Cherokee was introduced in mid-1992 (as an early 1993 model), Jeep marketing people decided to reshuffle the Cherokee model lineup. For 1992, Cherokee offered three models: Base, SE, and the new Cherokee Country, which replaced the Cherokee Limited model. The Cherokee Country was considered to be an upscale model, but its level of trim and equipment didn't compare to the Limited, and the price was lower as well. With the introduction of the Grand Cherokee, Jeep management envisioned the Cherokee XJ's new role to be that of a value-priced series.

814 By 1996, Jeep could brag that the stalwart Cherokee XJ was truly a world-class vehicle because it was being sold in more than 100 countries around the globe. It was so well designed that it could be offered in foreign markets with only minor modifications to meet local laws and regulations.

815 After being in production for 13 years with only moderate changes and upgrades, the Cherokee XJ was given a major freshening for the 1997 model year. It cost Chrysler a reported $215 million (nearly as much as the original tooling expense) and was meant to completely update the vehicle so that it could remain in production for several more years.

816 Continuing its efforts to expand the Cherokee model lineup, for 1998 Jeep introduced the Cherokee Classic. The Classic was considered a "value model" and came equipped with the 4-speed automatic transmission as standard equipment, along with sharp 15x7-inch cast-aluminum wheels that were painted Dark Quartz, standard power mirrors, a roof rack, a leather-wrapped steering wheel, floor mats front and rear, plus a rear wiper/washer. The Classic was meant to be an easy way for consumers to step up from the base SE model and into something that had more comprehensive equipment features and a value price tag.

817 Also for 1998 came the reintroduction of the Jeep Cherokee Limited in answer to the thousands of people who wanted a luxury Jeep that was more upscale than the Cherokee Country and didn't want to pop for a Grand Cherokee. The Cherokee Limited's standard features included 7-inch Luxury cast-aluminum wheels with P225/70R15 Goodyear Eagle GA OWL tires, Selec-Trac full-time four-wheel drive (on four-wheel-drive versions), air-conditioning, a six-way power driver's seat, a rear defogger, an overhead console with compass and trip computer, speed control, a keyless entry system, plus power windows, locks, and mirrors. When the Cherokee Limited debuted, the Cherokee Country was dropped.

Body and Interior

818 The XJ series introduced the biggest innovation in sport utility vehicles since the 1963 Wagoneer: unibody construction. In this construction, the traditional ladder frame was discarded in favor of a framework of stressed steel body and chassis members that were welded together to create a lighter yet stronger body structure. In addition, XJs had a computer-designed, thick sheet metal frame welded directly to the undercarriage to

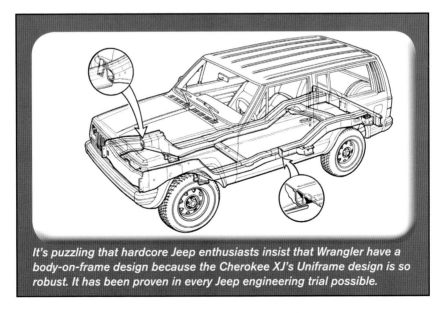

It's puzzling that hardcore Jeep enthusiasts insist that Wrangler have a body-on-frame design because the Cherokee XJ's Uniframe design is so robust. It has been proven in every Jeep engineering trial possible.

ensure it was extremely rigid and durable enough for the toughest off-roading.

It was a brilliant move. The XJ models weighed on average more than 700 pounds less than the J-series vehicles. Jeep called its version of the unibody "Uniframe" to reassure off-roaders worried about the lack of a conventional frame.

819 When it came to designing unibody vehicles, AMC had more experience than any other American automaker, and it had the added advantage of its engineers' nearly religious fervor about maintaining Jeep's off-road capability. They tested the Jeep XJs mercilessly to ensure that they would perform better than even the highest expectations of buyers.

820 Because of the smaller size of the new Jeeps and their outstanding fuel economy, the standard fuel tank on the XJ was a smallish 13.5 gallons, although a 20.2-gallon tank was available as an option. Skid plates were offered, of course.

821 One huge innovation by the Cherokee XJ was that it was offered in both two- and four-door models (the Wagoneer XJ came only as a four-door). The compact SUV competition (the Ford Bronco II and Chevy Blazer) both offered only two-door models. The public was a lot more interested in four-door models than Ford and Chevy management had realized, so Jeep profited handsomely from the extra sales volume that the four doors provided.

Following Jeep's grand tradition of innovation in the sport utility and four-wheel-drive market, the new XJ models were the first four-door compact SUVs.

822 The Jeep XJ wheelbase was 101 inches, which was much longer than the competition, allowing interior room for five passengers. Both the Ford Bronco and Chevy ST-Blazer could hold only four passengers.

823 The new Cherokee two-door models also had doors that were 4 inches wider than on the Bronco II and 2 inches wider than on the S10 Blazer, which provided easier access to the rear seat area. The Jeep XJs also offered more passenger room and greater cargo room that either Chevy or Ford.

824 Rather than retain the old-type fold-down station wagon tailgate, the new XJs were designed with a fold-up hatchback. In addition, because the J-series had suffered rust problems in the tailgate area, the XJ's hatchback door was made of fiberglass. A rear window wiper and washer was available as an option, as was an electric rear window defroster.

825 In XJs, for the first time in any Jeep vehicle, the heating, ventilation, and air-conditioning (HVAC) system was fully integrated into the vehicle's instrument panel for a neater appearance and much better performance. The HVAC system even included rear seat heating ducts, a first for Jeep.

826 Talk about clever ideas: To provide greater rear seat footroom, both of the XJ's front seats were of the pedestal type, a design that was copied from the Renault Alliance. The design consisted of a central pedestal mount for each front seat, which allowed rear seat passengers to place their feet underneath the front seat for greater "stretch-out" comfort.

827 When it came time to design the exterior styling of the XJ, exterior design chief Bob Nixon felt that to try to make the new vehicles look like the J-series would be the wrong approach. After all, the new XJs were going to benefit from every bit of modern technology possible, and Nixon wanted to give them a fresh, modern appearance rather than recycle the styling of the dated J-series vehicles.

Hundreds of design renderings and scores of clay models were produced as the team slowly developed the look that went into production. In the end, what they created was a rare thing; a modern, timeless design that looked so absolutely right that it became an instant classic. More than 35 years later, the Cherokee XJ still looks

sleek, modern, and beautiful. In comparison, the Blazers and Bronco IIs of that era look lumpy and dated.

828 When compared to the J-series wagons, the new XJs were a full 21 inches shorter in overall length, 6 inches narrower, and 4 inches lower in height. The Jeep designers made sure to use crisp, angular body lines; large, squared-off wheel openings; massive slotted grilles; and bold spoke-type road wheels, all of which were traditional Jeep style marks. Because of this, the XJ models were instantly recognizable as Jeep vehicles even though their exterior styling did not resemble the J-series vehicles.

829 The Jeep XJs were the first Jeep vehicles to use curved side-glass windows, which provided better aerodynamics to reduce wind noise and improve real-world fuel economy. The design also provided greater interior room. As another sign of how modern the new vehicle's design was, it was also the first Jeep that had its styling refined in a wind tunnel.

830 Designers chose large, rugged door handles for the XJs, and then they tested opening them while wearing heavy winter snow gloves, just one of dozens of ways that they made sure the new vehicles would be as customer friendly as possible.

831 All of the Jeep XJs for 1984 came with a tachometer in the instrument panel as standard equipment. In addition, all of the XJs ordered with the standard 4-cylinder engine and 4-speed manual transmission also came with a dashboard-mounted upshift light to help drivers maximize their fuel economy.

832 For the first year of Wagoneer XJ production, the grille was designed to have a similar appearance to the Cherokee; not exactly the same look, but similar in theme. For 1986, the Wagoneer XJ was treated to a new grille that featured stacked quad headlamps, a look that was surprisingly similar to the 1965 Rambler Ambassador. But perhaps it wasn't surprising after all because both grilles were designed by essentially the same design team.

For 1986, the Wagoneer XJ was restyled with a new grille and quad head-lamps.

833 Jeep introduced the new Comanche pickup for 1986. It was the first unibody pickup from an American producer and also the first unibody pickup with four-wheel drive. So, how were the Jeep designers sure that the Comanche's unibody design would work? An AMC design team led by Jim Alexander had secretly designed a Jeep compact pickup during 1972 called the

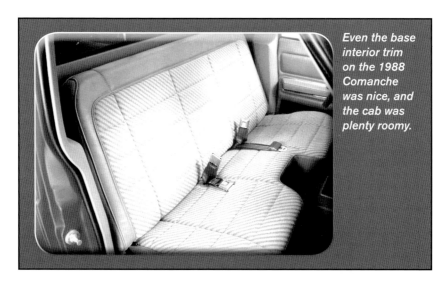

Even the base interior trim on the 1988 Comanche was nice, and the cab was plenty roomy.

Cowboy. It featured a unibody design, although it specified a rear stub frame to carry the pickup bed, which the Comanche didn't have; it was a full Uniframe design. Two Cowboy pickup prototypes were built and were extensively tested in the Utah desert. They performed like a Jeep should. One of the Cowboy prototypes still exists.

In addition to matchless horsepower, Comanche offered a lot of cargo space, especially in the long-bed version.

834 For 1987, Jeep added to the Comanche line by introducing a short-bed Comanche riding on a 113-inch wheelbase and fitted with a 6-foot cargo bed. The long-wheelbase Comanche (riding on a 119.6-inch wheelbase) with a 7-foot bed continued in production.

835 The Cherokee Limited luxury model proved to be so popular that for 1988 the company added a two-door

version of it. The Jeep Cherokee XJ was now offered in Base, Pioneer, Chief, Laredo, and Limited models, which was the most extensive Cherokee lineup ever.

836 Also in 1988, Jeep released a pair of limited-edition XJ vehicles to celebrate America's Olympic Team. The Jeep Comanche and Cherokee Olympic Editions were equipped with 6-cylinder engines, special exterior striping and trim, and stylish alloy wheels.

837 The base Cherokee XJ models were fairly stripped vehicles as far as standard trim and equipment. The floor covering on these models was old-fashioned color-keyed rubber until the 1992 model year, when full carpeting was finally made standard equipment.

838 One of the weirder Cherokee XJ variations was the 1992 Cherokee Police vehicle. The reason that it was introduced was to serve as a replacement for Chrysler's Dodge Diplomat–based police cars, which had been extremely success-

One of the more unusual versions of the Cherokee XJ was the police car. This is a 1994 model.

ful for many years but were now going out of production. The Police Cherokee was offered in both two- and four-wheel-drive versions. Special equipment on them included a reinforced suspension as standard, plus antilock brakes, larger tires, a 120-mph speedometer, and (get this) a column-mounted gear-shift lever for the automatic transmission.

839 Starting with the 1994 models, all Cherokee XJs were given a redesigned roof structure that was sturdier and designed to provide better crush resistance in a rollover accident. In addition, roof-mounted rear speakers were a new option.

840 Also for the 1994 model year, a new right-hand-drive Cherokee Postal Carrier group option was available for the first time on two- and four-door Cherokee models ordered with either two-wheel or four-wheel drive. These roomy vehicles proved to be surprisingly popular with postal route drivers.

841 During 1994, an extra cost Silver Two-Tone Country Exterior Appearance option for the Cherokee included a silver lower body side treatment with plastic body cladding,

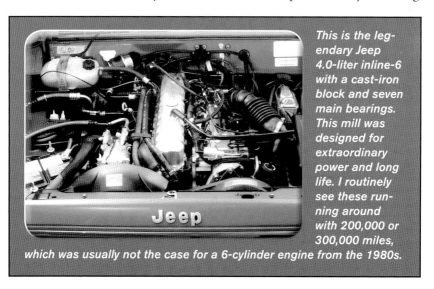

This is the legendary Jeep 4.0-liter inline-6 with a cast-iron block and seven main bearings. This mill was designed for extraordinary power and long life. I routinely see these running around with 200,000 or 300,000 miles, which was usually not the case for a 6-cylinder engine from the 1980s.

fender flares, bumpers and endcaps in silver, along with a body-color grille and headlamp bezels and tape stripes on the liftgate.

842 Jeep continued to pioneer new safety features in the four-wheel-drive market. Effective with the 1995 model year, all Cherokees came with a standard driver-side airbag. Many engineers felt that because of their off-road usage, SUVs couldn't be designed with airbags because jostling around off-road would cause the bags to go off. Jeep proved that it could be done, and today most SUVs have a number of airbags as standard equipment including front, rear, side, and knee airbags.

843 As part of a general upgrading of the XJ vehicles, a new automatic transmission and brake pedal interlock system became a standard feature for the 1996 models, along with intermittent windshield wipers, plus a heavy-duty battery and heavy-duty alternator.

844 When Jeep management ordered a major freshening of the XJ Cherokee for 1997, the vehicles were treated to an all-new interior, including new trim and a new instrument panel incorporating a passenger-side airbag. The redesigned instrument panel featured a clever "center stack" design to allow for production of both right- and left-hand-drive versions of the Cherokee. This was an important move because by that time Jeep had developed a significant overseas business in right-hand-drive markets including Japan, the United Kingdom, South Africa, and Australia, to name just a few.

845 Other interior features introduced on the 1997 XJ Cherokee were its comfortable and stylish wingback bucket seats that were copied from the Grand Cherokee, along with new interior door panels and a sharp new overhead console.

846 Also new was a "between the seats" floor console for the 1997 model year. It included the obligatory cup holders (can't do without them, right?) along with clever heater ducts

on the back that could channel both air-conditioning and heat as desired to the rear seat area.

847 The 1997 Cherokee instrument panel was also redesigned to use multiplex wiring for the first time, an important move that greatly reduced behind-dash complexity and improved functionality all while allowing for easier servicing.

848 Chrysler spent $215 million upgrading the Cherokee XJ for 1997, and you get a lot of change for that amount of investment. In addition to mechanical upgrades, exterior body changes included an attractive new grille, new headlamp bezels, new bumper end caps both front and rear, and new body side moldings.

849 Jeep XJ body changes for 1997 also included elimination of the fixed (non-opening) "vent window" on the front doors, a subtle change that most people don't notice, but which is a good aid in identifying model years. It was done to improve the vehicle's styling and reduce wind noise and potential water leaks. Improved doors seals were fitted as well to reduce dust and water leaks around the door openings.

850 In a surprise move, the revised 1997 Cherokee was given a stamped steel tailgate to replace the fiberglass one that it had used since its introduction for 1984. The reason the change was made was to improve door fit and appearance while also reducing the need to slam it shut to ensure that it latched properly. The new tailgate really did fit much better and was a great deal easier to use. It's one of the few times steel was used to replace a fiberglass part.

851 Jeep loves to remind people that it is the most awarded four-wheel-drive vehicle in history. Continuing this tradition, the redesigned 1997 Cherokee XJ was named Four-Wheeler of the Year by *Four-Wheeler* magazine, which was quite an honor for a vehicle in its 14th year of production. The many

refinements it received for 1997 made it feel almost like a completely new vehicle.

852 For the 1998 model year, the Cherokee XJ line was offered in four distinct trim levels: base SE, Sport, Classic, and Limited. The new Cherokee Classic was a well-equipped four-door with a monochromatic paint scheme, the 4.0-liter six, and lots of standard features. The Cherokee Limited came only as a four-wheel-drive model for this year.

Even after 15 years in production, the Cherokee was still the best-looking and best-performing compact SUV in the world. This is a 1998 Cherokee Limited.

853 The final year for production of the Cherokee XJ was 2001, and it was scheduled to halt in November 2000 after building a fairly small number of vehicles. However, demand remained so strong that management decided to continue building them. The final Jeep Cherokee XJ was built on June 22, 2001, in the Toledo plant. Its replacement received a new name, but it failed to attract anything like the deep reverence people have for the XJs.

FOR ONCE THE NAME BRAND COSTS LESS THAN THE GENERIC.

JEEP. CHEROKEE

Aspirin, toothpaste, sandwich bags. When you're at the local supermarket, it might not matter whether you buy name brand or generic. But when you're out in the wilderness, you can bet you are going to need the one

brand that stands above all others. Jeep.

Take Jeep Cherokee Sport for example. It's the adventure vehicle—the one that started a revolu 4x4s. With Cherokee Sport, you get legendary off-road capability along with features you do extra for. Like air conditioning, power windo

Jeep is a registered trademark of DaimlerChrysler.

This ad from 2000 spells out the unique advantages of the Cherokee: superior performance and a low price. It was an unbeatable combination. The XJs have held their resale value remarkably well.

The final year for the XJ series in the United States was 2001, and it was still selling well even then. No other Jeep wagon since the XJ has been able to attract so much enthusiasm or respect.

854 The Cherokee XJ was in production for 18 years (since mid-1983) and sold an estimated 2,707,645 units. In terms of sales, it is one of the most successful Jeeps ever.

Engine and Drivetrain

855 The Jeep XJs were designed from the beginning (the 1984 model year) to be able to offer decent performance with a standard 4-cylinder engine. (Jeep didn't release horsepower information for the XJs that year, but some generally reliable sources claim that the four produced 105 hp). Because the 4-cylinders were expected to be the volume models, AMC developed its own four to replace the Iron Duke that it had been using in the CJ series.

Dubbed the Hurricane, the new 150-ci AMC four was specifically designed as a truck engine and thus had to pass durability standards that were far more difficult than for any passenger car. The result was a compact, extremely durable 4-cylinder engine that (believe it or not) could out-accelerate the 6-cylinder Chevy Blazer. Full economy ratings for the four with a manual 4-speed transmission were 24 mpg in the city and 30 mpg on the highway, which was outstanding for that era, especially one fitted with a single-barrel carburetor.

856 Optional on all XJs was a GM-sourced 2.8-liter 173-ci V-6 engine that was rated at 115 hp, which produced about 10 more horses than the AMC four-banger. The V-6 engine also boasted more torque and, importantly, it peaked at a much lower RPM range; the V-6 producing 145 ft-lbs at 2,400 rpm versus the four's output of 134 ft-lbs at 3,500 rpm. Thus the V-6 mill provided greater low-end power, and much greater smoothness, not to mention increased towing ability.

857 The base transmission on the Cherokee XJ was a 4-speed manual, with a 5-speed manual or Chrysler 904 3-speed automatic optional. The front axle was a Dana Model 30 Hypoid; the rear axle was also a hypoid, this one manufactured by American Motors. Final-drive ratio was 3.31:1 with the automatic and 3.73:1 with the stick shift.

858 The Jeep XJ transfer cases were produced by New Process Gear. Vehicles with the automatic transmission were given the NP229 transfer case, while the manual transmission-equipped models received the NP207 transfer case. Both of these were two-speed Hi/Lo units. The torque split in either of the cases was a straight 50-50 front and rear.

859 The XJ's 2.5-liter 4-cylinder engine was based on the American Motors 258-ci 6-cylinder, an engine noted for its outstanding reliability. The 2.5-liter four was the first 4-cylinder engine designed and built by AMC. It was also the last, as the company was swallowed up by Chrysler Corporation in 1987.

860 The standard four-wheel-drive system used on the XJs was Jeep's all-new Command-Trac part-time system that featured shift-on-the-fly capability. That was quite an innovation at the time. Optional on the XJs was Jeep's outstanding Selec-Trac full-time four-wheel-drive system, which could be operated in either two-wheel drive or all-surface four-wheel drive. Jeep was the only company offering two distinct four-wheel-drive systems on its vehicles.

The Cherokee Laredo for 1988 boasted this stylish bright grille rather than the blacked-out grille seen on the Sport models.

861 Like the J-series Jeeps, the new XJs were designed from the ground up to be four-wheel-drive vehicles. Unlike the Js, the XJs didn't offer a two-wheel-drive version initially; that came later. Although all the design and engineering work was performed by Jeep engineers (because they had more expertise than anyone on the planet), its "partner" Renault "proved" the designs by using finite element analysis technology, particularly in the critical chassis structure.

862 Although purists would probably condemn the act today, in mid-1985 Jeep introduced a two-wheel-drive version of the Cherokee

Only in a Jeep.
2-Wheel Drive Jeep Cherokee.
The Intelligent Choice.

In response to a growing trend in Southern states, Jeep soon added two-wheel-drive versions of the XJ series. This is a base model 1985 Cherokee.

XJ. The reason was simple: The competition was doing it quite successfully, especially in warm-weather markets. Jeep management saw that the Chevy, Ford, and GMC two-wheel-drive sport utilities were selling well, especially in the South, where four-wheel drive often wasn't needed as much as in the North. In fact, the market for two-wheel-drive SUVs had actually quadrupled in the previous four years. The only way Jeep could compete against vehicles having the price advantage of two-wheel drive was to offer the same thing in a Cherokee. Not surprisingly, the two-wheel-drive Cherokee sold pretty well.

863 Two-wheel drive on a Jeep? The very idea enrages purist Jeep owners. But the truth is, Jeep has offered two-wheel-drive models in the United States almost every year that it has been in business. In the early days, the two-wheel-drive Jeeps were the station wagons and pickups, and later the DJ series and the FJ postal vans were added. Today, almost every model of Jeep can be purchased as a two-wheeler because some people want a Jeep but don't want (or need) four-wheel drive. Accept it and move on.

864 For 1985, the XJ Cherokee and Wagoneer offered an optional 2.1 Turbo Diesel engine (except in California). Designed and built by Renault, the Turbo Diesel was rated at 85 hp with peak torque of

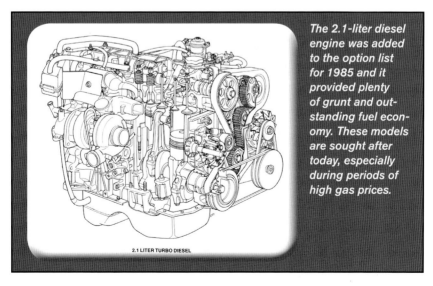

The 2.1-liter diesel engine was added to the option list for 1985 and it provided plenty of grunt and outstanding fuel economy. These models are sought after today, especially during periods of high gas prices.

2.1 LITER TURBO DIESEL

132 ft-lbs at 2,700 rpm. Not available on the base XJ models, the new engine was EPA rated at 31 mpg in the city and 36 mpg on the highway with manual transmission. The Turbo Diesel could also be ordered with automatic transmission. These models are sought after by diesel enthusiasts today, especially any time fuel prices go way up.

865 The Cherokee XJ included a standard 4-speed manual transmission from 1984 to 1988, with a 5-speed manual available as an extra-cost option. Also optional at extra cost was an automatic transmission. For the 1989 model year, the Cherokee series was upgraded when the 5-speed stick was made standard equipment.

866 In the 1986 model year, the XJ's 4-cylinder engine was upgraded with standard throttle body fuel injection, raising horsepower to 112 and offering improved drivability, smoothness, and a sharp increase in fuel efficiency.

867 Jeep's trademark Trac-Lok limited-slip rear differential had long been offered only in conjunction with the Command-Trac part-time four-wheel-drive system. For 1986, the company now also offered it combined with the Selec-Trac full-time system, making a great four-wheel-drive system even better.

868 For 1987, American Motors Corporation introduced a new version of its longtime inline 6-cylinder engine. Designed specifically for the Jeep XJ vehicles, it was a new type of high-output six, displacing 4.0 liters (242 ci). This revolutionary mill produced a surprisingly potent 173 net hp along with 220 ft-lbs of torque, making it the most powerful engine in its class by a good margin.

It was a phenomenal leap in engine technology, representing more than a 50-percent gain in horsepower, despite being 16 ci smaller than the engine it replaced. Powered by the new 4.0 engine, the Jeep XJs could now accelerate 0–60 mph in under 10 seconds and tow up to 5,000 pounds. If that wasn't enough, the new engine also provided better gasoline economy while running on regular-grade gasoline.

The 1989 Jeep Cherokee Sport continued to be a top-selling model because its combination of popular features and a value-oriented price tag made it an unbeatable bargain.

869 A Jeep Comanche equipped with the new 4.0-liter six managed to set 13 new speed records at the Bonneville Salt Flats during 1987, including a top speed of 144 mph, and running the quarter-mile in 16.97 seconds. And remember, this was with a 6-cylinder engine!

870 The 1987 American Motors/Jeep 2.5-liter 4-cylinder engine that was standard equipment in the XJ series was upgraded to a 121-hp rating simply by fitting it with the air cleaner from the 6-cylinder engine. The improved breathing alone boosted power that much.

871 According to an engineer at American Motor's Mexican affiliate, Vehiculos Automores Mexicanos (VAM), the idea of stuffing the inline-6 into the XJ chassis originated with VAM. That company was much smaller than American Motors, and it

had only one engine in production: the AMC inline 6-cylinder. So when the new Jeep XJs were being readied for production at the Mexico plant, VAM engineers were told they had to make the engine fit inside the XJ's engine compartment or the company wouldn't be able to produce the vehicles. Somehow they managed to shoehorn a 258-ci six under the hood.

When AMC's US engineers saw that it could be done, they decided to do it for the US market so that they wouldn't have to buy engines from General Motors. Along the way, they ended up redesigning the engine to create the powerful new 4.0-liter.

872 The 1987 XJ vehicles also were treated to a great new transmission option: a wide-ratio 4-speed automatic with an overdrive fourth gear. The new transmission was electronically controlled, and it featured a lock-up torque converter to improve fuel economy and reduce noise. It also came with dual-shift modes: one for more power and one for better fuel economy. Built by Aisin-Seki, the new 4-speed automatic was standard equipment on the Wagoneer XJ and optional at extra cost on the Cherokee. It could be ordered in conjunction with either the 4-cylinder or new 6-cylinder engine.

873 For 1988, the Jeep 4.0-liter six, which had already been tweaked a bit and was now rated at 177 hp, was made standard equipment on Jeep Wagoneer Limited and Cherokee Limited models. The combination of reasonable fuel economy and class-leading performance made the awesome 4.0-liter six the engine of choice for most people anyway, so it made sense to standardize them on the topline XJ models.

874 For the 1990 model year, Jeep finally offered a four-wheel-drive version of the popular Comanche Eliminator sport truck. The Comanche Chief model was dropped. The Comanche lineup now consisted of base, Pioneer, Laredo, and Eliminator models.

875 On March 22, 1990, the one-millionth Jeep XJ rolled off the assembly line. It was a beautiful, bright red Cherokee Limited. It was obvious by that landmark production that the Jeep Cherokee had become one of the most beloved Jeeps in history. Designer Bob Nixon, who'd fought so hard for the design he created, must have felt vindicated.

876 For 1991, the 4.0-liter six was goosed up to 190 hp for the version used in the XJ-series vehicles. With more room for a larger exhaust system, the XJ 4.0-liter had much better breathing than the Wrangler 4.0, which that year was rated at 180 hp. The XJ's 2.5-liter four was now rated at 130 hp, which was 7 more than the version used in the Jeep Wrangler.

877 American Motors/Jeep continued to improve and upgrade its engines. For the 1993 model year, the Cherokee XJ 2.5-liter four was given Sequential Multi-Port Fuel Injection (SMPI) for smoother operation and improved fuel economy.

878 Improved and enhanced for 1996, the Jeep 4.0-liter six used in the Cherokee XJ was now rated a whopping 225 ft-lbs of torque, which now was developed at 3,000 rpm, or a full 1,000 rpm lower than previously. The engine also boasted a stiffer block, a revised camshaft profile, and new state-of-the-art aluminum pistons that made it quieter running and smoother as well. Towing capacity was rated at up to 5,000 pounds.

879 Although by 1996 it had been years since Jeep had offered a diesel engine for US-market Cherokees, the 2.5-liter Turbo Diesel was still offered in overseas markets, where the demand was much stronger. These export diesel Cherokees were produced at the massive Jeep Toledo, Ohio, factory.

880 The 1996 XJ models also featured a new On-Board Diagnostic (OBD II) system for all powertrains, along with a new JTEC Powertrain Control Module. A returnless fuel supply system also debuted this year.

881 For its final season in production, the 2001 model Jeep Cherokees (now in its 18th model year) finally were given the sturdy 4.0-liter 6-cylinder engine as standard equipment on all models. The old four-banger, which was never very popular once the amazing 4.0 became available, was quietly dropped from the line.

Suspension and Brakes

882 The XJ series introduced a new and very innovative front suspension called Quadra-Link. It consisted of a solid front axle to provide maximum strength, along with four specially designed locating arms plus coil springs for a smooth ride on-road, and a panhard rod for maximum handling control. In addition, the Haltenberger-type steering linkage

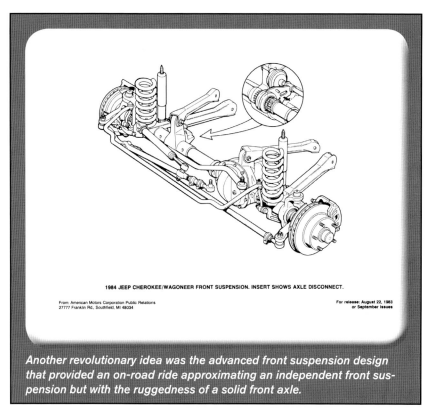

1984 JEEP CHEROKEE/WAGONEER FRONT SUSPENSION. INSERT SHOWS AXLE DISCONNECT.

From: American Motors Corporation Public Relations
27777 Franklin Rd., Southfield, MI 48034

For release: August 22, 1983
or September Issues

Another revolutionary idea was the advanced front suspension design that provided an on-road ride approximating an independent front suspension but with the ruggedness of a solid front axle.

enabled Jeep engineers to keep the linkage entirely ahead of the front axle to allow better turning angles. The new Quadra-Link suspension provided on-road ride and handling that was equal to an independent front suspension yet had the durability of a solid-axle system.

883 The Jeep Cherokee and Wagoneer XJ constant (dynamic) ground clearance was a full 7.6 inches, which was more than an inch greater than the competitive Ford Bronco II or Chevy T Blazer sport utility wagons, both of which had clearance of just 6.5 inches. Also, unlike the competitors, the Jeep XJ's proving ground was the rugged Rubicon Trail.

884 For 1984, the new Jeep XJs were offered with three tire sizes: P195/75 R15, P205/75 R15, and P215/75 R15. All of these were of steel-belted-radial design. Two road wheels were offered: 15x6 and 15x7 inches. A compact spare tire was standard equipment, but a full-size tire could be had for an extra charge. Steel wheels with small hub caps were standard with styled alloy wheels optional at extra cost.

885 The 1984 XJs used a recirculating ball type of steering system, which Jeep engineers felt was better for an off-road-capable vehicle. The steering box was sourced from the GM Saginaw Division. The power steering provided excellent road feel and required just 3.5 turns lock to lock; the XJ's standard manual steering required 4.8 turns lock to lock. Stabilizer bars were standard equipment on both the front and the rear.

886 For the 1986 model year, the Cherokee XJ offered a new Off-Highway Vehicle package that included premium high-pressure-gas shock absorbers (which were painted yellow), five P225/75R15 OWL Wrangler tires, white-spoke wheels, a skid-plate package, a 4.10:1 axle ratio, tow hooks, and a high ground clearance suspension.

887 The biggest innovation in sport utility vehicle braking systems was introduced by Jeep on the 1989 Cherokee and Wagoneer Limited XJ models: a four-wheel antilock brake system that worked in both two-wheel-drive mode and when switched over to four-wheel-drive mode. This type of system is now standard equipment on pretty much all four-wheel-drive sport utility vehicles sold in the United States, but it took years for the rest of the industry to follow Jeep's lead.

Numbers Crunching and Press Commentary

888 The all-new 1984 Jeep Cherokee and Wagoneer XJ models retained 90 percent of the interior space of the J-series Wagoneer and Cherokee while at the same time shedding nearly 1,000 pounds in excess weight. The curb weight of the basic 4-cylinder XJ was a remarkable 2,886 pounds, which was about the same as the subcompact AMC Spirit, a much smaller vehicle. The 6-cylinder XJ's curb weight was 2,971 pounds, still a remarkable achievement.

889 For 1984, an optional rear-mounted spare tire carrier was offered for Cherokee, but for some reason it was restricted to two-door models only. Both two-door and four-door XJs rode on the same wheelbase and were the same length overall, so it's puzzling why Jeep chose to restrict the outside spare to the two-door models.

890 During 1984, Cherokee was named 4x4 of the Year by Petersen's *4 Wheel & Off-Road* magazine, *Off-Road* magazine, and *4-Wheeler* magazine. This was the first time in history that a four-wheel-drive vehicle won the award from all three magazines in the same year. Jeep dubbed the new Cherokee a "Triple Crown" winner.

891 To celebrate being chosen as 4x4 of the year, Jeep introduced a special Cherokee 4 X 4 of the Year model in March 1984. Offered in both two-door and four-door Cherokee models, the package included Charcoal Gray Metallic exterior paint with Charcoal Gray fender flares, lower body side moldings, a chrome Sport

Grille, 15x7-inch aluminum wheels, and dual pinstripes. Inside were Garnet checkered fabric wing-back bucket seats, a console with armrest, and a brushed pewter instrument panel overlay. A "4WD Award" decal was placed in the rear window. Jeep didn't disclose how many were built, only that there was a limited supply.

892 What effect did the new XJ have on Jeep retail sales for 1984? Plenty. In fact, total sales of Jeep vehicles in the United States more than doubled for the year. Export sales also showed a strong increase.

893 When the Comanche pickup debuted for 1986, it boasted the longest wheelbase of any compact truck (119.7 inches) on the market. It also boasted of a greater payload capacity than either the Chevy S-10 or Ford Ranger pickups. The new Comanche also offered a wider pickup box than any other truck in its class, along with industry-exclusive 15-inch wheels as standard equipment on both two-wheel-drive and four-wheel-drive models. In my opinion, the Comanche was also a much better-looking truck than any of its competitors.

894 For some reason, the Jeep Wagoneer XJ base model never sold in the expected volumes; buyers at that end of the market usually decided to spring for the more expensive and much more luxurious XJ Wagoneer Limited. To simplify its production scheduling, the company dropped the base Wagoneer from the lineup at the end of the 1987 model year.

895 The first "package" model developed under Chrysler for a Jeep vehicle was the 1988½ Cherokee Sport two-door, which was a high-value model aimed at expanding Jeep's market share by offering most of the equipment that people were looking for at a bargain price. Included with the Cherokee Sport were the 4.0-liter six, a 5-speed manual transmission, power steering, full floor carpeting, P225/75 OWL tires, unique aluminum wheels, and unique body stripes. Pricing was pegged at $12,265 for a two-wheel-drive model and $13,727 for one with four-wheel drive. Automatic transmission was available at extra cost.

The 1988 Cherokee Sport two-door was a value-priced model and boasted very stylish wheels and a 4.0-liter engine.

896 The Jeep Wagoneer and Wagoneer Limited XJ were never anywhere near as popular as the Cherokee, and the last year they were offered was 1990. Their replacement, a dressed-up Cherokee four-door with woodgrain side trim, called the Cherokee Briarwood, debuted for the 1991 model year.

897 The two-millionth Jeep Cherokee XJ was produced on August 27, 1996. It was big news in the auto industry, and President Bill Clinton traveled to Toledo to be on hand for the celebration.

898 The 1996 Jeep Cherokee XJ was assembled in Toledo, Ohio, as well as Thailand, Malaysia, Venezuela, Egypt, and China. Export versions were offered in both left- and right-hand-drive versions and could be purchased with gasoline or diesel engines.

899 During 1998, Bob Eaton, the Chrysler chairman who replaced Lee Iacocca, negotiated a merger of Chrysler Corporation

with Daimler-Benz, the maker of Mercedes-Benz cars. Eaton claimed it to be a "merger of equals," but in later conversations with the press, his German counterpart, Jurgen Schrempp, bragged that he had lied to Eaton (who swallowed it hook, line, and sinker) and that Daimler-Benz was taking full control and there was to be no equality of management. Eaton didn't seem to care; he walked away with a big check and a permanent blot on his reputation.

900 What were Jeep Cherokee's big product changes for 2001, its final year on the market? Elimination of the 4-cylinder engine and introduction of exactly one new paint color: Steel Blue. It was clear that Daimler-Benz loathed investing money in the Jeep line until it absolutely had to. For the following few years, Daimler-Benz introduced new Jeeps based on passenger car chassis while starving the rest of the line.

901 Jeep finally replaced the beloved Cherokee XJ in mid-2001, when it introduced the all-new Liberty as a 2002 model. Although it was a true SUV (not based on a passenger car plat-form), many longtime Jeep enthusiasts were shocked. They felt that the Cherokee was still relevant, and they weren't particularly impressed with the new Liberty.

Chapter 9

Jeep Grand Cherokees

Legends and Lore

902 As soon as design work was completed on the Cherokee XJ, Jeep designers were given a new project: begin designing a larger, heavier Jeep sport utility to replace the XJ once it had run its course. The job was given to the brilliant Jeep design chief Bob Nixon, but he was forced to compete with several European design firms because AMC's new owner, Renault, felt that it knew more about SUV design than any American. However, when the various designs were submitted to a market-test review by ordinary consumers, Nixon's design was the overwhelming favorite. Believe it or not, Renault executives were actually ticked off that an American won the contest.

903 The Grand Cherokee design was essentially complete by 1987, and AMC styling director Vince Geraci had a team work overtime to create a trio of hand-built prototypes to show to Chrysler's chief executives, who were just taking over AMC. Lee Iacocca and Bob Lutz were astounded at how perfect the designs were.

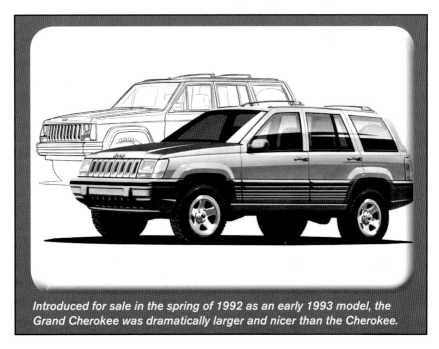

Introduced for sale in the spring of 1992 as an early 1993 model, the Grand Cherokee was dramatically larger and nicer than the Cherokee.

904 Chrysler was pinched for money, so Iacocca decided to delay the introduction of the Grand Cherokee until 1992. Amazingly, although the design was by that point almost five years old, it was an instant success.

905 The new Jeep that became the Grand Cherokee carried an internal model designation as the ZJ; that was decided simply by its place in the ongoing Jeep alphabet model-name list. First came the Cherokee XJ, then the Wrangler YJ, and then the Grand Cherokee ZJ.

906 The 1993 Grand Cherokee made its official debut at the 1992 North American International Auto Show in Detroit, when a Grand Cherokee was driven up the steps of the Cobo Center and right through a plate-glass window as stunned journalists looked on. It was the most dramatic new car introduction in Detroit history.

The all-new Jeep ZJ (aka the Grand Cherokee) debuted at the 1992 Detroit Auto Show by triumphantly bursting through the plate-glass window to Cobo Center, where the show was held. No reporter who was there ever forgot that introduction!

907 The new Grand Cherokee was built in an all-new factory on Jefferson Avenue in Detroit. Dubbed the Jefferson North plant, it cost the company $1 billion to construct.

908 When it was launched as a 1993 model, the all-new Jeep Grand Cherokee became the world's first sport utility vehicle to include a driver-side airbag as standard equipment. It was another sign of Jeep's relentless product pioneering and innovation. Today, airbags are standard on all vehicles sold in the United States.

909 Chrysler made a veiled threat to the Jeep dealer network when it speculated to the press that if it were unable to "sell out the plant" on the Grand Cherokee, a Dodge version would be created for sale through the Dodge dealer network. Legendary Jeep designer Bob Nixon was instructed to come up with a design for the Dodge/Jeep, and photos of it have survived.

910 As many people know, most Jeep vehicles are produced in Toledo, Ohio, at the huge Jeep plant there. However, the Grand Cherokee was (and is) the only Jeep vehicle manufactured in Detroit. Grand Cherokee has also been produced in Austria and Venezuela, but only for the local markets.

911 Jeep sales began to fall in 2000, one year after the company was taken over by Daimler-Benz. The reason? Daimler-Benz, maker of the Mercedes-Benz automobiles, didn't understand the US mass market. That company felt that it was unbecoming to offer big rebates and "deals" to sell vehicles, so it cut back on both. Believe it or not, the executives were actually surprised when sales dropped like a stone.

912 The Grand Cherokee added three new models for 2002: the Sport, which was a Laredo upgraded with a 10-disc CD player, trip computer, and fog lamps; the Special Edition, a Laredo with power passenger seat, 10-disc CD player, and an array of minor convenience items; and the Overland, which became the new top model. The Overland came with unique leather interior, 10-way power seats, real redwood trim, a standard 4.7-liter V-8, 5-speed automatic, Quadra-Drive, Up-Country suspension, skid plate, and tow hooks.

913 For 2003, Jeep launched the new Freedom Editions in all lines. The Grand Cherokee Freedom Edition included a silver front facia accent, bright-silver roof rack, chrome tow hooks, and OWL Goodyear P235/65R-17 Wrangler SR-A all-terrain tires mounted on 17-inch graphite-painted cast aluminum wheels. Inside were Micro-Tech instrument panel accents, Dark Slate cloth seats, slush mats, and a molded rear cargo tray.

914 There were many times in Jeep's history when the company allowed other vehicle builders to assemble Jeeps under contract for their local markets. Jeep earned its profits from royalty payments for each vehicle that was built and by selling CKD kits to the assemblers. But in the case of the Grand Cherokee, the company contracted with Steyr-Daimler-Puch Fahrzeugtechnik AG to produce Grand Cherokees to sell in international markets in both left- and right-hand-drive four-wheel-drive versions. Those Grand Cherokee were produced at an assembly plant in Graz, Austria.

915 Occupant safety was vastly improved on the 2003 Grand Cherokee when available ceiling-mounted side-curtain airbags were offered to provide additional head protection during a collision for both the front seat occupants and both rear outboard occupants.

916 Over the years, Jeep designers have created scores of concept vehicles, some merely dress-up packages, others completely new designs. Several were controversial, some outlandish. Without a doubt, the absolute weirdest Jeep concept vehicle ever was the 2003 Jeep Treo, a bug-like three-passenger vehicle that was designed for Asian markets.

917 For 2004, Jeep introduced its new Trail-Rated standard, which it said was developed "to communicate to consumers the extensive level of off-road requirements that all Jeep 4x4 vehicles must meet." In retrospect, Jeep was laying the groundwork for a new generation of Jeep vehicles that, even with four-wheel drive, might not be able to handle heavy-duty off-roading like the Rubicon Trail, which new Jeep designs traditionally had to be able to conquer before being released to the public.

ALL 4x4s SHOULD TAKE A SIMILAR ROUTE TO GET TO YOUR DRIVEWAY.

Photo taken from NATC testing

Traction	Articulation	Ground Clearance	Maneuverability	Water Fording

THE JEEP TRAIL RATED™ SYSTEM. The path to becoming a TRAIL RATED Jeep 4x4 is long and difficult. It requires numerous trips through a series of grueling off-road test courses. The result? Unmatched go-anywhere, do-anything capability. And a remarkable feeling of safety and security on the most treacherous trails of all: paved ones. Learn all about the TRAIL RATED Jeep 4x4s and their impressive 7-year/70,000-mile Powertrain Limited Warranty* at jeep.com/trailrated **IF IT'S NOT TRAIL RATED, IT'S NOT A JEEP 4x4.**

ONLY IN A

JEEP.COM

Jeep and Trail Rated are trademarks of DaimlerChrysler Corporation.
*See dealer for a copy of this limited warranty. Transferable to second owner with fee. A deductible applies.

The new Jeep Trail-Rated designation was an early sign that the day was approaching when not every four-wheel-drive Jeep would be capable of traversing the tough Rubicon Trail; only the Trail-Rated models would be that capable.

918 To earn the Trail-Rated designation, a Jeep vehicle had to meet strict capability standards in traction, ground clearance, maneuverability, articulation, and water fording. At the time that the standards were released, nearly every Jeep vehicle could meet them. Once the Patriot and Compass arrived, not every Jeep was Trail-Rated.

919 The Grand Cherokee offered a limited-production Rocky Mountain edition for 2005 with a sticker price of $31,230 for the two-wheel-drive model and $33,200 for the four-wheel-drive version. Introduced in an innovative electronic newsletter to 240,000 existing Jeep owners, the Rocky Mountain Grand Cherokee featured upgraded exterior trim and special badging.

920 For 2006, Jeep reintroduced the Grand Cherokee Overland model at the top of the Grand Cherokee line. The new Overland featured the awesome 5.7-liter Hemi engine producing 330 hp at 5,000 rpm and 375 ft-lbs at 4,000 rpm hooked up to Quadra-Drive II, the ultimate four-wheel-drive system.

Overland boasted platinum accents placed on the front grille, body side, beltline moldings, 17-inch platinum-clad wheels, roof-rack side rails, lift-gate light bar, sideview mirrors, and rear bumper. Other standard Overland features were a real wood steering wheel, wood door trim and console trim bezels, side airbags, ParkSense, TPM, trailer tow group, navigation radio, Sirius Satellite Radio, two-tone seats with ultra-suede and leather-trimmed seats, leather-wrapped center console armrest, and "Overland" logo embroidered on the front seat backs. A rear DVD player, off-road package, and engine block heater were options.

921 Also for 2006, Jeep introduced another instant legend: the all-new Grand Cherokee SRT8. It was the quickest, most powerful Jeep vehicle ever built to that point. Featuring a 6.1-liter Hemi V-8 engine, the Jeep Grand Cherokee SRT8 was the first four-wheel-drive SRT vehicle ever produced, as well as the first Jeep-branded vehicle in the renowned SRT series from Chrysler.

922 In April 2017, Jeep introduced yet another instant legend: the 2018 Grand Cherokee Trackhawk. Boasting an incredible 707 hp (courtesy of a supercharged 6.2-liter V-8 engine), the Grand Cherokee, already the most awarded SUV ever and the most capable full-size SUV on the planet, was now also the most powerful and quickest SUV ever built.

The new Chrysler-developed benchmark 707-hp supercharged engine, combined with a beefed-up high-torque capacity TorqueFlite 8-speed automatic transmission and vastly enhanced chassis to create a world-class on-road driving experience. Brembo high-performance disc brakes delivered a whole new level of stopping power.

Trackhawk performance was insane: How does 0–60 mph in 3.5 seconds sound? Or how about running the quarter-mile in 11.6 seconds at 116 mph? Trackhawk performance included a top speed of 180 mph, the ability to achieve a 60–0 mph braking distance of just 114 feet, and a true 0.88-g capability on the skid pad.

Mike Manley, who at the time was head of Jeep, said, "Long recognized as the full-size SUV capability leader, the Jeep Grand Cherokee is now the most powerful and quickest SUV as well, with the introduction of our new 707-hp Trackhawk. The new Grand Cherokee Trackhawk delivers astounding performance numbers, backed by renowned SRT engineering that combines world-class on-road driving dynamics with luxury, refinement, and an array of innovative advanced technology." Manley is now the head of FCA following the untimely and unfortunate death of former CEO Sergio Marchionne.

923 As of 2019, Jeep vehicles are manufactured in the following countries: United States, Mexico, Brazil, Italy, China, and India. To my surprise, the Grand Cherokee is still being built in Venezuela, although nowadays they are assembled from CKD kits rather than being manufactured there. Years ago, Venezuela was a big market for new Jeep vehicles, but in its longtime economic downturn it no longer is.

Body and Interior

924 Originally, the Grand Cherokee was going to be offered in two bodystyles: a two-door and a four-door. Full-size mockups were made, and if AMC had continued as an independent company, they probably would have gone into production. But Chrysler delayed the program so long that by the time the Grand Cherokee did go into production, demand for two-door SUVs had fallen dramatically.

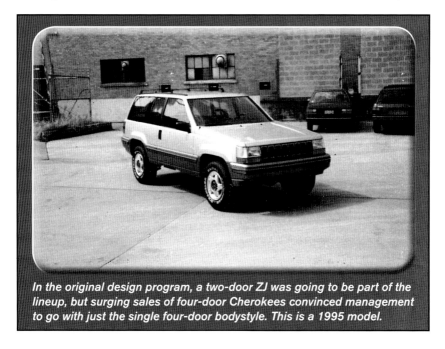

In the original design program, a two-door ZJ was going to be part of the lineup, but surging sales of four-door Cherokees convinced management to go with just the single four-door bodystyle. This is a 1995 model.

925 A seldom-seen model in the initial Grand Cherokee line was the base model, which came with steel wheels and no body side cladding. It's hard to find a photo of one! The more popular models for 1993 were the Laredo and Limited.

926 According to documents taken from the files of Jeep styling, the original Grand Cherokee ZJ program was to include a pickup truck on a 119-inch wheelbase. Targeting the Ford Ranger and Chevy S10, it was planned to seat three people and offer a maximum payload of 2,205 pounds.

927 Like the Cherokee XJ, the Grand Cherokee used modern unibody construction to provide a lighter, tighter platform with outstanding durability and safety. Because of this, the Grand Cherokee had the lowest curb weight of any vehicle in its class. It was years later that other companies switched to a unibody for their SUVs.

928 Another benefit of the Grand Cherokee's advanced unibody design was that it was much stiffer than that of previous Jeep vehicles. In fact, the new Grand Cherokee boasted the highest torsional rigidity in its class, which in turn provided it with superb ride and handling. At the time it was being designed, many engineers were still not aware of the benefits of a stiffer chassis.

929 One complaint about the Jeep Cherokee XJ was its narrow rear door opening. In designing the new 1993 Grand Cherokee ZJs, designers addressed the problem of the XJ's narrow rear door opening by providing a door that was 4.3 inches wider. The Grand Cherokee also offered 7.4 cubic feet more cargo space.

930 The 1993 Grand Cherokee was the first sport utility vehicle to use environmentally friendly R134A refrigerant in the air-conditioning system. It was also the only vehicle in its class to offer an automatic temperature-control air-conditioning system.

931 In another safety innovation, Jeep engineers pointed out that the Grand Cherokee included as standard equipment both lap and shoulder belts for all outboard passengers. This was unusual at the time, but it eventually became standard on all cars and trucks.

932 For 1994, the Grand Cherokee base model was renamed the SE and still did not offer the ubiquitous body side cladding that was standard equipment on the Grand Chero-

kee Laredo and Limited models. Apparently, the cladding was something people wanted because sales of the base Grand Cherokee were never very high.

933 For the 1995 model year, Jeep expanded the Grand Cherokee offerings by the addition of the special Orvis Edition, a high-luxury version that included all the features of the

During the 1995 model year, Jeep added this special Orvis Edition to the Grand Cherokee lineup. The Orvis Edition included all the features of the Grand Cherokee Limited along with special Moss Green exterior paint. The Champagne interior trim boasted Dark Green and Roan red accents. Standard features on the Orvis Edition also included Up Country suspension and Trailer Tow Prep. Jeep bragged that it was "the Official vehicle of Orvis."

Limited. It also added Moss Green exterior paint, Champagne with Dark Green and Roan red interior trim, Up Country suspension, and Trailer Tow Prep.

934 The 1996 Grand Cherokee was given an all-new interior with Euro-styling and greatly improved finishes, as befitted a luxury-class sport utility vehicle. Only two models were offered for 1996: the Laredo and Limited. The slow-selling SE base model was dropped.

935 The all-new 1999 Grand Cherokee interior boasted an overhead console with 14 programmable features, heated seats, memory-seat programming, and infrared dual-zone climate control that could even detect when a passenger was running a fever and adjust the temperature to make him or her more comfortable.

936 Sometimes it's the little things that count. The 1999 Grand Cherokee had its spare tire nestled underneath the rear floor. Every other SUV in its class had theirs hanging underneath the vehicle, where they became wet and dirty.

937 For the 2000 model year, the Jeep Grand Cherokee introduced a new option dubbed the Mopar Navigation System, which was one of the very first factory-installed GPS systems, and the first to be offered in a Jeep vehicle. Onboard navigation systems have since become extremely popular with car buyers.

938 For 2004, Jeep expanded the Grand Cherokee lineup to five models: Laredo, Special, Freedom, Limited, and Overland. The range was made even broader because all models were now offered in two-wheel and four-wheel-drive versions.

939 Besides the five basic models for 2004, the Jeep Grand Cherokee offered a special Columbia Edition featuring 17-inch platinum wheels, graphite fascia and trim, sunroof,

fog lamps, and more. Inside were special Dark Slate and Taupe two-tone seats with the Columbia logo. Named for the famous sportswear company, the special model was priced at $30,375.

940 The 2004 Grand Cherokee Special featured the monochromatic exterior design cues of the Limited. Four-wheel-drive Specials came with fog lamps, Quadra-Trac II, and AM/FM/Cassette with a 10-disc CD player. The similar two-wheel-drive version had slightly different equipment.

941 The Grand Cherokee was all new for 2005; the company made it larger and more luxurious because Jeep was losing market share to competitors that offered a smoother ride and more luxury features. To focus attention on the improvements, the company came up with the advertising slogan "The Off-Road Legend Continues. The On-Road Legend Begins."

942 All of the new Grand Cherokee models for 2005 (Laredo and Limited 4x2 and 4x4 models) were built with Jeep's famous Uniframe chassis construction, a new aluminum hood, front air dam, and new front fascia, grille, and body side moldings.

Larger, handsomer, and still trim and agile, the new 2005 Grand Cherokee was a marked improvement.

Engine and Drivetrain

943 When it debuted, the Grand Cherokee boasted the most powerful engine in its class, the 190-hp 4.0 six. It was the only one to offer three distinct four-wheel-drive systems: conventional part-time, Selec-Trac full-time, and all-new Quadra-Trac all-time four-wheel drive. The new Quadra-Trac included a center-mounted viscous coupling that could automatically lock the center differential as needed.

944 Although at introduction the Grand Cherokee offered only a standard 4.0-liter 6-cylinder engine, within a few months Jeep added a 5.2-liter V-8 option with 220 hp. In one of the greatest auto ads of all time, a headline announced "The Good News is Jeep Grand Cherokee is now available with a V-8. There is no bad news."

945 The Grand Cherokees introduced in early 1992 were badged as 1993 models, but they had another introduction in the fall, along with the rest of the 1993 Jeep line. At that time, a 5-speed manual transmission became available with the 4.0-liter six.

946 Also for the fall 1992 introduction period, a two-wheel-drive version of the Grand Cherokee became available in both SE and Laredo trim, but could be ordered only with the 4.0-liter 6-cylinder engine. Demand for the two-wheel-drive Jeep Grand Cherokee proved to be surprisingly robust.

947 Due to the popularity of the two-wheel drive Laredo and SE, for 1995 a two-wheel-drive Grand Cherokee Limited was made available. It was mainly popular in warm-weather states.

948 The 1995 Grand Cherokee 4.0-liter 6-cylinder engine produced an impressive 190 hp. The newly improved 5.2-liter V-8 engine was now rated at 220 hp and provided 300 ft-lbs of torque for improved acceleration and greater towing capacity.

During the 1995 model year, Jeep introduced the ZJ Orvis Edition, a high-trim model.

949 For 1996, Grand Cherokees equipped with the 5.2-liter V-8 engine were given an all-new wide-ratio automatic transmission that provided better response and improved fuel economy. Grand Cherokees equipped with the standard 4.0-liter six were given a higher stall torque ratio torque converter.

950 During the 1998 model year, Jeep wore the crown as the world's fastest sport utility vehicle with the recently introduced Grand Cherokee 5.9 Limited. A top-of-the-line model powered by a 5.9-liter V-8 engine producing 245 hp and 335 ft-lbs of torque, the Grand Cherokee 5.9 Limited's acceleration time of 0–60 mph in 7.3 seconds was best-in-class by a big margin.

951 The 1998 Grand Cherokee 5.9 Limited was so powerful that Jeep had to use a beefed-up NV249 transfer case. Trak-Loc axles came standard.

952 In 1999, Jeep advanced the state-of-the-art four-wheel drive yet again when it debuted the Quadra-Drive system that worked through a new Quadra-Trac II on-demand transfer case to direct torque from rear to front and side to side as required to maintain maximum traction. The moment a rear wheel lost grip, a gerotor coupling in the rear axle transferred torque to the other rear wheel. If that wheel couldn't maintain traction, a gerotor pump in the transfer case sent torque to the all-new Vari-Lok progressive front axle, where a gerotor coupling had the ability to transfer 100 percent of the torque to just one wheel if necessary. All this was done silently, smoothly, and in mere microseconds.

953 There were some teething problems with the new progressive axles; not all of them were quiet. A number of complaints were lodged about noise and harshness. It turned out that they were the result of minor manufacturing errors, and Jeep fixed the affected vehicles and corrected the problem in assembly.

954 How important was the new Quadra-Drive system? *Automotive Industries* magazine said, "The introduction of the Quadra-Drive System . . . changes the rules of four-wheel-drive so dramatically, it may never be the same."

955 The Grand Cherokee WJ offered three four-wheel-drive systems: Selec-Trac was standard on Laredo sixes. Quadra-Trac II was standard on Laredo V-8 and optional on the six. Limiteds came with Quadra-Drive.

956 The Grand Cherokee for 1999 also debuted a very interesting transmission. Officially it was a 4-speed automatic, but in reality it had five speeds because there were two second gear ratios: 1.5:1 and 1.67:1. The transmission decided which second gear to use based on vehicle speed and throttle position.

957 Also debuting on the 1999 Grand Cherokee was a low-emissions 16-valve 4.7-liter V-8 that provided more power, better fuel efficiency, and lower emissions than the 5.2-liter it replaced. Power

output of the new engine was 235 hp at 4,800 rpm and 295 ft-lbs of torque at a mere 3,200 rpm, where it's most useful for off-roading.

958 Dana Corporation, the manufacturer of Jeep's Spicer-brand axles, helped to promote the 1999 Grand Cherokee by releasing a brochure that explained the superiority of the Spicer Hydra-Lok intelligent axles that were fitted to the new Jeep. They provided greatly improved off-road capability.

959 For 2001, the Grand Cherokee came with a new 5-speed automatic transmission. It still had the two-step second gear but now also had a second overdrive top gear. This was a 0.67:1 ratio for maximum fuel economy and a quieter engine.

960 The last year for the legendary 4.0-liter six in the Grand Cherokee was 2004. When an all-new Grand Cherokee arrived for 2005, it had a 3.7-liter 210-hp single overhead cam (SOHC) V-6 engine. Also available was an updated version of the 4.7-liter V-8 offering 230 hp.

961 The big news for Jeep lovers in 2005 was the availability for the first time of the 5.7-liter Hemi V-8 pumping out 325 hp and 370 ft-lbs of torque for best-in-class power. An incredible 90 percent of peak torque came between 2,400 and 5,100 rpm.

Available in the 2005 Grand Cherokee was the Chrysler 5.7-liter Hemi V-8 engine, which this particular unit has.

962 The new Hemi V-8 included a multi-displacement system that deactivated four cylinders when not needed, such as cruising on the highway at a steady speed. The result was much better gas mileage. I've driven various examples thousands of miles, and the system works seamlessly.

963 The 2005 Grand Cherokee also introduced a 5-speed automatic transmission, the 545RFE, with smoother shifts and optimum fuel economy. It was also beefier to allow for greater towing capacity.

ALL NEW JEEP GRAND CHEROKEE.
THE OFF-ROAD LEGEND CONTINUES...ON-ROAD.

Now you can make the most of every journey, no matter what the terrain. The new Trail Rated Jeep Grand Cherokee features a 330-hp 5.7L HEMI V8, the most powerful engine in its class, an Electronic Stability Program, and Quadra-Drive II, our most advanced four-wheel-drive system ever. Visit jeep.com **Jeep**

Jeep, Trail Rated, and HEMI are registered trademarks of DaimlerChrysler Corporation. *Only available on Limited 4x4 model. †Based on 2004 Ward's Middle/Sport Utility Segment and published industry information. †Available.

One fact has always been true: Jeep owners are more likely to take their vehicles off-road than owners of any other four-wheel-drive vehicle. It's a Jeep thing, and you understand it.

964 Also for 2005 was a new NV245 transfer case for Quadra-Trac II and Quadra-Drive II four-wheel-drive systems. The NV245 uses inputs from a variety of sensors to determine tire slip at the earliest possible moment and take immediate action to maximize traction before a slip can occur.

965 The new Quadra-Drive II system included front and rear electronic limited-slip differentials (ELSD) for the industry-leading traction and control. Offering the ultimate in off-road capability, the Quadra-Drive II differentials used electronically controlled clutch packs to automatically vary from slip to lock at each axle to maximize traction.

966 For 2006, Jeep topped itself when it introduced the exciting Grand Cherokee SRT8 model. Powered by an incredible 6.1-liter Hemi V-8, it produced 420 hp and 420 ft-lbs of torque, which was 90 more horses and 25 percent more power than the 5.7-liter Hemi–equipped 2006 Jeep Grand Cherokee. The Grand Cherokee SRT8 performance numbers included the ability to accelerate 0–60 mph in less than 5 seconds, and 0–100–0 mph in the low-19-second range.

967 To create the first SRT vehicle with full-time four-wheel drive, SRT engineers developed a drive system that was lightweight yet robust enough to handle massive amounts of horsepower and torque from the SRT8 powertrain. They created a new transfer case, combining housing components from two existing units with the upgrades needed to make it SRT capable.

The engineers opted to use the front half of a Jeep transfer case for its capability and light weight. They mated it to the rear half of a heavier-duty case, which was chosen for its ruggedness and ability to house the electronic full-time four-wheel-drive system components. The transfer case output shaft was also upgraded to handle the high torque generated by 6.1-liter Hemi. The resulting unique transfer case provided the necessary power-handling capabilities for the Jeep Grand Cherokee SRT8 while weighing 60 pounds less than a Jeep heavy-duty case.

Under normal driving conditions, from 5 to 10 percent of torque was directed to the front wheels, but as much of the 6.1-liter Hemi's torque as needed could be redirected. The remaining torque was sent via a heavy-duty driveshaft designed for the European Grand Cherokee diesel model to a Dana 44 rear differential upgraded with a larger ring gear within a new axle housing.

968 By 2018, the SRT had been surpassed by an incredible machine dubbed the Grand Cherokee Trackhawk. Built in Detroit at the Jefferson North Assembly Plant, the 2018 Grand Cherokee Trackhawk was powered by a breakthrough supercharged engine designed and manufactured using only the strongest and most durable materials. Its cast-iron block featured water jackets between the cylinders for optimal cooling. A forged-steel crankshaft with induction-hardened bearing surfaces was so strong that it could easily withstand firing pressures of nearly 1,600 psi (110 bar), which is the equivalent of five family sedans standing on each piston, every two revolutions.

The unique, specially tuned crankshaft damper was burst tested to 13,000 rpm. In addition, high-strength forged-alloy pistons (developed using advanced telemetry measurement) were coupled to powder-forged connecting rods with high-load-capacity bushings and diamond-like carbon-coated piston pins. Premium grade, heat-treated aluminum-alloy cylinder heads were optimized for superior thermal conductivity. Sodium-cooled exhaust valves featured hollow-stem construction and special steel-alloy heads that stand up to temperatures as high as 1,652 degrees Fahrenheit. The supercharger, of course, included integral charge-air coolers, along with an integrated electronic bypass valve to regulate boost pressure to a maximum of 11.6 psi.

Suspension and Brakes

969 The Grand Cherokee raised the bar in SUV suspension systems because it featured Jeep's all-new Quadra-Coil multilink front and rear suspension that included solid axles and coil springs at all four wheels, which provided better durability, improved on-

road ride and handling, and provided greater off-road capability than ever before. In testing, it proved to be superior to the competitors' suspensions.

970 From the very start, the Grand Cherokee came with four-wheel antilock brakes as standard equipment, unusual in the SUV market segment. The system included front disc and rear drum brakes.

971 Road testers of the day always remarked on how well the Grand Cherokee handled and cornered in on-road driving. That's not surprising, given that the company hired renowned race car driver Emerson "Emmo" Fittipaldi as a consultant and tester. Emmo made sure that the new Jeep could handle like a BMW. Oddly enough, the Grand Cherokee used conventional recirculating-ball steering rather than rack and pinion.

972 Each of the three Grand Cherokee models for 1993 had a different standard wheel. The base models received stamped steel wheels, the Laredo came with full-face steel wheels, and the Limited had cast-aluminum wheels.

973 To replace the discontinued Grand Wagoneer, Jeep introduced a loaded version of the Grand Cherokee with wood-grain sides and called it the Grand Wagoneer. It didn't catch on and was dropped by 1994.

974 For 1994, Jeep introduced a new top-line model called the Grand Cherokee Limited, with four-wheel antilock disc brakes as standard equipment. The Grand Cherokee Limited also included leather interior fabric with vinyl-trimmed bolsters, a 60-40 split rear bench seat, automatic temperature control air-conditioning, and front and rear adjustable headrests.

975 For 1995, four-wheel antilock disc brakes became standard on all Grand Cherokee models. It had already been standard equipment on the Grand Cherokee Limited models, but it now was

added to the standard equipment on the base SE model and mid-range Laredo as well.

976 As good as the Grand Cherokee was, Jeep engineers were able to improve its suspension effective with the 1996 model year. The deflected-disc shock absorbers were re-valved for more linear damping under all driving conditions, and a new front sway bar boasted ball stud joints for improved durability, response, and stability.

977 New in the 1996 Grand Cherokee was Speed-Proportional Variable Ratio steering that progressively increased or reduced the amount of steering assist in proportion to vehicle speed. Also new were stiffer steering column mounts.

978 New standard equipment for the 1996 Grand Cherokee Limited models were premium Goodyear Eagle LS all-season performance radial tires. The size was P225/70r16, marking the first time that 16-inch tires were factory fitted to the Grand Cherokee.

979 For 1997, Jeep introduced a sport performance version of the Grand Cherokee, the TSi. Although the standard engine

The 1997 Grand Cherokee came with a new wheel design.

was the 4.0-liter six, most were ordered with the 220-hp 5.2-liter V-8. Road-gripping 16-inch Goodyear Eagle ES performance tires mounted on unique five-spoke alloy wheels were standard. The Quadra-Coil touring suspension provided outstanding handling.

980 As mentioned earlier, the Jeep Grand Cherokee was given four-wheel antilock disc brakes as standard equipment on all models in 1995. Not content to rest on its laurels, for 1999 the all-new Grand Cherokee debuted a new antilock brake system that featured massive 12-inch rotors and dual-piston front calipers that in testing proved to be best-in-class in braking ability. Jeep has always been determined to keep Grand Cherokee at the forefront of technological development.

981 And so it started: In 2001, the Grand Cherokee gained optional 17-inch wheels, which seemed outrageously big at the time. They were standard on Limiteds and optional on Laredos.

982 Jeep was the first sport utility vehicle to offer a tire pressure monitoring system with the 2002 model. Sensors mounted in the valve stem of each tire, including the spare, transmitted information to the vehicle's overhead console. A warning message displayed on the overhead console alerted the driver when the tire pressure exceeded or fell below set thresholds.

983 The 2003 Grand Cherokee boasted improved brake feel and lower "effort." Reduced brake-pedal effort allowing shorter stopping distances during braking maneuvers was accomplished by increasing the master cylinder output pressure for a "lighter" brake pedal feel. New brake calipers for 2003 also helped provide lighter brake pedal feel, providing smoother and more linear braking.

984 The Grand Cherokee had an even better ride for 2003, and reduced steering effort was part of the Chrysler Group's continuous improvement process. The 2003 Jeep Grand Cherokee suspension featured reduced-pressure shocks for improvements in overall ride comfort. Jeep engineers also reduced steering effort

both on- and off-center by a very noticeable 20 percent through the use of a revised steering gear torsion bar.

985 As good as the Grand Cherokee's ride was, by 2005 it needed to improve to outshine competitors. An all-new short-long arm (SLA) front suspension was introduced that improved both on-road ride and off-road capability. Included were nodular iron lower control arms and forged upper control arms plus coilover shocks.

986 As fast as the 2006 Grand Cherokee could accelerate, it could stop in extremely short distances. It boasted a 60–0 mph braking distance of less than 125 feet, courtesy of four-wheel brakes featuring four-piston performance brake calipers developed by Brembo and finished in gloss black. While braking, the calipers clamped down on 360x32-mm vented rotors up front. The 350x28-mm vented rotors in the rear provided rapid, straight deceleration.

987 The 2006 SRT8 was also endowed with SRT world-class ride and handling across a dynamic range. The chassis setup was aimed at balanced performance with SRT-tuned dampers, unique sway bars, and specially tailored spring rates and suspension bushings. New front suspension knuckles featured a camber angle calibrated for optimum suspension performance. The ride height of the 2006 Jeep Grand Cherokee SRT8 was 1 inch lower than the Jeep Grand Cherokee to reduce aerodynamic drag.

Numbers Crunching and Press Commentary

988 In order to obtain the highest possible quality in the new Grand Cherokee, Jeep built a huge, all-new factory on Jefferson Avenue in downtown Detroit. It was one of the most advanced auto-making facilities in the world with robotic subassembly, its own waste-water treatment plant, and capacity to build more than 300,000 vehicles annually.

989 Spurred by the Grand Cherokee, Jeep sales for 1993 totaled more than 408,000 vehicles in the United States, setting a new record. From 1991 to 1993, Jeep sales in the United States more than doubled.

990 Compared to the Cherokee XJ, the 1993 Grand Cherokee was 8 inches longer overall, rode a wheelbase that was 4.5 inches longer, and had 3 inches more front shoulder room.

991 In 1994, workers at the big Grand Cherokee plant on Jefferson Avenue in Detroit agreed to the addition of a third shift, which boosted output to 315,000 Grand Cherokees per year and reduced the heavy overtime schedules that they'd been working.

992 In 1996, Jeep annual sales exceeded half a million units for the first time, and that was just in the United States! The company sold another 28,000 units outside the country. At the time, Jeep had just three models: Wrangler, Cherokee, and Grand Cherokee. The Grand Cherokee was the biggest-volume seller.

993 Jeep introduced a completely new Grand Cherokee for the 1999 model year. At the January 1998 Detroit Auto show, Chrysler Corporation displayed the upcoming vehicle's new powertrain and four-wheel-drive system. Chairman Bob Eaton held up a small sack and told journalists that it held the only parts carried over from the old vehicle. He said that most of the 127 parts were screws and fasteners.

994 The all-new 1999 Grand Cherokee was introduced in August 1998. At the introduction, chairman Bob Eaton noted that Jeep was having a hard time keeping up with international demand for the Grand Cherokee. The plan was to produce 350,000 Grand Cherokees in Detroit (many of which would go to export markets) and another 80,000 in plants in Austria, Venezuela, Argentina, and Thailand.

This is an all-new Grand Cherokee for 1999. Only 127 parts were carried over from the previous generation.

995 During development, Jeep benchmarked the all-new Grand Cherokee's chassis performance against 23 competitors and didn't stop development until the new Jeep was the overwhelmingly superior vehicle.

996 *Four-Wheeler* magazine and Petersen's *4 Wheel & Off-Road* magazine named the 1999 Grand Cherokee "4x4 of the Year." In announcing the award, Petersen's *4 Wheel & Off-Road* magazine said this: "Whether it is on-road performance and handling or its capability in treacherous off-road terrain, the 1999 Jeep Grand Cherokee masters it all."

997 An independent testing company compared the 1999 Jeep Grand Cherokee with the Hummer, Mercedes-Benz ML320, Isuzu Amigo and Trooper, Range Rover, Lexus LX470, Chevy Tahoe and Blazer, Ford Explorer, and Toyota 4Runner. The vehicles were tested for acceleration 0–60, 40–70, and the quarter-mile; braking and cornering; and off-road traction.

The Grand Cherokee came in first in all of the categories. That became the basis of Jeep's claim that the Grand Cherokee was the "Most Capable Sport Utility Ever."

998 Even though the 1999 Grand Cherokee WJ series had more power and better acceleration than previous Grand Cherokees, the EPA fuel economy estimates were even higher with ratings of 15 mpg city and 19 mpg highway versus 14 mpg city and 17 mpg highway for the outgoing Grand Cherokee ZJ model. To boost power is a good accomplishment; to do it while also boosting fuel economy is a great accomplishment.

999 During 1999, a Jeep Grand Cherokee made it onto the list of Top Ten Selling Vehicles in the US for the first time, with 300,031 units sold at retail. It came in just behind the Honda Civic at 318,308 units. Jeep sold 554,466 vehicles in the United States that year. The incredible thing is that the division built just over 635,000 vehicles for the year (many were sold overseas), even though Jeep still offered just three models: Wrangler, Cherokee, and Grand Cherokee.

1000 Dan Knott, director of Chrysler's Street and Racing Technology (SRT) Group had this to say about the 2006 Grand Cherokee SRT8: "When we set out to create the quickest, most powerful Jeep vehicle ever, the Grand Cherokee presented us with an incredibly capable starting point. With an infusion of SRT DNA, the 2006 Jeep Grand Cherokee SRT8 is the new benchmark performance SUV. It has the raw power to outperform the Porsche Cayenne Turbo, while providing exceptional ride and handling, world-class braking, race-inspired interior appointments and functional, performance-oriented exterior enhancements."

1001 Here's one fact that is indisputable: There are just two kinds of people in the world: those who own Jeeps and those who wish they owned Jeeps.

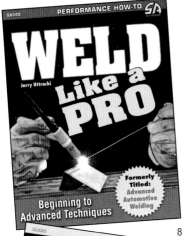

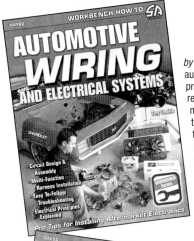

1001 JEEP FACTS

CarTech®

PATRICK FOSTE

1001 JEEP FACTS